NEUTRAL IRELAND AND THE THIRD REICH

John P. Duggan

NEUTRAL IRELAND AND THE THIRD REICH

GILL AND MACMILLAN
Dublin

BARNES AND NOBLE
Totowa, New Jersey

Published in Ireland by
Gill and Macmillan Ltd
Goldenbridge
Dublin 8
with associated companies in
Auckland, Dallas, Delhi, Hong Kong,
Johannesburg, Lagos, London, Manzini,
Melbourne, Nairobi, New York, Singapore,
Tokyo, Washington
© John Duggan, 1985
7171 1384 1

British Library Cataloguing in Publication Data
Duggan, John
    Neutral Ireland and the Third Reich.
    1. World War, 1939-1945 — Diplomatic history
    2. Ireland — Foreign relations — Germany
    3. Germany — Foreign relations — Ireland
    I. Title
    327.417043   DA964.G3
    ISBN 0-7171-1384-1

First published in the USA 1985 by
Barnes & Noble Books
81 Adams Drive,
Totowa, New Jersey, 07512

Library of Congress Cataloging in Publication Data
Duggan, John P.
    Neutral Ireland and the Third Reich.
    Bibliography: p.
    Includes Index.
    1. World War, 1939-1945 — Diplomatic History. 2. Ireland — Foreign Relations
— Germany. 3. Germany — Foreign Relations — Ireland. 4. Great Britain — Foreign
Relations — Ireland. 5. Ireland — Foreign Relations — Great Britain. 6. Neutrality.
7. Ireland — Foreign Relations — 1922-. 8. Germany — Foreign Relations — 1933-
1945. I. Title.
D754. I5D84 1985 940.53'2 85-18678
ISBN 0-389-20598-2

Print origination in Ireland by Galaxy Reproductions Ltd, Dublin
Printed in Great Britain by
Biddles Ltd, Guildford and King's Lynn

Contents

To
Anglo-Irish-German
understanding

Preface

In any future world war the Republic of Ireland will have to resolve the problem of whom to be neutral against. In the last war, de Valera's 'certain consideration for Britain' tipped the scales of neutrality in favour of the Allies and against the Third Reich. There was no existing code in international law to contain all the variations in that neutrality theme which is nowadays, inaccurately but conveniently, described in Ireland as traditional neutrality.

Eire's considerations were not given out of any special love for the Allies or any initial animosity towards the Third Reich. They arose from national self-interest: they were essential for survival. Acting in the national self-interest is the norm for nation states. As de Valera pointed out, none of the powerful nations like the United States went crusading until they were forced into it by circumstances. The justification of the nation lies in its unified pursuit of self-interest against the outside world. In time of war the essence of this pragmatic pursuit is unity, and wars result in the drawing and re-drawing of national frontiers.

In time of global nuclear war frontiers would be obliterated, not reshaped. There would no longer be a next time to worry about. There is, however, much to ponder on before that dread moment is reached. This account of Irish wartime neutrality, based mainly on extracts from contemporary archival material, will, it is hoped, throw new light on a perennially fascinating subject. It offers neither solutions nor blueprints, but it may help to clarify some of the ambiguities surrounding an historical episode in which political and military concerns were mixed in a unique blend.

Acknowledgments

It is difficult to know where to begin or end in acknowledging the generous help I received from a wide range of people in my efforts to chronicle this aspect of modern history. In the beginning, on a recommendation from Rev. Professor F. X. Martin o.s.a., Professor Basil Chubb and Professor Patrick Keatinge admitted me, a very 'mature' student, to do an M.Litt. degree in Trinity College. Professor Desmond Williams of U.C.D. kindly suggested the theme: 'Herr Hempel at the German Legation in Dublin 1937-1945'. I appreciate the facility with which a late vocation was received into the absorbing world of archival scholarship. The assistance I received in the British Foreign Office Archives and Public Record Offices; in the Imperial War Museum; and the archives in Bonn, Koblenz and Freiburg (where I started) was a revelation to me. Irish archives cannot match those institutions in resources but they certainly can in co-operation. Courtesy and patience seem to be the hallmarks of archivists. Queries to U.S. archives were dealt with promptly without, however, locating the Bewley Papers I was after. A query to the Public Records Office, Four Courts, Dublin was answered by return of post. I am most grateful to all the archivists whose paths I crossed.

The thesis would not have fallen into an appropriate mould without the guidance of Dr Patrick Keatinge. The gulf in style between thesis and book could not have been bridged without the apt advice of Mr Fergal Tobin of Gill and Macmillan. It was Anthony Marecco who first suggested turning the thesis into a book. Mr John Keegan's assessment proved to be a turning point and Mr Joe McGeogh, very kindly, gave the project the essential kick-start that got it moving.

Colonel Dan Bryan, the most effective Chief of Intelligence during the War, was forbearance itself: my last marathon interview with him lasted up to seven hours and ran to six tapes (with numerous blank stretches, I hasten to add). Frau Hempel very kindly gave me three full days of her time in her sister's Kensington flat, while we combed the thesis line by line, pausing only to drink cups of coffee, to ensure that her husband's reputation was not traduced unfairly. She would, however, hardly recognise the book from the thesis: for that reason I did not dedicate it to her. The form is changed. The material has been melted down and recast. I ask indulgence for this, especially from Frau Hempel. In spite of Frank McDermot's gratuitous observation in his 'Dear Patricia' letters that she was 'extravagantly' pro-Nazi, I found her to be a woman of immense integrity and great charm.

I drew encouragement from sitting at the feet of Professor D. A. Binchy for a few informal chats. Interviews played an important part in providing ingredients and orientation and I would like to thank most sincerely all those who gave of their time and experience. Some meetings were fleeting; some contacts and conversations casual: in view of the informal atmosphere in which most of the interviews were conducted I must stress that responsibility for recall, impressions and interpretation and for any views and conclusions expressed is mine alone. A list of interviews, letters and conversations (mostly carried out, it must also be emphasised, in the context of reserarch for the original thesis, not this book) is included as an inadequate expression of appreciation in the Bibliography.

List of Principal Characters

Aiken.   Frank Aiken (1909-1983) was born in Co. Armagh. Chief of Staff, IRA 1923-5. De Valera's right-hand man, he served as Minister for Defence, 1933-9, and Minister for Co-ordination of Defensive Measures, 1939-45.

Bewley.   Charles Bewley (1888-1969) was the maverick son of an established Dublin family. He succeeded D. A. Binchy in 1933 as Irish minister in Berlin. Before the outbreak of war, de Valera got rid of him and he retired to Italy. Captured by the Allies towards the end of the war, he was lucky not to have been executed as a spy.

Binchy.   D. A. Binchy (b. 1900) was the first Irish minister to Berlin. A very distinguished scholar, he had little enthusiasm for diplomatic life, and he returned to academic life at the first possible opportunity.

Boland.   Frederick H. Boland (b. 1904) was Assistant Secretary in the Irish Department of External Affairs, 1938-46. He later had a career of outstanding distinction in the Irish diplomatic service.

Bryan.   Colonel Dan Bryan (b. 1900) was the highly successful director of intelligence (G2) in the Irish army. He was single-minded in his professionalism and was highly regarded by his peers, particularly in Britain.

Butler.   Colonel Eamon Butler (de Buitléir; 1902-81), Bryan's assistant as director of intelligence. Differences of temperament and approach between the two men led to a strained working relationship.

Costello.   Lieutenant-General   Michael   J.   ('Mickey   Joe')

Costello (b. 1904) commanded the first ('Thunderbolt') division in the south of Ireland. A charismatic leader, he whipped his division into a high pitch of combat readiness for whom down-to-earth soldiering became a religion. He later had a highly successful business career.

de Valera.   Eamon de Valera (1882-1975), the last surviving commandant of 1916, architect of the constitution, and implementer of neutrality, was Taoiseach and leader of the Irish people during the Emergency.

Goertz.   Dr Hermann Goertz (1890-1947) was an Abwehr spy. He parachuted into Co. Meath in May 1940 and remained at large for eighteen months. His mission achieved little.

Gogan.   Liam Gogan (1891-1979) was a veteran of 1916 and a relative of Patrick Pearse. He and Hempel were close friends during the envoy's time in Dublin and he was regarded by Berlin as an authority on the IRA.

Gray.   David Gray (1870-1968) was the American minister to Ireland during the Emergency. He was not a professional diplomat. He was gauche and assertive and de Valera found him extremely difficult to deal with.

Hempel.   Eduard Hempel (1887-1972) was the Minister Plenipotentiary for the Third Reich to Eire, 1937-45. A formal and correct diplomat of the old school, the propriety of his conduct was in sharp contrast to that of Gray.

Kerney.   Leopold Kerney (1881-1962) was Irish minister to Spain during the Second World War. He failed to keep in touch with the changing nuances of de Valera's neutrality policy and consequently assumed it to be less flexible and more anglophobic than it actually was.

MacNeill.   Major-General Hugo MacNeill (1900-63) commanded the second ('Spearhead') division of the Irish army which was deployed in the area north of the river Boyne. He was mercurial, controversial and given to intriguing.

Maffey.   Sir John Maffey (Lord Rugby; 1894-1969). United Kingdom representative to Eire, 1939-49. An old colonial administrator, he was considerably less abrasive than Gray and his relations with de Valera were generally even-tempered. He did, however, vent his frustrations with the Taoiseach in private memoranda to London.

O'Donovan. Jim O'Donovan (1897-1980) was the chief Abwehr agent in Ireland. He had fought in the War of Independence and had taken the republican side in the Civil War. In 1941 he was arrested and interned for three years in the Curragh.

Thomsen. Henning Thomsen (d. 1975) was Hempel's second in command at the German legation in Dublin and was commonly regarded as a Nazi overseer. He maintained a close professional relationship with Hempel.

Veesenmayer. Edmund Veesenmayer (d. 1978) was one of the Nazi party's most accomplished *coup d'état* specialists and was specially selected by Ribbentrop to foment rebellion in Ireland. He had proved his ruthless efficiency in liquidating Jews in Hungary and Czechoslovakia, for which he was sentenced to seven years imprisonment by the Nuremburg tribunal. He constantly exaggerated the IRA's ability to precipitate a revolution in Ireland.

Walshe. Joe Walshe (1886-1956) was the Secretary of the Department of Foreign Affairs, 1922-46.

Warnock. William Warnock (b. 1911) ran the Irish legation in Berlin from the time of Bewley's dismissal until 1944. In his quiet way he complemented Hempel's work in Dublin in keeping Irish-German relations on an even keel during an extraordinarily difficult period.

Chronology

1927   • Fianna Fáil break with Sinn Féin, take their seats in the Dáil and, in Lemass's words, become 'a slightly constitutional party'.

1929-32   • Professor D. A. Binchy appointed first Minister for the Irish Free State in Berlin.

1932   • Fianna Fáil emerge as the largest party in the Dáil. Elected with support of IRA sympathisers, they took over government with the help of the Labour Party.
   • Binchy resigns as Minister in Berlin.

1933   • In a snap election, de Valera secures overall majority.
   • Hitler comes to power in Germany.
   • After a hiatus, Bewley succeeds Binchy in Berlin.

1936   • Abdication crisis in Britain.
   • De Valera introduces his External Relations Bill.
   • The king retained for certain functions in external affairs: the Commonwealth link remains.
   • Civil war in Spain. De Valera supports non-intervention. Blueshirt leader General O'Duffy recruits a so-called Irish brigade to fight for Franco.

1937   • Hempel, through the king, accredited Envoy Extraordinary and Minister Plenipotentiary in Dublin for the Third Reich. He acts as official observer and generally speaking, intelligence agent.
   • New constitution approved by Dáil Éireann and endorsed by plebiscite.

1938   • Ports handed back: Irish neutrality now possible.

1939   • *January:* IRA bombing campaign begins in Britain.
   • *February:* Abwehr agent Oskar K. Pfaus makes

contact in Dublin with IRA. Sean Russell selects
Jim O'Donovan for liaison with Abwehr.

- *June:* Offences against the State Bill becomes law
in Eire to prevent the IRA usurping the authority
of the state.
- *August:* De Valera finally sacks Bewley.
- *September:* Hitler invades Poland; Britain declares
war on Germany. Ireland opts for benevolent
neutrality and passes emergency legislation to
cope with the consequences. Reservists and Volunteer Force called out on permanent service.
Sir John Maffey appointed British Representative
to Eire.
- *December:* The Magazine Fort raid by the IRA.

1940
- *January:* Francis Stuart returns to Berlin.
- *February:* Abwehr agent Ernst Weber-Drohl landed
from submarine on south-east Irish coast.
- *March:* David Gray appointed American Minister
to Ireland.
Abwehr II select Dr Herman Goertz for Operation
Mainau mission to Ireland.
Dr Edmund Veesenmayer selected by Ribbentrop
to foment rebellion in Ireland.
- *May:* Goertz parachutes into Co. Meath.
De Valera condemns German invasion of Belgium
and Holland.
- *June:* The Stephen Hayes 'confessions'.
Ribbentrop spells out for de Valera the type of
compliant neutrality expected.
Two more agents, Simon and Preetz, landed in
Dublin from U boat.
Government declares that a state of emergency
exists. The Defence Forces Act amended to
authorise the enlistment of personnel for the dur-
ation of the Emergency.
- *July/August:* Three further agents landed on the
Cork coast and promptly arrested.
Frank Ryan handed over to Germans by Spanish
authorities. With Sean Russell he prepares for
intervention in Ireland concurrently with 'Oper-

ation *Grün*', a putative plan for German invasion. MacNeill intriguing with Goertz.

Germans sinking Irish ships and dropping bombs on Irish soil (Campile creamery).

Crisis point of German invasion threat to neutrality.

- *December:* In Irish eyes invasion imminent. On the ground not clear whether main threat is German or British at this particular point.

1941
- *March:* Schultz parachutes into Co. Wexford; quickly arrested.
- *May:* Dublin's North Strand bombed by Germans.
- *June:* With invasion of Russia, fears of German invasion of British Isles recedes.
- *July:* Another Abwehr agent, the Irishman Lenihan, parachutes into Co. Meath. Surrendered across the border to the British; released by them and disappears.
- *September:* Hempel's meeting with Goertz.
  Allied pressures to abandon neutrality mount.
- *November:* Goertz captured and interned. Allies mollified but aggrieved. Clissmann has meetings with Kerney.
- *December:* Churchill's telegraphic exhortation to de Valera that the historic moment to trade neutrality for Irish unity had now arrived. Rejected by de Valera.

1942
- Veesenmayer goes to see Kerney himself.
- Large scale Irish army manoeuvres; high point of combat readiness reached.
- Allied victories cause neutrals to review their positions.
- Loss of Irish ports felt in Battle of Atlantic.
- Hempel factor in failure of Dieppe raid.

1943
- Veesenmayer disillusioned with Kerney.
- *December:* Two more Abwehr parachutists, O'Reilly and Kenny, land in Co. Clare complete with transmitter sets.

1944
- De Valera rejects Gray's 'American Note' and subsequently wins general election.
- Hempel factor in Battle of Arnhem.

- De Valera intervenes with Hempel to save Rome being bombed.
- German defeat inevitable. Allies demand 'unconditional surrender'.

1945
- Hitler's death. De Valera expresses condolences; grants the Hempels asylum.
- Legation wound up and taken over by Gray.

1947
- De Valera at last accommodates Allies on repatriation of the agents. Goertz commits suicide.

Foreword

An Englishman of Irish descent reads John Duggan's account of his ancestral country's relations with his homeland's principal enemy during the crisis of the Second World War with fascination. The personal context is important here (the personal context, some Englishmen would wearily say, is always important where anything Irish is concerned). My maternal grandfather was born in Co. Limerick in 1882, came to England in 1900, and lived there until he died. He remained distinctively Irish all his life but settled happily to English ways and, in the end, preferred this side of the water to that. In politics he was a moderate nationalist, a Home Ruler and a Redmondite. On my father's side, the family had come a generation earlier, refugees from the famine. Their links with Co. Armagh had been lost, and all outward traces of their Irishness. Perhaps for that reason — American students of immigration are familiar with the pattern — my father was much more strongly nationalist than my grandfather, had sympathised with Sinn Féin as a young man, and had spent one of his leaves from the Western Front in Dublin, hobnobbing with people who had nothing but hard words for the British army. He saw no inconsistency, of course, in being simultaneously a fierce English patriot and ardent Irish nationalist; England, indeed, for him could do almost no wrong — except where Ireland was concerned.

Something of what both my grandfather and my father felt for their twin countries has come down to me. Certainly I understand that it is possible to see that England has rights and Ireland wrongs, and that the two may weigh equally on the same mind. I confess that they do on mine. But could Churchill understand that? Or de Valera? Could anyone as

Irish as de Valera grasp what command of the North Atlantic meant to a maritime people fighting 'freedom's battle' against a continental dictator? Could anyone as English as Churchill being to hear how flawed the word 'freedom' sounded on the tongue of a British prime minister to Irish ears? That, in essence, is the theme of John Duggan's fascinating and original book. It is the story of how de Valera resolved to make and keep Ireland neutral during the Second World War, and how he succeeded in doing so, in the face of British efforts to win from her facilities to wage the Atlantic war and German efforts to subvert her nationalism for Nazi purposes.

The principal source for the author's investigations have been the official reports of the German Ambassador to Dublin, Eduard Hempel, which have never previously been used. They show us a sorely troubled man at work. For poor Hempel — and John Duggan sympathises with him tenderly — was a man in the middle, and with a vengeance. Indeed, his lot would have less unenviable if he had been grist between millstones. But he had nothing as solid against which to push. True, the word from Berlin was harsh and uncompromising. Thence Ribbentrop and his Irish 'specialist', Veesenmayer, who had all the subtlety for which Ribbentrop's regional experts were noted, demanded crude results — particularly opportunities for German agents to operate from Irish soil against England. The message from Dublin was altogether less easy to grasp. 'Hempel's problem with de Valera — one that he shared with many others — was that of trying to decipher the Taoiseach's ambiguous and delphic utterances. De Valera's was a mind of exceptional subtlety and his words could never be taken at their face value. The major interest centred on the tension which Hempel, mesmerised on occasion by de Valera, experienced between the two requirements of his job. He was the principal means of inter-governmental communication at a time when other sources of communication were restricted and yet the need for communication was great . . . [Yet] like all diplomats, he was also a source of intelligence for his own government.'

Frankly, Hempel was no good at the intelligence side, because he quite rightly thought the aggressive espionage and subversion which Berlin wanted him to foster no part of an ambassador's duties. But he was not really very much better at telling Berlin what was most currently in de Valera's mind, because he very often could not puzzle his way through the labyrinth. Like de Gaulle, with whom he did not merely share great height and a particular and fierce physical courage, de Valera had the gift of saying one thing which did not simply mean another, but meant different things to different people, sometimes several different things at once.

It was a trait that drove Churchill — who said of de Gaulle that the heaviest cross he had to bear during the war was the Cross of Lorraine — almost to distraction. Nothing perhaps better sums up the absolute incompatibility of his and de Valera's temperaments than the telegram launched from London to Dublin on the day after Pearl Harbor: 'Now is your chance. Now or never. "A Nation once again". Am ready to meet you at any time.' De Valera rightly construed this wild message to be a demand for the one thing Churchill wanted from Ireland at that stage of the war — an end to her neutrality — in exchange for the one thing he calculated might bring it about: unification. De Valera appears to have been struck almost dumb by the sensationalism of the approach, so contrary to every one of his political instincts. He returned a simple refusal, no doubt with the thought that Churchill must have understood the North as little as he did the South if he believed he could railroad the pair of them simultaneously.

De Valera's policy, in a sense, was to be railroaded by no one. He was determined to maintain Irish neutrality because he was an Irish patriot first and foremost. Yet, as John Duggan admirably succeeds in demonstrating, his Irish patriotism had an English dimension. He believed that neutrality was right for Ireland, but he also believed that Irish neutrality was the best Irish policy for England. He had, as the author puts it time and again, 'a consideration for England', not always best served by giving the English what they thought they wanted.

What they really want of Ireland, and what the Irish want of them, not even those who have both countries in their bones can really understand. But we can all think and talk and read and hope and pray, and books like John Duggan's will help us on the way. My feeling for both countries has been amplified by reading it.

John Keegan

Introduction

In the Second World War Eire remained neutral. It did not claim its policy to be one of principled neutrality.

For historical reasons British influences and interests in Ireland were pervasive and impossible to uproot. It was difficult therefore for Eire to implement a policy of perfect absolute neutrality. Unlike Switzerland, she was not neutralised by special treaties. Furthermore, consideration for Britain's position had, inescapably, to be the other side of the coin of Irish-German relations. This was particularly the case when Britain's adversary was as ruthless and implacable as the Third Reich. For Ireland, the emotive term 'mainland', implying linkage of some description, did not apply to a fragmented Europe, no matter how far the legends of the Wild Geese were stretched. But historical justification could be invoked for applying it to Britain.

Geography had ordained that Britain and Ireland were close neighbours: history saw to it that they did not become loving ones. In the 1720s, Swift railed at British economic exploitation of Ireland: what he was really concerned about was the constitutional relationship between Ireland and Great Britain. Two centuries later, the same relationship vexed Eamon de Valera. The inheritor of the separatist tradition, he regarded neutrality as a prime factor in that relationship. Neutrality had become interwoven with traditional Irish nationalism.

He took pains, however, to show consideration for the British position: the German position did not arise initially. In 1922 he was concerned that his alternative to the Anglo-Irish Treaty — Document No. 2 — would look as like the

Treaty document as possible: the British, he felt, would not go to war over the slight difference between them. In the event the British did not have to go to war over them; the Irish fought a civil war instead.

De Valera had been ready to grant Northern Ireland every right it wished for, short of sovereignty. Delusional myths are at the heart of concepts of sovereignty. De Valera never fully appreciated how crucial the *unequivocal* link with the Crown was to the Ulster Protestants. Tenuous links were not enough, and de Valera's rickety device of external association was regarded as an affront, a threat to their British identity: their heritage. The Taoiseach's tireless constitutional juggling left them cold. They were convinced that it was all a confidence trick to undo them: a cosmetic exercise to throw dust in their eyes. It hardened their siege mentality. They had no trust in de Valera, although as far back as 1921 he had revised his ideas about them from expulsion or coercion to assimilation, seeking to accommodate them within a wide variety of options. But they had demonised him and his 'Fenians' and they would give no consideration, good or bad, to the lengths to which he was prepared to go to appease them.

He had them in mind in his liberal approach to the 1936 British abdication crisis when he favoured the king's marriage taking place without abdication, but without Mrs Simpson becoming Queen. He then introduced the External Relations Act at once instead of waiting for the completion of the new constitution which he had in hand. This Act, again with the Unionists in mind, retained the king in foreign affairs. His hope was that this recognition of the king would one day smooth the path towards the reunification of Ireland. The previous political unity of the island had been under the crown.

While conciliatory to the Unionists, de Valera tantalised the British Foreign Office by dragging his feet in introducing the External Relations Bill after the abdication. A lapse of time between the British and Irish Acts would have left an interval during which the Germanophile Edward VIII would still be king in Ireland but not in the UK.

The Treaty ports were handed back in 1938 on the understanding that, in time of war, the Irish attitude to Great

Britain would be one of friendly neutrality. In international law the necessary attitude of impartiality was not incompatible with sympathy for one belligerent and antipathy towards the other, so long as these feelings did not find expression in actions violating impartiality. Public opinion and the press of a neutral state could show sympathy to one party or another without thereby violating neutrality. There was a loophole in the law here, a vent for letting off steam, but de Valera stood this aspect of international law on its head: his anti-partition rhetoric was anti-British but his actions continued to show a certain consideration for Britain.

Friendly neutrality in an absolute sense is a contradiction in terms. The added paradox was that major trouble for de Valera arose from the party he was being friendly to in deed if not in word, and the implementation of his version of neutrality was to be severely tested in that quarter.

Subconsciously there was a general impression that neutrality would be guaranteed by British naval supremacy in the Atlantic. After the victories in the Great War that supremacy was taken for granted. Things changed dramatically in June 1940 after the fall of France. Reeling Britain was now in mortal danger, with her shipping routes south of Ireland more exposed to German surface submarine and air attacks. It was not until September 1944, when the Americans liberated the French ports in Normandy, that the Allies were able to resume the use of those traditional southern routes. They had to rely during that life-or-death interim on the remaining route around the north coast. They had been able to keep that lifeline open only because they had retained a hold on Northern Ireland and Iceland. The temptation to secure the southern Irish ports had an understandable but simplistic appeal in some British appreciations of that situation.

After the ports' settlement, the British still hoped to promote the closest consultation with Ireland on defence matters. But for de Valera the fact was that Ireland could now make her own decisions regarding peace and war and he recognised that such a course could not possibly please everyone. Since national interest had to remain paramount it was necessary to take account of the British position and point of view. He realised that geographically, commercially, and socially the destinies of the two islands were in many ways inseparable. He did not see his consideration as being incompatible with the maintenance of a neutrality in the event of war; nor, in his view, did it affect Ireland's fundamental right to control her own territory. It was clear to him, however, that Irish territory could in no guise be used as a base or as an instrument for action detrimental to British interests. There was a realisation that the United Kingdom and Eire were bound by their common strategic and economic necessities. He was statesman enough in 1939 to see what the realities were and to navigate the ship of state accordingly. Both Britain and Germany contributed to making it a perilous voyage.

Officially, Britain took an unsympathetic view of de Valera's efforts: they tended wilfully to misunderstand and misrepresent. The Third Reich's ambiguous attitude was more difficult to discern. Officially they received full and regular reports from their representative in Dublin. They did not always heed them. They were sometimes, to the chagrin of their official representative, Hempel, influenced by inconsistent information from unofficial sources. Furthermore, they continued to harbour a sneaking regard for England. Their Dublin representative was accredited through Britain.

Herr Dr Eduard Hempel was the German Minister in Ireland from 1937 to 1945. He was a career diplomat. His apologists insist that he was never a Nazi. This is an eccentric point of view: pre-war Germany as a whole was at best ambivalent towards the Nazis. The fact remains that Hempel was the official representative of Hitler's Third Reich, although the Nazi habit of minimum disclosure to diplomats of the old school modified that status to some degree. Hempel had to contend quickly with radically different accounts of de Valera's character. To his Civil War adversaries the Taoiseach was Mephistopheles incarnate. To his own following he was a mystic and messiah. His consideration for Britain was not enough for pro-British elements but it was too much for extreme republicans and more enigmatic diehard characters like Charles Bewley, former Irish Minister in Berlin. Bewley's main concern was that any consideration that was going should be given to the Third Reich.

De Valera's own ambiguous attitude contributed at times

to the rise of conflicting expectations. He had let it be known that the position of the Sudeten Germans was such that he felt that there was some justification in Hitler's claims to the territory. He claimed to see parallels between the Sudetenland and Northern Ireland. He also recognised that the short-sighted Treaty of Versailles had created problems. But at that point, any identity of views between de Valera and Hitler ended.

Berlin's opinions of de Valera were based on superficial out-dated stereotypes. Ireland in any case was peripheral to the Führer's expansionist plans. It would be readily dispensed with if an accommodation with Britain were attainable. Hitler needed quick, cheap conquests. Britain and France were his main obstacle. France, the more hated of these two enemies, could be dealt with; but the British cousins presented a more elusive problem. Hitler was a great admirer of the British Empire. He attributed British successes to their Germanic racial strains, relating them to his old master race theories.

Ideally, especially with a view to making use of their naval expertise, it would be better, in Hitler's opinion, to have Britain harnessed in partnership to German dreams and aspirations. At one stage the Führer was convinced of British non-participation in the looming war. The Irish Department of External Affairs never doubted that Hitler would happily compromise Irish independence in pursuit of a patched-up peace with Great Britain. When Hess (who was later said not to be insane but suffering from hysterical amnesia) landed in Scotland on 10 May 1941, in a wild effort to make peace with England, he is said to have stressed that the Führer entertained no designs against the British. Questioned about Ireland, he retorted that in all his conversations with the Führer the subject of Ireland only cropped up incidentally. He said that as Ireland had done nothing for Germany, Hitler would not concern himself in Anglo-Irish relations. Ireland was part of the United Kingdom as far as Germany was concerned: and Germany was willing to have peace with Britain. The difficulty of reconciling the wishes of Northern and Southern Ireland was not a matter that would bother them greatly. They would, however, be bound to be concerned with any undue consideration for Britain by de Valera in war-time. That was a different matter.

If Britain continued to refuse to co-operate, Hitler was of the opinion that their Empire was not invincible. This is where Ireland and Hempel and de Valera came in. Hempel cited Ireland's struggle for independence; constitutional disputes with India; Japan's erosion of the British position in the Far East; Italian infringement of British interests in the Mediterranean and Africa; and upheavals in the Moslem world as significant pointers to the vulnerability of the Empire. It fell to Hempel to handle the problem of how best to make use of Ireland's neutrality in pursuit of German war aims.

Initially Irish postures on neutrality, with reservations, were tolerable to the Germans as well as to the British: both hoped to make that policy work to their own advantage. It was in fact precast to work to Britain's advantage. That is how de Valera's certain consideration translated. The Third Reich never wholly grasped the full extent of their handicap, in spite of Hempel's painstaking portrayals. They never got the full picture; neither did the Irish people; neither did the British beneficiaries. Diplomacy does not flower under arc-lights.

A retrospective focus on Hempel's reports leaves intriguing characters like Bewley and Veesenmayer in the shadows. Bewley's activities in Italy during the period require major examination while Veesenmayer's relations with Leopold Kerney, the Irish Minister in Spain, merits a separate sensitive study.

Kerney's predicament carries many lessons for diplomats of emerging states. His problem was in keeping abreast, while abroad, of the subtleties of de Valera's neutrality. In contrast to Bewley, he seemed to have regarded the Taoiseach's nationalism as cast irrevocably in traditional anti-British moulds, unaffected by the ebb and flow on the battlefields.

On the other hand, Hempel's problem with de Valera — one that he shared with many others — was that of trying to decipher the Taoiseach's ambiguous and delphic utterances. De Valera's was a mind of exceptional subtlety and his words could never be taken at face value. The major interest is centred on the tension which Hempel, mesmerised on occasion by de Valera, experienced because of a conflict between the two requirements of his job. He was the principal means of inter-governmental communication at a time when other sources of communication were restricted and yet the need for communication was great. Therefore, he had to establish personal credibility with both governments, keep official channels open and recognise and avoid misunderstandings, all within the constraints of established diplomatic conventions. Like all diplomats, he was also a source of intelligence for his own government. In part this function was met by establishing official sources and by generally processing and transmitting information via normal diplomatic channels. However, because non-governmental groups were significant in Ireland and because policy-making in Nazi Germany was in such a state of confusion, he gravitated into the grey fringe areas of spying and subversion.

Hempel had neither the training nor the inclination to indulge in such cloak-and-dagger activities. His job was to keep Ireland out of the war, a task which suited his character and a role which he was grateful to play in times of hate and aggression. His punctilious attention to protocol was, in his eyes, nothing more than the employment of the essential tool of diplomacy.

The diplomat's dilemma was heightened by trying to reconcile Berlin's idea of de Valera, as a revolutionary biding his time to settle old scores with Britain, with his own increasing but inconstant awareness of the Taoiseach as an ardent constitutionalist, whose greatest achievements were to be in the fields of incremental constitutional innovation and foreign policy. De Valera was a constitutionalist almost by stealth and he shrouded in secrecy and republican rhetoric each *demarche*. Hempel could not always reconcile his rhetoric with his actions.

One way in which the Envoy sought to resolve the tensions in this conflict was to try to achieve what appeared to be an impossible objectivity in his reporting, to try to see all sides of the question. This would have been his normal approach, whereas Nazi officials reported what they reckoned their masters in Berlin wanted to hear. Hempel's ambidextrous but basically honest style of reporting exasperated, and to some extent, frustrated officials in Berlin, particularly Ribbentrop, Veesenmayer and Haller.

Recollecting these experiences many years later, Frau Hempel was quick to point out that it did not frustrate the professional diplomats like Weizsächer and Woermann. The reporting, she held, achieved the desired result: it aided the accomplishment of the mission of keeping Ireland neutral, or at any rate out of the close collaborative embraces of the Allies. She was contemptuous of Veesenmayer's and Haller's derogatory remarks about her husband.

In the opinion of the Abwehr officer Haller, Hempel was nothing more or less than a typical arid bureaucrat, without initiative or enterprise. But this very dryness was, ironically, an essential element in making the implementation of de Valera's neutrality policy credible and possible. The German representative's pedantry, his penchant for protocol, conventional correctness, and keeping himself covered were crucial factors in enabling de Valera successfully to steer a course of pursuing a policy of neutrality with a certain consideration for a disgruntled Britain and a lesser one for Germany.

Relations with Germany were aggravated by human factors. Unless de Valera and Hempel had an implicit understanding it is doubtful if this adulterated Irish neutrality could have been so successful. At its conception both men had expressed doubts about its viability. What price a policy of neutrality that was not merely pacifist at heart, but actually professed its readiness to take on any would-be aggressor on a first-come, first-served basis! British and German military planners counted the cost of invading Ireland: they both found that the price in terms of men and materials was too high. In the German case control of the sea, the achievement of air superiority, time and space difficulties for reinforcements: all complicated the position. Yet these impediments did not deter them from irresponsibly dropping agents into Ireland with subversive missions which would have undermined neutrality. These agents bedevilled Irish-German relations and were a constant source of harassment to Hempel and de Valera, who also had his hands full with the British.

In layman's language, without pretending omniscience in the business of war, it was clear to de Valera that, in the final analysis, Irish neutrality was also the best thing for Britain. It was politically impossible at home for him to use plain words to spell out that military reality. In Britain a few of the more thoughtful politicians agreed. In 1938 the professional soldier-ly appreciation of the British chiefs of staff effectively coin-cided with that assessment, although the grim statistics of the Battle of the Atlantic later provided food for second thoughts.

The bulk of British politicians had no need for any second thoughts. Inflamed by Churchill, they simply saw Irish neutrality in black and white terms. Jingoism obscured any deeper analysis. Unionist politicians, predictably, compul-sorily, made capital and mischief out of the paradoxes.

It is necessary therefore to note the background of British policy towards Ireland, and in particular Churchill's public and private representation of his own aims. These outbursts on the 'so-called neutrality of so-called Eire' coloured the Third Reich's perception of de Valera's performance.

The nature of German diplomacy is looked at through the eyes of its officials, mainly Hempel's, in the context of the Third Reich's responses towards a country with a com-plex and by no means unified attitude to the war. As the war progressed, de Valera's opinion hardened that in a future war neutrality for a small strategically located island could not work.

His great achievement was to make it work during a war which originated as a European civil war waged to destroy Hitlerism and to liberate the continent. Like every other responsible statesman he was motivated fundamentally and unashamedly by a concern to protect the national self-interest, while openly acknowledging a certain consider-ation for Britain. The Third Reich, constrained by its cap-abilities, found de Valera's presentation of neutrality toler-able for most of the time. He managed to reconcile pragmatism with principle and to square what, in balance, were pro-Allied practices with the popular perception of neutrality as a national stand, the ultimate proclamation of independence. Moreover, he could present himself to Fianna Fáil ard-fheiseanna (party conferences) as the man who was twisting the British Lion's tail.

To appease British fears, to allay German suspicions and to keep down internal trouble meant that de Valera had to tread warily. Hempel was a help to him in maintaining his precarious balance; Maffey in general was supportive; but Gray, the petulant American Minister, was unhelpful. Through it all de Valera managed to give the Irish people the only type of neutrality that was attainable, the type of neutrality that suited them. It was no mean feat. No one else could have done it. The neutrality policy which, unabashed, he labelled *'ad hoc'* is now enshrined as traditional. Such rigidity would have been inimical to his essentially pragmatic programme for survival, carried through in the teeth of enemies of all kinds, foreign and domestic.

ONE

Backgrounds

The personality and concepts of Eamon de Valera strongly influenced the pattern of events in Ireland from 1916 to 1937, the year of the arrival in Dublin of Herr Eduard Hempel as the diplomatic representative of Adolf Hitler's Third Reich. By 1927 he had succeeded in persuading himself and the party he had founded — Fianna Fáil (the Republican Party) — to take their seats in the Dáil. Although this involved a break between him and the Sinn Féin Party of Miss Mary MacSwiney, it did not entail a complete severance with the IRA, who shared objectives, idealism, sympathies and a common social-political background with Fianna Fáil. Fianna Fáil was republicanism by parliamentary means. Sean Lemass, de Valera's second in command, defined Fianna Fáil as a slightly constitutional party. Nevertheless, its entry into Leinster House was regarded as a great turning point in the history of parliamentary government in Ireland: it consolidated Irish political democracy.

By 1932 the Cumann na nGaedheal government had become stubbornly and almost obsessively a law and order government. There was, therefore, substantial IRA backing for de Valera to put Cosgrave out. Soon afterwards Fianna Fáil reached a position of strength from which they were no longer dependent to the same extent on IRA support. The focus of their attack on the Cumann na nGaedheal government under its leader W. T. Cosgrave had been the question of the oath of allegiance — an oath which Dáil deputies were then required to take to the British king. In office the Fianna Fáil government abrogated that parliamentary oath; in addition, the right of appeal to the judicial committee of the British privy council was abolished and Irish citizens ceased to be regarded in Irish law as British subjects (Irish Nationality and Citizenship Act 1935). Advantage was taken of the abdication crisis in Britain in 1936 to substitute de Valera's concept of external association for membership of the Commonwealth. An 'economic war' had been fought with Britain and the opportunity used to pursue a policy of economic self-sufficiency. By 1937 a draft constitution had been prepared which deleted reference to the crown in internal Irish politics and laid *de jure* claim to the territory of Northern Ireland.

In Germany in the corresponding period another charismatic leader, Adolf Hitler, was leaving an even larger mark on events. A major difference between Germany and Ireland was that while Hitler operated a rigged dictatorship, de Valera's activities and ambitions were tempered by the democratic processes of open government. A series of circumstances had combined in Germany to create a climate from which Hitler's National Socialists emerged as a strong party, filling the vacuum left when the world economic crisis destroyed the Weimar Republic. The 'Versailles Humiliation' was also remembered with bitterness. Hitler restored feelings of national pride. He articulated frustrations felt by all classes of society. The pull of the party was felt by workers, middle class and members of the nobility alike. He prescribed remedies that satisfied yearnings for order. Anti-semitism and other over-simplifications were accepted as part and parcel of the panacea. Atrocities were camouflaged. Under the swastika a career was promised for everyone; for all Germans, that is. Dr Hans Frank told a convention of lawyers in 1936 that there was in Germany only one authority, and that was the authority of the Führer. By 1937 Hitler had used that authority to eliminate opposition, to regiment the state and to repress individual freedom. At home he cloaked this by abolishing unemployment and by getting the wheels of industry and commerce turning again. Abroad he was content, for the time being, to leave the surface, day-to-day running of foreign policy in the hands of the professional diplomats.

But well before Hitler came to power — from the foundation of the Free State in fact — the Irish found difficulty in dealing with German career diplomats, who were labouring under a sort of superiority complex. Some of the difficulties had their roots in the well known deference paid by German Foreign Ministry officials to their British counterparts in the Foreign Office, a deference traceable back to the days of Victoria and Albert and the then emerging German Foreign Service which looked up to the British for example. It was a deference that paradoxically persisted even in wartime and British hauteur to the fledgling Free State parvenu may have influenced German attitudes.

Until 1929 the Irish Free State, as a member of the British Commonwealth of Nations, was represented in Berlin by the British ambassador. It was useful for the new state to avail of an established experienced service. In a draft of a commercial convention between the Irish Free State and Germany (1926) the preamble named as their respective plenipotentiaries:

> His Majesty, the King of the United Kingdom of Great Britain and Ireland and of the British Dominions beyond the seas, Emperor of India
>
> AND
>
> The President of the German Reich

The correspondence of the time conveys the tone and tenor of the negotiations which culminated in the appointment in 1929 of Professor D. A. Binchy as Irish Minister to Germany in Berlin.[1] The British insisted that he be designated as 'Minister for the Irish Free State' and not as 'Irish Minister'. Binchy resigned in 1932 after two and a half years of office, preferring to return to the academic world. He subsequently wrote an article on Hitler[2] that put him permanently in the black books with the Nazis. It was a prophetic analysis of the phenomenon of Hitler and demonstrated that the Irish government had a well-informed and perceptive Minister in Berlin between 1929 and 1932. It illustrated that, unlike his controversial successor, Bewley, one senior[3] Irish Minister at least had few illusions about Hitler. Another penetrating article on Hindenburg[4] analysed the pathos of the very old and very tired venerable field marshal playing into Hitler's hands. Hitler accepted all the conditions and broke them all

in turn. Binchy's caustic conclusion was that the president
had not read *Mein Kampf.*

The appointment of an Irish Minister did not abate German
high handed attitudes. British insistence on trimming the title
of the appointment encouraged their boorish behaviour. Inflexible attitudes continued to be struck in exploring the
possibilities of establishing an export trade with Ireland in
live cattle and sheep, pigs, bacon and eggs, even though the
balance of trade was very much in Germany's favour. Their
line was that, as far as they were concerned, the Irish Free
State had only dominion status and should therefore get only
the same treatment as New Zealand. Moreover, Danish opinion
had to be taken into account. In 1932 Dieckhoff put it
specifically: 'nothing was to be done with regard to the Irish
Free State that might be prejudicial to the interests of German
relations with England'. They continued to talk down to
Leo T. McCauley, the acting representative for a year and a
half following Binchy's resignation.[5]

German-Irish trade relations continued to be influenced by
relations with England and the gold standard devaluation of
the pound. By 1935, Anglo-Irish trade relations were im-
proving, following a thaw in the economic war. A German
overseas organisation — in effect the foreign organisation of
the Nazi party — known as the *Auslandsorganisation,*[6] reacted
and addressed itself to promoting trade in Ireland to
Germany's advantage. There was much haggling over quotas,
however, and on 28 February 1936 the German Economic
Office in Dublin (W. Hahn of 69 Fitzwilliam Square) attributed the failure in economic negotiations to a recently concluded British-Irish trade treaty. De Valera had earlier declared
that his policy, directed towards freeing Ireland from economic domination by Britain, did not mean a complete severance in relations between the two states.

Ireland remained dependent on Britain and exports to
Germany continued to be difficult. By May 1937 the Irish
cabinet were still giving consideration to the problems of
exporting cattle to Germany and agreeing that in the event
of the Minister for Agriculture being unable to secure better
terms he might accept prices which might not, as far as could
be foreseen, cover the costs of the shipments which he would

be required under the contract to export to Germany. Germany's efforts in the first years of Nazism to achieve a good understanding with England were not matched by corresponding efforts to facilitate Ireland.

The Führer's 'Grand Design' may have been another explanation for a continuation of this dismissive German policy towards Ireland. Hitler had been able to get Germany's industry moving again because he had it geared towards the erection of a mighty military machine which would be used as an instrument to enable him to achieve his foreign policy goals. The Clausewitz theory of war as an extension of diplomacy by other means was being followed.

Hitler's *'Stufenplan'* was not a radically new departure. It merely gave a new lease of life to deep-rooted German myths and aspirations. Traditional territorial demands were given a new dimension in the expansionist strategy of the Third Reich. This plan aimed firstly to restore to her prewar eminence Germany's status as a great power; then to achieve pre-eminence in Western Europe prior to subjugating the Soviet Union in order to secure continental hegemony and *Lebensraum* in the East; and finally Hitler would lead this 'Greater German Reich of the German Nation' to overseas global expansion. The essence of Hitler's megalomaniac conceptions could have been deduced from *Mein Kampf* and the *Second Book* (1928).

There is no specific reference to Ireland in *Mein Kampf* though Hitler had a knowledge of relations between Great Britain and Ireland. He had pinned his hopes on an alliance with Britain for his projects and particularly so on Neville Chamberlain who in May 1937 had succeeded Stanley Baldwin as Prime Minister. Chamberlain's obsessive preoccupation was with the preservation of the British Empire: the interest of peoples in Central Europe took second place to these attentions. In this period of wooing England, Berlin looked askance at Irish attitudes in the economic war. But what the Germans did not notice was that by May 1936 the new British Dominions Secretary, Malcolm MacDonald, had renewed attempts to reach an understanding with the Irish in security, defence, trade, and industry.

Contemporary political controversy in Ireland had produced a foreign policy that tended towards confrontation with Britain; the very opposite of early Nazi aspirations and attempts to seek an alliance and an accommodation with the British Empire. In 1932 de Valera orated:

> What now of the treaty imposed under threat 'of immediate and terrible war'? What about the governor-general residing in the old viceregal lodge and symbolising the presence of the crown in the constitution? What about Irish neutrality with the Treaty ports in British hands? What about the right of secession itself?

The right of secession and neutrality had been preoccupations of de Valera for a long time, going back to 1917 at least and linked with Casement's case for guaranteed neutrality. In an interview given to the *Westminster Gazette* in February 1920 he had suggested the example of the 1901 Treaty between the United States and Cuba to Britain as a means of safeguarding herself against foreign attack. He suggested that a British declaration of the Monroe Doctrine for the two neighbouring islands would produce wholehearted co-operation by the Irish side: they would co-operate 'with their whole soul', he said dramatically.[7]

In 1927 he had stated that in the event of war the right of maintaining Irish neutrality should be insisted on. Neutrality was an ongoing question preoccupying politicians' minds. It had yet to be thought through. It was a hypothetical question while the Treaty ports were in British hands. The German representative for Ireland, von Dehn-Schmidt, reported in 1927 that in view of her geographical situation he doubted Ireland's ability to remain neutral in the event of Britain becoming involved in a war. He also referred to the Dáil debates of 16 February 1927 where the question of co-operation between the British and Irish forces in the event of an attack by a third party was considered. He quoted the then Minister for Defence, Desmond FitzGerald, as saying that the two armies must co-operate and that it was out of the question that the Irish army would ever become involved in combat with Great Britain.

De Valera's rise to power caused anxiety in British official circles, for such assurances as given by FitzGerald now seemed worthless. In 1932 J. H. Thomas, Secretary of State for Dominion Affairs, stated in Ottawa that their hopes lay in the newly formed opposition — the Army Comrades Association — triumphing in a civil war in Ireland so that then Britain would be dealing with a different government. M16 had reported that Fianna Fáil's prospects were not good. On 6 June 1932, when Thomas arrived in Dublin, he was rather ominously accompanied by Lord Hailsham, the Secretary of State for War. The subjects under dispute were the oath of allegiance; land annuity payments; partition; British occupation of the three Treaty ports, and finance in general. The British considered financial reprisals. Relations deteriorated and led to the 'economic war'. The passage of routine secret information between the Foreign Office and Dublin was restricted and certain categories of information were withheld.

By 1936, however, the clumsy German efforts to seek a British accommodation, as spearheaded by Ribbentrop — the German Ambassador to London from 1936 to 1938 — revealed gaps that were to prove unbridgeable. On the other hand, the pressures of the international situation, geographical contiguity and historical links moved Anglo-Irish relations, under the guiding hand of Malcolm MacDonald, towards a mutual recognition of the need for a *modus vivendi*. These drifts — they can hardly be more definitively described — inevitably coloured policies which were in the process of evolution. Nevertheless, on 24 March 1936 a note by the British Secretary of State on a conversation with de Valera remarked: 'Naturally he has keen sympathy with Germany in her struggle to establish equality with other nations.' MacDonald felt that de Valera had been greatly comforted by the British failure to react to Hitler's reoccupation of the Rhineland in 1936 and felt that it could have given him encouragement to think that he too could face the British with a *fait accompli* on the ports and partition.

That reaction, as outlined by MacDonald, did not imply that there was universal Irish approbation for German foreign policy. The internal policy of the Nazis towards the Jews — denying them office and citizenship — did not provoke noticeable Irish public reaction: Ireland after all, in spite of de Valera's care to foster relations with the non-Catholic section of the population, did herself have occasional anti-Semitic outbursts; Limerick was a controversial case in point.[8] But Germany's anti-Catholicism was another matter.

It had been reported on 14 January 1934 that the Gospel of St John had been revised in Germany to make it more acceptable to the National Socialists. It was anti-Jewish in tone and contained no Hebrew words. The author (Bishop Weidemann of Bremen) sought to modify Christian teaching to bring it into harmony with the Nazi world outlook based on 'blood and soil'. Care was taken to distinguish between the Jews and Jesus.

Mit brennender Sorge — with burning anxiety — Pope Pius XI opened his encyclical of 14 March 1937 on the condition of the Catholic Church in Germany. It condemned the persecution of the Church, the new neo-paganism and the campaign against denominational schools which had been guaranteed by the 1933 concordat. The failure of the concordat was attributed to 'machinations that from the beginning had no other aim than a war of extermination'. Tension between Germany and the Holy See had been heightened. The Archbishop of Chicago, Cardinal Mundelein, spoke out in support of the Vatican:

> Perhaps you will ask how it is that a nation of 60 million intelligent people will submit in fear and servitude to an alien, an Austrian paper hanger, and a poor one at that, and a few associates like Goebbels and Göring who dictate every move of the peoples' lives . . . American Catholics must fight back.

Irish-Americans constituted an influential section of the American Catholic population. The reactions of Irish public opinion were also reflected. The *Irish Independent* of 1 July 1937 sympathetically reported the strong protests by the Catholic Bishop of Berlin on behalf of the German episcopacy against 'the flood of filth' which had filled the German press in connection with the trials of priests on charges of immorality.

The *Irish Press* of 12 July gave coverage to Cardinal Pacelli's (later Pope Pius XII) comparison between Pope Pius XI's stricture on Nazi Germany and the manner in which St Ambrose imposed penance on the Emperor Theodosius.[9]

The *Irish Times* of 16 July commented that no folly seemed to be too extreme for the leaders of the Nazi party. The reference was to the arrest of Dr Otto Niemöller, pastor of the famous Protestant Church in Dahlen, one of Germany's popular U-Boat war heroes and an outspoken opponent of the Nazi campaign against the Christian Churches. He was lodged in Moabit prison, an institution that was remembered well by many Irish prisoners of war.[10]

Attitudes to the Christian Churches worked a fundamental divergence between the two regimes. The draft constitution in preparation in Ireland was acknowledged to be based on the papal encyclicals and had indeed gone so far as to accord recognition to the special position of the Catholic Church.[11] This is not to imply that there was no disagreement in Irish affairs: but, under the influence of de Valera's personality cult, dichotomy on expressed policy was not discernible to any great extent among members of the government.

The German legation sent a cutting from the *Irish Times* (31 July 1936) quoting 'The Three Voices', de Valera, Sean T. O'Kelly, and General Eoin O'Duffy on the subject of 'Britain in Time of War'. They were all seeking the ending of partition in varying tones of militancy. Koester, who signed the report, doubted the efficacy of these protestations. His opinion was that the retention of the ports and Northern Ireland would serve, initially at any rate, to secure Ireland for Britain in the event of war. He did not see any significant reaction from the British to the argument that in war Ireland would place facilities willingly at Britain's disposal on condition that her national aspirations were first fulfilled. Koester's finger was not on the quickening pulse of *rapprochement* between Britain and Ireland which was bringing the economic war to a close. Mutual self-interest was gradually impelling the British and Irish towards reconciling their differences. The British problem was how to deal with an Irish Republic outside the Commonwealth, assuming, that 'the 26 Counties' was what was meant by an Irish Republic.

The special act passed in December 1936 after the abdication of Edward VIII changed fundamentally the relations between the Free State and the Commonwealth. As a result of the new act the king no longer figured in the Free State constitution. The British chose to look on the brighter side of this and observe that for the first time in Irish history an English king had been recognised spontaneously by the people of southern Ireland. De Valera by his own free will had chosen to keep the Free State in the Commonwealth, albeit for external purposes only. The king would still have to accredit and receive diplomatic representatives to and from Ireland, including representatives from the Third Reich.

German reports from the Dublin legation did not reflect this trend. They indicated growing cleavages in Anglo-Irish relations. Their reports were based on Ireland's intention to remain neutral in the event of a European conflict (30 January 1936); Irish refusal to attend the coronation celebrations (1 August 1936); Ireland and the Oath of Allegiance (25 February 1937); de Valera's broadcast to Australia on Anglo-Irish relations and the wrong of partition (17 March 1937); and on de Valera's declaration regarding Ireland's non-participation in the Imperial Conference. The rhetoric misled the Germans.

It was against this background that the cabinet approved on 21 May 1937 the proposed appointment by the German government of Herr Eduard Hempel as Envoy Extraordinary and Minister Plenipotentiary of the Third Reich at Dublin; the Minister for External Affairs (de Valera himself) was authorised to advise the king accordingly. Hempel was to take over from the unattached legation counsellor, Schroetter, who had been acting temporarily as a chargé d'affaires since the death of the previous representative, von Kuhlmann.

There were a lot of loose ends for Hempel to tie up. The first German representative, von Dehn, had been maladroit. His mishandling of matters almost justified the snobbish sneer of his Foreign Ministry colleagues about his flawed pedigree. Like Ribbentrop's similar requisition, the 'von' prefix had been appropriated from a neighbour who had adopted him. His own name was Schmidt; his father was a veterinary surgeon. The old guard with Junker pretensions never let him forget where he came from. They would never call him 'von Dehn' but always referred derisively to him as 'Der Schmidt'.

He had been the German representative in Liverpool from where initially he also dealt with matters affecting the Free State. Reflecting that notorious obsequiousness of all Foreign Ministry grades to the British Foreign Office, he advised caution in dealing with the new Free State: he felt that they might be getting too big for their boots. This type of condescension evoked a favourable response from Robert Smylie, the editor of the *Irish Times*, who was pro-British and proud of it.

But not everyone got on as well with von Dehn as Smylie did. In 1928, when the Irish Minister for Defence asked him for a prototype German army helmet, he curtly turned down the request, citing prohibiting regulations. An order was subsequently placed in Vickers (London) for 5,000 of them. So another symptomatic anomaly was added to Anglo-Irish-German relations: the Irish army was equipped with German-style helmets, made in Britain! He was not very popular.

Nevertheless when the time came in 1929 to reciprocate Binchy's Berlin posting with the appointment of a German Minister in Ireland the Irish Minister for External Affairs, McGilligan,[12] would not hear of anyone else for the job but von Dehn. Irish officials in Berlin had been favourably impressed by a diplomat of the old school, a Catholic from Wurtenburg, Baron Ow Wachendorf. The Baron's talented wife also charmed all who met her. Soundings were made. But McGilligan insisted: it had to be von Dehn. Binchy dutifully informed the German Foreign Office accordingly and von Dehn became the first German Minister to Ireland.

The newly appointed Minister got on very well with the Cosgrave administration. Its pro-British mien appealed to him. He reacted differently to Fianna Fáil. They matched the original image of an upstart government which he had at the foundation of the Free State. His outspoken criticism of the change of government did not endear him to de Valera.

Tact and political perception were not von Dehn's strong points: the more perceptive saw through him. At a luncheon he was regaling Monsignor Boylan, the well known biblical scholar, about his visit to the Bishop of Köln. The conversation was in German and the Monsignor finally remarked that the way he was going von Dehn would end up a 'Roman' and then having judged a pause for von Dehn to preen himself, added with quite pricking mockery 'in the interests of the Reich of course'.

His 'Roman' friends unwittingly were a source of misfortune for him. Before leaving Dublin in 1934 to take up an appointment in Bucharest he paid a courtesy call on the Papal Nuncio and a chance photograph was taken of him kissing the Nuncio's ring. Adolf Mahr, the chief of the *Auslandsorganisation* in Dublin, saw to it that the photograph was reproduced in Jew-baiter Julius Streicher's paper *Stürmer*. When Hitler saw the photograph, he was furious. Von Dehn was summarily recalled from his post in Bucharest and instantly dismissed. Grovelling to a Papal Nuncio was considered to be conduct unbecoming a representative of the Third Reich. Frau Hempel, however, saw the point in the Reich's disciplinary action: it was not the done thing to kiss the ring, she held.

When he fell from grace the loyal Smylie visited him in Germany. He found the banished diplomat a broken man; a social outcast. Von Dehn later died unexpectedly in hospital following a minor operation.

His successor, von Kuhlmann, was also dogged by bad luck. He was seriously ill when he was appointed Minister in October 1934. To add to his troubles his mother died in a fire at his home in Brennanstown, Cabinteely. He himself died after a long illness in Wiesbaden in January 1937.

His reports had not brought much joy to Berlin. He had to report a rash of 'Down with Hitler' slogans and a parade of protesting women in Dublin carrying 'Free Thalman' placards. The Irish government had expressed regret for these incidents. During von Kuhlmann's time in Dublin the Nazi regime was virulently but unsurprisingly criticised in Ireland by the left-wing press. *The Worker* reported that Rudolf Claus, the working-class leader and communist deputy, was 'beheaded by the Nazi butchers'. The *Irish Workers Voice* attacked also:

> The Nazis are keeping up their propaganda in Dublin. Hardly a week goes by now without some speech-making or social function to attract the serried ranks of 'seoininism'.[13] They

took over the Metropole last week for another dance graced by von Kuhlmann, Sean MacEntee and Alfie.[14] And the Tricolour and the Swastika of the fascist murder gang were draped in unholy matrimony in the ballroom. But where oh where were the 'young men' of the CYMS[15] that they made no protest here against the dictatorship that had outlawed all religious association and is arresting clergymen of every denomination.

In the same issue Sean Nolan accused the German colony in Dublin[16] of being the mouthpiece of propaganda for Hitler's fascism and castigated the *Independent* for vilifying the 'workers' Russia . . . the country of real freedom', while remaining silent on Hitler's jailing of priests and boosting 'Mussolini's war of plunder in Abyssinia'.

During von Kuhlmann's sick leave in Germany he was represented by Schroetter, who also was unfortunate and who, like von Dehn, was also undermined by the *Auslandsorganisation*. Schroetter called himself a chargés d'affaires and the newspaper reports referred to him as such. The Foreign Ministry corrected that and described him as an 'unattached legation counsellor charged with temporary representation of the legation'.

Schroetter's undoing was an index of the growing power of the *Auslandsorganisation*. Masterminded in Berlin by its ambitious intriguing chief, Bohle, they were now attempting to make policy of their own. Toadying to this trend, Adolf Mahr reported adversely on Schroetter as he had done on von Dehn. There were no specific accusations but Schroetter did have a Greek wife and this undoubtedly offended the Nazi racial purists. Schroetter had reported in a hand-washing detached manner the Irish government's misgivings about suspected espionage activities of a German national residing in Ireland who was head of the German Academic Exchange Service, Helmut Clissmann. When the head of the *Auslandsorganisation* in London coldly thanked Schroetter for this report, he advised him to be more benevolently disposed, pointing out Clissmann's adroitness and reliability in carrying out his mission. The DA (*Gesellschaft der Berliner Freunde der Deutschen Akademie*) chimed in with a mention of the need to protect Clissmann from intrigues. The upshot of the affair left the official finger pointing at Schroetter. It was another scalp for the *Auslandsorganisation*.

An intriguing exercise in duplicity followed. Having sown the seeds for Schroetter's downfall, Mahr then proceeded to compliment him personally, saying that it was a shame that he had to go. For this double-dealing Mahr received a peremptory rebuke from an aggrieved Gauleiter Bohle in Berlin: it was, after all, Mahr who had prompted him to remove Schroetter![17] Mahr was ordered to have no further correspondence whatsoever with the Legation.

This clipping of the *Auslandsorganisation*'s wings coincided with Hempel's arrival in Dublin. As he must have been cleared by them on party loyalty grounds in order to get the appointment in the first place, it is unlikely that the new German Minister would have been unduly apprehensive or that he would be conscious of the *Auslandsorganisation*'s machinations in undermining von Dehn and Schroetter. He had nothing to fear from them, apparently, though he knew he would have to watch his step and be wary of party invigilation.

There had been a rumour that de Valera had informed German sources that the Irish government would not favour the appointment of a Nazi as German Minister in Ireland. It was alleged that when Hempel arrived in Dun Laoghaire where he was met by the members of the Legation he discovered that he was the only non-party man among them. This gossip had it that, although a patriotic German, he was never a Nazi and that his diplomatic training before the advent of Hitler ensured that he would follow normal diplomatic procedure in loyally serving his government, but would do so free from Nazism.

There was no indication as to how this exercise in ambivalence was to be achieved. It does not answer the question of how he could have satisfied the *Auslandsorganisation* with proofs of his proper National Socialist attitudes before being appointed. It was whispered that family connections may have had an influence in procuring the Dublin post for Hempel. There does not seem to have been any substance in this; rumours that Frau Hempel's brother held the Nazi

Blut Orden decoration are vehemently contradicted by her; the inference had been that this connection could have influenced the venal von Neurath to recommend the appointment.

Frau Hempel also felt that it was unfair to label von Neurath 'venal': 'weak' maybe, she conceded; 'sychophantic' she did not strenuously deny. Her version was that her husband had already indicated his intention to quit the service but that Weizächer and von Neurath had prevailed on him to stay on. Weizächer, she maintained, was anti-Nazi from the start but sought to work from within the service to try to counter Hitler's influence. Nevertheless, both he and Hempel passed the scrutiny of the *Auslandsorganisation*. That achievement was no recommendation in de Valera's eyes.

There may have been an assessment in Berlin as to how Hempel might get on with de Valera. His greatest asset was his decency: he was untainted by the Nazi manoeuverings for power; but the inescapable fact remains that the *Auslands-organisation* must have rated him as suitable for the appointment. They did not oppose him at any rate: if they had he would not have got the job. They may have applied different criteria in Hempel's case, although it is also just conceivable that he might have slipped through their sieving processes.

Herr Henning Thomsen, who was transferred to Dublin on 25 October 1938 and appointed First Secretary on 20 November, explained the Nazi party connection thus: Hitler, unexpectedly but very cleverly, did not touch the Foreign Service initially. Later, however, German diplomats abroad were given the option of joining the Nazi party or leaving the service. Refusal to join would have barred the person concerned from any post in the public service, and very likely qualified them for 're-education'.[18] So both Hempel and Thomsen joined.

Thomsen acknowledged that he had for some time previously belonged to the Mounted SS. He explained that there were two versions of the party badge; one, he compared in size with a five shilling piece;[19] in black and white on red with a big swastika in the centre: the other — the so-called *Hoheitsabzeichen* in silver — was about half the size as that worn on every military cap. Members of the legation (according to Thomsen), including Hempel, preferred the less eye-catching silver *Hoheitsabzeichen*. This reticence may have been due more to prudence than to modesty. Hitler had cautioned Hempel of hostile feelings in Ireland to the Third Reich's treatment of religion. There was no point in flaunting Nazi emblems. Hempel fully realised that it was his job to get on well with his Irish counterparts and he was determined to give no unnecessary offence.

His Irish counterparts were drawn principally from the so-called Clongowes Mafia, notwithstanding the barbed comment that the change of government in 1932 had seen a substitution of Clongowes boys by Christian Brothers boys. The Clongowes fellows were not to be dislodged that easily: they were too well entrenched. Clongowes men had ruled the roost in the first Cumann na nGaedheal government. Prominent Clongownian ministers in that government were Paddy McGilligan (Industry and Commerce and External Affairs), Kevin O'Higgins (Justice), Paddy Hogan (Agriculture), Seamus Burke (Lands), and the great John Marcus O'Sullivan (Education). With the possible exception of Burke, they happened to be men of uncommonly high ability. Hogan had the reputation, endorsed by the Tory whip Lord Newton, of being the most progressive Agriculture Minister in Europe. Clongowes men who reached the top in the civil service were Joseph Brennan (Secretary, Department of Finance), Joe Walshe (Secretary, Department of External Affairs) and his Number Two, Sean Murphy, who eventually succeeded him.

Walshe had taught Binchy French at Clongowes.[20] McGilligan and O'Sullivan succeeded in persuading a reluctant Binchy to let his name go forward as the first Irish representative in Berlin. Binchy in turn inducted another Clongowes man, Freddy Boland,[21] into External Affairs to join the Clongowes club of himself, McGilligan, Walshe, Murphy and Count O'Kelly.

Clongowes Wood College had been founded in 1814 to cater for the emerging Catholic middle classes. It was a school for the well off though the less well-heeled like James Joyce also managed to get in there. The apotheosis of Clongowes was represented by its triumphalist reception in 1914 of past pupil John Redmond as a guest of honour after the Home Rule Bill had been passed. This was Redmond's apotheosis too. The college was pro-British only to the extent that on the outbreak of war in August 1914 it flocked to Redmond's recruiting call. The boastful peer-comparison was that Clongowes sent more boys to the front than Eton did. By then the Home Rule Bill had been put on the statute book accompanied, however, by a suspensory act which post-poned its operation until the end of the war. But by then, everything had been transformed by the 1916 Rising.

In the new Irish Free State of the 1920s, the pro-Treaty Cumann na nGaedheal party drew its grass roots support from the big farmers, bourgeois and professional classes who could afford to send their sons to Clongowes. Their affluence dictated that it was politic to move forward in accommodation rather than in confrontation with Britain. Fianna Fáil was later to brand this pragmatism as little short of treachery. The Cumann na nGaedheal government, however, saw no dividends in bucking the British so they tried to get along with them. Part of McGilligan's and O'Sullivan's motivation in urging Binchy to accept the Berlin post stemmed from a desire not to offend the British: Charles Bewley's openly pro-German proclivities could have been an embarrassment.

McGilligan's antipathy to the former non-Catholic[22] might have had some Ulster sectarian roots: Bewley's anti-British sentiments were not revealed at this time. He had been in fact aggressively pro-Treaty and, as far as republican sentiments went, he proclaimed that Erskine Childers[23] had got what was coming to him when he was executed during the civil war in 1922. On the other hand, Binchy admired Childers. Distinctions were blurred: they were more personal than political.

Binchy told John Marcus O'Sullivan that he was reluctant to go as Minister to Berlin because he did not like the Germans. 'That's exactly why you should go', O'Sullivan snapped, making a comparison apparently between Binchy's mannerly discretion and Bewley's incipient fascism.

Sean T. O'Kelly, who was later under de Valera to become the great anti-British whip cracker, had also opposed the appointment of Bewley while skilfully managing not to mention him by name. Bewley had gainfully prosecuted republican prisoners during the civil war. That might explain O'Kelly's opposition to his getting the Berlin appointment or indeed any diplomatic post.

However, none of this deterred de Valera from later appointing Bewley to succeed Binchy. Bewley had captivated de Valera during the latter's visit to Rome in 1933. In any event, de Valera's awareness of a McGilligan opposition to Bewley inclined de Valera in Bewley's favour, Sean T. O'Kelly notwithstanding. McGilligan loathed de Valera with a black, northern bitterness and de Valera knew it. Any overtures made or contacts initiated with Fianna Fáil were regarded by 'Tody' McGilligan as acts of apostasy, the works of a renegade. Just as his friendly disposition to von Dehn had been the worst possible recommendation for the German representative in the eyes of the new Fianna Fáil government, his opposition to Bewley did the latter no damage when de Valera took power. In the final analysis, however, it was probably Bewley's charming of de Valera in Italy that was decisive in getting him the Berlin appointment after Binchy had resigned. There was also support for Bewley from John A. Costello SC[24] with whom he had worked during the civil war trials. Von Dehn also supported him.

Costello's support indicates that Bewley was not without friends. His relatives and various maiden aunts also left him well provided for in their wills, which gave him the means to indulge his inveterate snobberies and move in aristocratic circles, playing bridge with Italian princesses.

But Bewley did not need politics to make himself unpopular. For all his social graces he repelled many. In small things he had a habit of rubbing people the wrong way. Although he had plenty of money he could be extremely mean. He contrived a personal invitation from Binchy to visit Berlin and gratuitously quartered himself, his chauffeur and his valet on Binchy for the duration of his stay. Frau Hempel thought that part of his problem arose from being assexual, an ambiguous condition, although the passing thought also occurred to Binchy that in his younger days Bewley may have had a disgusting sexual experience that had turned him off women.

He did not, in general, appeal to the opposite sex. But there was no denying his social ease and assurance. The British, who set store by public school manners,[25] were not ill-disposed to him initially. Later, in Hitler's Germany, they came to regard him as a thorn in their side. In 1933 before feelings had hardened, a Foreign Office official had minuted:

> The son of a Dublin doctor, Mr Bewley was educated at New College, Oxford. At Oxford he won the Newdigate prize. He was called to the Irish Bar and become K.C.
>
> When the Cosgrave government decided to establish relations with the Vatican Mr Bewley was selected as the first minister. He was transferred to Berlin this year. He is a quick-witted, cultivated man, with a good knowledge of German, French and Italian. He is an admirer of German culture and has been working for some time, he admits, to obtain his present post. His work is, I imagine, presumably concerned with the development of trade relations.

He had also escaped the brunt of British ire in the protocol confusion which surrounded his recall from the Vatican in 1933. Pope Pius XI chose Cardinal Bourne as his agent to send a personal letter in Latin, noting Bewley's recall, to King George V. The Foreign Office found this a curious channel of communication. The king found it all very complicated and there were caustic comments on the Pope's bad Latin. The way out was to treat the Pope's communication not as a letter of credential. The attitude of the new Fianna Fáil government to the crown was blamed for it all, and it was even speculated that de Valera — this time the real villain of the piece in the Foreign Office eyes — would protest at the king having opened the letter!

A subsequent bestowal of a papal decoration on Bewley without asking whether this would be agreeable to the king or not added fuel to the fire. Anger increased at an awareness that the Irish government would presumably not take any steps to obtain His Majesty's permission to wear the decoration. This was at a time when the Department of Defence in Dublin found it necessary to issue an official denial of a statement that an officer of the Free State army had honoured the toast of the king at a recent dinner in Trinity College.

But, without leaving de Valera off the hook, Bewley's failure to attend the king's jubilee celebrations in Berlin in 1935 put the Irish Free State minister firmly in the dock. The Irish minister's name became mud in the Foreign Office. 'Mr Bewley is a good disciple of his master Mr de Valera', wrote Sir E. Phipps to Mr Bland. 'It would have cost him nothing to be polite even if it be assumed that his non-acceptance of the jubilee invitation from H. M. Embassy was the result of instructions from Dublin.' Bland observed that Phipps was 'wonderfully restrained in his comment on this revolting piece of bad manners'. Another Foreign Office official added: 'I am not surprised altogether to hear that Mr Bewley's manners had deteriorated from his residence at the Vatican to that at Berlin. At the former post I understand that he was fairly friendly personally but difficult officially. He has the reputation of being very pro-German and anti-Jewish and so having got to Berlin he no doubt feels he can let himself go.'

Bland laid before his superiors what he termed 'the distasteful morsel' of Bewley's refusal. Among the top echelons of the Foreign Office it engendered 'a feeling of such acute nausea' that Bland was instructed to express to the Berlin embassy his hope that after 'this piece of impertinence and bad manners' Bewley be invited 'no more to anything' as it was intolerable that the embassy be treated in this way, particularly by Bewley who was now regarded as 'irreclaimable'.

They had earlier said that his transfer of allegiance from the Cosgrave to the de Valera party was motivated by a desire to bag the Berlin post for himself, noting that for internal political reasons, he was careful to associate himself as little as possible with the British embassy, and observing that, although a professed admirer of Germany, he was not popular at the German Ministry for Foreign Affairs where he was described in a Foreign Office report of 1938 as being too sharp witted and anxious to drive a hard bargain. The only hint that the Foreign Office was aware at that point that Bewley did not see eye to eye with de Valera in all things was a reference in a report that Bewley had declared his intention to resign if Mr de Valera had, in the September 1938 crisis, joined Great Britain in a war against Germany.

They did not separate Bewley from de Valera. As far as they were concerned he was still the puppet of de Valera's malignant anglophobia. This was compounded in their eyes by Bewley's identification with the Third Reich. John Marcus O'Sullivan's original foreboding about appointing him to Berlin had been borne out.

Eventually Bewley had to be replaced because deteriorating relations between him and the Department of External Affairs meant that he could no longer function to their satisfaction as an effective instrument of de Valera's policy. His anti-British antics embarrassed the realistic Taoiseach. His Nazi predilections caused disquiet. He made little effort now to conceal his insubordination and insolence.

Nazi struttings and simplifications had a profound influence on him and he found de Valera's prosaic approach to Britain difficult to swallow. To anyone who would care to listen he denounced the Taoiseach for sacrificing republican ideals to political expediency. His extreme republicanism contrasted strangely with his prosecution during the civil war of de Valera's republican followers.

De Valera did not brook Bewley's conduct. He had the recalcitrant Minister repatriated and reduced in rank. There was nothing left to Bewley but to offer his resignation. De Valera accepted it. Bewley got no pension or gratuity in spite of having had fifteen years service. The general opinion was that the brilliant but erratic Wykehamist had deserved his come-uppance.

After leaving the service, Bewley wrote waspish reports and poisonous little notes on his former colleagues: Walshe; Count O'Kelly; Ó Briain; Murphy; Kerney; MacWhite; McCauley; L. N. Cremins; Dulanty; Brennan; Boland; Lester and Kiernan. One of his reports accused Walshe of running the Department with unbelievable incompetence. No Minister was adequately briefed on foreign policy, it said, and Walshe did not read the reports of his colleagues from other capitals; requests for instructions in certain cases were either not answered or were regarded as an intrusion into the private affairs of the Secretary. The report said that de Valera condoned this type of inefficiency because he was too penny-pinching to engage a couple of extra typists. Walshe was also

accused of currying favours with minor British officials who
treated him with a condescending friendship which seemed to
impress him. The further accusations were that he was
enthusiastic for the Jewish cause and travelled to Palestine
at Jewish expense; and that he was hostile to Irish independence, having boasted that he had weaned de Valera
away from the notion of a republic.

Hempel later drew on these reports in his attempts to
explain the making of Irish foreign policy which from 1932
was concentrated in de Valera's hands, since he had, as head
of government, also assumed direct responsibility for the
External Affairs portfolio.

In contrast to W. T. Cosgrave's reluctance to become involved in the formulation of foreign policy — feeling that
significant developments in this sphere were more properly
left to the British — de Valera was the conceiver and the
implementer of his own brand of policy which was obsessed
with constitutional readjustments with Britain, particularly
in regard to partition. The previous preoccupation had been
with establishing legations to encourage trade.

Joe Walshe had experience of both these worlds. Born in
Limerick in 1889, he initially intended a career in the church
but had to leave the Jesuits for health reasons: he had done
eight out of the twelve years training necessary for ordin-
ation. It was during this time that he had taught Binchy
French at Clongowes. He had never actually filled a diplomatic post abroad and augmented his knowledge of international affairs from his experience as a member of the
League of Nations delegation. There are many stories to
indicate that his relations with his staff were uneasy and
prickly though he developed a rapport with Miss Sheila
Murphy, a third secretary, whom, according to contem-
poraries, he should have married. He had a reputation in
intelligence circles for blowing hot and blowing cold. It was
during the early days of Hempel's representation in November
1937 that the Envoy made the following remark in the context of reporting a conversation with Walshe: 'It is customary here to say agreeable things without meaning everything
that is said.'

Hempel needed to learn about the oblique ways of Irish

diplomatic language. Furthermore, he would have to appreciate the reservoir of genuine national feeling that lay behind the slogan 'Up Dev'. It was not good enough for Hempel privately to dismiss de Valera's political aspirations as anachronistic and arcadian; a more sympathetic, and indeed more comprehensive grasp of Irish nationalism was required if he was to understand the basis of the country's neutrality. He had to accept that Irish neutrality was not a doctrine that lent itself to definition. It was not, in de Valera's own words, an 'adherence to some theoretical, abstract idea of neutrality or anything like that'. In time it was to develop a mythology of its own that defied literal interpretation. 'Who are we neutral against?' was an off-repeated Irish bull that never ceased to baffle the German Envoy.

Bewley on the other hand had fixed in his own mind what de Valera was up to. He regarded the Taoiseach's expedient consideration for Britain as giving the game away on his sinister pro-British designs, and paradoxically (considering his own connections with the British establishment: Bewley had a brother in the British Treasury and his uncle, Sir Arthur Pim, was a retired colonial administrator living near Oxford) he affected an uncompromising antagonism to the Taoiseach on that account. This antipathy went back a long way. In 1922 he had gloatingly drawn Binchy's attention, during their student days in Munich, to a caricature in the *Volkisher Beobachter* portraying de Valera as a Jew.

During the war he retreated to the Italian wings. He identified with the Third Reich and meddled in Irish affairs. His interventions irritated Hempel who saw them as undermining his position. Bewley did not think twice about going over Hempel's head or behind de Valera's back to thwart and, if possible, to abort a neutrality he correctly perceived to be weighted to favour the British.

It is difficult to reconcile Berlin's *idée fixe* of de Valera the revolutionary biding his time to best the British with Bewley's perceptions and contributions. It provides a symptom of the confusions and contradictions in the appreciations of the Third Reich.

Binchy by comparison took a balanced view: he saw the sense of de Valera's policy and appreciated the problem.

Though of differing party political persuasion he was well disposed to the Taoiseach, if only because his advent to power provided him with the opportunity to put behind him that 'strange interlude' in the distasteful artificial world of diplomacy and to return to his beloved scholastic groves. He had none of Bewley's hang-ups or McGilligan's hatreds towards de Valera. He would also willingly have swapped his plum appointment in Berlin with Bewley, preferring as he did the Italians to the Germans. Later, having been elected Senior Fellow of an Oxford College, he was seconded for war service in the press section of the Foreign Office, where he was charged with reporting on Italian affairs. The Foreign Office felt that he was too biased to be asked to report on the Germans. The contrast between the attitudes to the Germans of the first two Irish Ministers to Berlin, while speaking for itself in one sense, tells perhaps more about the persons concerned than it does about policies.

De Valera's evolving neutrality was part of a policy continuum that coupled Commonwealth association to Irish independence. The initial British response was predictably blimpish, though in the end they evolved a working relationship that grasped the essentials of the situation. Bewley in his self-appointed role of keeper of the grail of unpolluted nationalism fumed at this growing British-Irish understanding. He disdained de Valera for what he saw as a sell-out and he dismissed Hempel as a nonentity. He was wrong on both counts.

TWO

Keeping the Reich Informed

Bewley's antics irritated Hempel, who resented the credence Berlin appeared to give to him. The Envoy felt that giving Bewley a hearing diminished his status as the accredited representative of the Third Reich. The accreditation had been marked with full pomp and ceremony.

In Berlin on 22 June 1937 Hempel's letter of credence was signed by the Reich Chancellor, Adolf Hitler, and the Foreign Minister, Freiherr von Neurath. It was addressed from Hitler to 'His Majesty, King of Great Britain, Ireland and the British Dominions beyond the Seas, Defender of the Faith, Emperor of India', and was couched in conventional terms. Hempel, as Envoy Extraordinary and Minister Plenipotentiary of the German government, was recommended on account of his proven personal qualities as a worthy successor to the late von Kuhlmann. The hope was expressed that Hempel would earn the good will of His Majesty and so strengthen and deepen the bonds between the two peoples (British and German). Hitler requested that the Envoy be given a good reception and that full credence be accorded to any undertakings he carried out in the name of the German government. The opportunity was availed of to assure His Majesty of Hitler's absolute esteem and sincere friendship and to express his best wishes for the well-being of His Majesty and the development and prosperity of the Irish Free State. A translated copy of this letter of credence was later presented to de Valera. Hempel's rank for his new appointment was Minister Class I.

In those circles in Berlin where Bewley was influential, Hempel's credentials did not seem to carry much weight.

Prior to the Dublin posting he had been concerned with the administration abroad of the property of the Foreign Ministry. His wife's opinion was that although he did not like that job very much it was nevertheless not uninteresting because it involved a lot of travel. He had no apprenticeship at all in the skulduggeries of Third Reich foreign policy.

Hitler saw Hempel before he left for Dublin and the Führer impressed him with the extent of his knowledge of Ireland. The German leader was well versed on the problems in Anglo-Irish relations and was well aware that the religious factor was a difficulty in German-Irish relations. Frau Hempel's opinion however was that there were no special instructions to the Envoy from Hitler. The meeting was not photographed: it was private. The fulsome phraseology in the letter of credence to the king cloaked a real deterioration in Anglo-German relations. Ireland on the other hand, conscious of the threat of war, was modifying its attitude towards Britain. There was a growing realisation of the need for a mutual understanding: the British were in a mood to respond. This turnabout developed largely out of the rapport established between Malcolm MacDonald and de Valera.

By comparison with the confusion and overlapping inevitably arising from the labyrinth of Nazi organisations, the German Minister found the smaller more compact Irish Department of External Affairs easier to come to grips with. The head of the government being the Minister for External Affairs also helped cohesion. Depending on the weight of the matter of the moment, Hempel dealt mainly with either the Minister (de Valera), the Secretary (Joe Walshe) or the Assistant Secretary, the comparatively youthful thirty-one year old Clongownian, F. H. Boland.

During 1937-9 Hempel's reports from Dublin outlined the emerging policy of improbable neutrality which was evolving tentatively. De Valera saw the likelihood of a European war and determined to resolve some outstanding Anglo-Irish problems prior to that event. The outstanding issues were partition, defence, agriculture and finance. Partition and defence were diplomatically linked in de Valera's mind. For this he was suspected in some quarters — notably by the IRA and of course by Bewley — as being too pro-British. Bewley compared de Valera adversely with John Redmond who, he said, at least had the courage to declare himself openly before the public whereas de Valera was keeping his policy dark even from his own followers. Neutrality was hardly yet in 1937 a firm policy, much less a doctrine. Northern Ireland and Anglo-Irish relations were two of the main factors circumscribing the neutrality concept and Hempel's reports dealt largely with matters relative to these areas. In that context the IRA inevitably obtruded and received his assessment. He appreciated them (the IRA and what he termed radical nationalist opinion) as potential allies, and acknowledged the US influence on Irish affairs. Up to 1939, Hempel concentrated mainly, if broadly, on those topics. He was reporting back to a government now firmly embarked on a *Lebensraum* policy which was to be achieved through military might and determination — a policy which recognised that Great Britain might well have to be regarded as an enemy. Mussolini's visit to Berlin in September 1937 had cemented the Axis. Lord Halifax's visit to Germany in November 1937 was a major step in Anglo-French appeasement. *Lebensraum* and strong-arm methods came increasingly to dominate German foreign policy.

Anglo-French appeasement did not allay the general underlying current of apprehension that war was inevitable, though von Ribbentrop and Hitler liked to pretend that Great Britain would never take on the risk of a large-scale war merely on account of a crisis in Central Europe.

In that situation the importance of Ireland to Germany lay in the context of her relations with Great Britain. Walshe told Hempel that he hoped that an easing of German-British tension would favourably affect the settlement of Anglo-Irish relations which could be expected sooner or later. In Walshe's opinion Britain was in a difficult situation and he believed that the Anti-Comintern pact was aimed at her. An understanding with Germany was essential for Britain, Walshe told Hempel, and, in his opinion, there were prospects that Germany's demand for a return of her colonies would be successful; that sooner or later the Sudeten German question must move towards a fundamental solution.

These Irish views, as articulated by Walshe and reported by

Hempel, must have made for reassuring reading in the Third Reich. That was the point where Hempel sounded his note of caution about the Irish: their assertions, he said, had to be taken with a grain of salt. The only observations of Walshe's which the Envoy reported that could have caused disquiet were the references to the Anglo-Catholic Lord Halifax being highly thought of in Ireland.

Hempel kept a close eye on de Valera and carefully reported Dáil and Senate debates on defence and neutrality. He recorded that de Valera saw parallels between British and Irish interests and had remarked that the 1938 Agreement which ended the economic war and returned the Treaty ports to Ireland was more worthwhile for Britain than for Ireland. On defence, de Valera was quoted as not wanting to have Ireland placed in an unsatisfactory position in the event of war, such as had been the case while the British had occupied the ports. The Envoy again expressed doubts about the practical possibilities of implementing a policy of neutrality, and noted further the importance of the Irish overseas in these matters when he reported de Valera's 1938 St Patrick's Day broadcast to them. The Irish overseas, notably in America, were an ever present factor in any Anglo-Irish negotiations affecting reunification. He reported the 1938 Agreement briefly and factually under three headings: the handing back of the ports; the settlement of the land annuities and the signing of a three-year trade agreement. The Minister subsequently urged an extension of the existing German-Irish trade agreement.

He later submitted a more comprehensive report. It was astonishing, he commented, how swiftly those two sister islands, who had been traditional enemies for centuries, reached accord, especially when de Valera's inflexible, doctrinaire obstinacy in the pursuit of his goals was taken into account. But, he observed, returning to an earlier theme, the fact had become obscured that de Valera had long wished for friendly co-operation and association with Britain in return for unification and that more than any of his countrymen de Valera was a champion of the ideals of western democracy. Hempel's judgment of de Valera's purpose was that Ireland, in return for reunification, would join a British-American-

Commonwealth camp. He retraced what he portrayed as de Valera's Machiavellian steps from the time the Taoiseach had seen his way free to introduce the External Relations Act: de Valera foresaw, Hempel said, the coming European War and with it the compromised position in which Ireland was placed as a result of the occupation by a Britain involved in such a war; this situation would render Irish aspirations towards neutrality illusory. But, continued Hempel, de Valera was concerned to protect Britain's interests. He did not share the IRA aspiration that 'England's difficulty was Ireland's opportunity'. He took the poor state of the country's economy and financial conditions into account. The report mentioned de Valera's old thesis that Britain and Ireland were both mother countries; that Ireland, as much as England, could be proud of commonwealth achievements and that both lands should rebuild a friendly partnership. In a long report Hempel relayed Chamberlain's and de Valera's denial that there was any secret understanding on matters of defence and touched on Ireland's position of being, next to the US and Canada, one of Britain's biggest suppliers. De Valera's hesitations about being able to implement a policy of neutrality in the event of a large-scale war were again recorded. Hempel granted de Valera popular acclaim for completing the 1938 Agreement but sounded a warning about IRA disenchantment with him: some of the latter, Hempel asserted, were idealists and adventurers but others were worthwhile types who, it might be assumed, would show a clear understanding towards a new Germany and her aims; although that remained to be seen. Hempel was more speculative than usual in this report.

He then got down to brass tacks and reported progress on the German-Irish trade agreement. It was de Valera's wish, he said, to expand trade with Germany, something that had been retarded during recent Anglo-Irish negotiations and which he now wished to redress. Hempel undertook to look into the matter during his coming holidays when he planned to visit Berlin.

During Hempel's absence, his representative — Marchtaler — submitted the clearest report to date on the evolution of a neutrality policy, which was to prove to be definitive in

linking neutrality and defence. Its clarity was due not merely
to an improvement on Hempel's circuitous style of reporting:
it was perhaps because de Valera was now clearer in his own
mind as to projected policy patterns. The report outlined de
Valera's replies to the opposition's questions on foreign
policy: he refuted vehemently the suggestion that Ireland's
League of Nations policy was dictated by the British; in reply
to General Mulcahy (Fine Gael), who asked if in a coming
war, as a result of the Agreement, Ireland would ally with
Britain or remain neutral, he answered comprehensively: Irish
policy in a future war was in no way firmly laid down; they
were fully free to act in the best interests of the country.
Ireland's first interest was to remain neutral, though the difficulties of carrying out this policy in a future war were recognised. It was not enough merely to wish for neutrality: the
other sides were required to recognise and respect that wish;
if they did not, Ireland would defend itself by every means
in its power. The report further gave de Valera's version of
the circumstances of Anglo-Irish relations: on the one hand,
the circumstances in which Ireland would seek British aid;
and on the other, circumstances in which Britain was the
aggressor. De Valera hoped that the latter situation would
never arise but if it did Ireland would make such aggression
as costly as possible for Britain. The fact was, however, that
Britain provided a bulwark for Ireland against an attack from
the continent and therefore it was in Ireland's interest that
Britain remained in a position to execute this defensive
function. A free and united Ireland would be better able to
co-operate, militarily, politically and psychologically with
Great Britain to achieve this end: therefore the removal of
partition — for which the Irish government would continue
to strive — was in Britain's interest. The report concluded
with de Valera's assertion that if they could remain neutral
they would still endeavour to continue to trade with all countries, and that included regularly sending supplies to England.

   In October 1938 Hempel interpreted Ireland's reaction to
the European crisis of the previous month. He reported a
widespread apprehension and a general desire to stay out of
any coming conflict between Britain and Germany, though
predictably the Anglo-Irish rallied to the British colours. An

appreciation was shown for the Sudetenland *coup*, analogies being drawn between that situation and the position in Northern Ireland; the transfer of population seemed to find acceptance as a solution. The conflict with the Catholic Church and, in particular, the plight of Cardinal Innitzer in Austria was looked on with disfavour. Hempel further reported rumours of a split in the cabinet with Sean T. O'Kelly taking a negative attitude towards Britain compared with de Valera who was alleged to be becoming more and more pro-British, while at the same time wishing to spare his country the horrors of war. The burning question, the report stated, was whether the supply of essential commodities to England such as food and petrol would constitute a breach of neutrality and if that in turn would bring counter-measures, such as an attack on Irish territory. Sean T. O'Kelly had blurted out to Hempel that he did not see how a policy of neutrality could be implemented. There were rumours, the report said, of Sean T., was he was popularly known, being shifted as ambassador to Paris on the one hand and on the other taking over External Affairs. This latter move by the Anglophobe O'Kelly would, Hempel thought, hardly please the British.

The Envoy's long report on de Valera's interview in the *Evening Standard* which labelled the partition of Ireland as a 'dangerous anachronism' and suggesting a devolved solution, construed this ploy as further evidence of de Valera's long-standing wish for an association with Britain. From Belfast, Lord Craigavon spat back 'No Surrender'. However Hempel was finding it difficult to make his reports labelling de Valera as absolutely pro-British sound wholly convincing. The following month he was reporting de Valera's speech to the Fianna Fáil ard-fheis in which the Taoiseach declaimed that as far as Ireland was concerned England was a foreign country: the association with England was not a statutory necessity; it was merely a gesture to a part of the Irish people. De Valera was keeping his options open as well as humouring his followers.

At the end of November 1938 he informed Hempel of his acceptance of the German proposal to extend the Irish-German trade agreement for a further period of one year as

from January 1939. The note concluded with the usual protestations of esteem for the German Minister and by extension the Third Reich. But maintaining cordial relations with
the Third Reich was not an easy option.

Towards the end of 1938 the Jewish question was making
an impact outside Germany and Hempel now reported an
unfavourable Irish reaction to the treatment of Jews in
Germany, following the assassination of the diplomat von
Rath. He circulated to German Jews living in Dublin the Nazi
edict that German male Jews must have 'Israel' inserted in
their passports as part of their first names: for females the
insertion was 'Sarah'. At least one Jewish refugee family in
Dublin at the time refused to comply though summoned to
the Legation in this connection, that of Professor Ernst
Lewy (formerly *b a o für Allgemeine Sprachwissenschaft*) who
had been summarily dismissed from his post in Berlin University and later, in 1937, had sought refuge in Ireland at his
wife's instigation; they just did not return from holidays.
Professor Lewy was an unworldly Jew and an extremely like-
able and good-natured character. The Nazis offered him back-
pay as compensation to return to his post in Berlin. This
would have meant a substantial amount of money for the
impecunious Professor and his family but, in principle, as
a protest against the Nazi regime, he declined the offer and
chose to eke out an existence in comparative poverty (£400
p.a.) in Ireland. The story that Hempel was rude to Lewy and
snubbed him is not substantiated by the Professor's son. On
the contrary, his recollection was that Hempel was liked by
the Dublin Jewish community and was far from being anti-
semetic. That recollection, however, included an impression
that Thomsen was the Gestapo man sent to keep an eye on
Hempel.[1]

The German Jews in Dublin were never invited to any
function in the legation. This was simply a matter of tact: the
Hempels did not even invite Germans whose anti-Nazi feelings
were known to them. Frau van Hoek, the German-born wife
of their friend, the well-known Dutch journalist Kees van
Hoek, was likewise not invited. Lines were being firmly
drawn: in January 1939 Ribbentrop forbade all social relations
between his subordinates and the American embassy in Berlin.

The question for Hempel was where Irish sympathies lay. He reported that de Valera was the only one in the League of Nations assembly who had welcomed Chamberlain's decision to go to Berchtesgaden. De Valera also told him — asking him to treat it in confidence — that he had been considering appealing directly to Hitler and Mussolini in a solo effort to preserve peace — not in his capacity as President of the League of Nations Assembly[2] but as Prime Minister of Eire. The German Minister seemed to have been singled out for 'confidences' by the Taoiseach who had previously requested that, no matter what happened, Irish-German relations should not be broken. Hempel promptly telegraphed the contents of de Valera's confidence to Berlin. Such a confidence had to be reported and de Valera would have expected it to have been reported.

From then until the outbreak of war the following September, Hempel continued to monitor the refinements and shades of meaning in de Valera's utterances on his neutrality policy; doubts were still raised as to the possibility of implementing it. The question of Northern Ireland and the attitudes of the Irish in America remained blurring factors. This situation was aggravated by the introduction of a more sinister factor which called into question the capability of the democratically elected government to govern. Its fundamental right of being the body in whom alone was vested the right to declare and wage war was being challenged by the IRA ultimatum of 12 January 1939 which formally opened their bombing campaign in England. Hempel reported his subsequent meeting with de Valera. The Taoiseach left him in no doubt as to his disapproval of alleged German links with the IRA, making the point that the government, as the legally constituted authority, would under no circumstances use illegal methods to resolve the Northern Ireland problem. He warned Hempel that it would be a mistake to overrate the IRA and he was convinced that inter-Irish strife, particularly in the context of a future European war, would have no decisive role against England: Ireland could only be interested in a strong Britain that would be prepared to defend the island if attacked. Hempel attempted to scotch the rumours of German involvement in the bombing in Britain and blamed the British press for circulating this smear.

Then on 16 February 1939 Hempel reported in detail the Dáil debate on the current army vote, together with army strength and the government's plans for recruiting for the army and the ARP (Air Raid Precautions). In spite of Frank Aiken's bouyant projections (including a statement that the preparations for the erection of an ammunition factory were completed) Hempel remained unconvinced: the provision of £3,200,600 as against the previous year's £2,000,000 would, in his opinion, only afford marginal strengthening of installations and personnel. He enclosed an *Irish Times* projection analysis of budget increases required for equipment and stores (£5,500,000); for the building and equipping of installations, airfields, and possibly a munitions factory, an expenditure of £4,200,000 was forecast.

As regards policy he reported the Minister for Defence's statement that the General Staff had drawn up plans based on the following guidelines:

1. That the sovereignty of Ireland as presently constituted by the 26 Counties is respected and internationally recognised.
2. That the Dáil as the assembly of the elected representatives of the people was the only body empowered to declare war.
3. That the government had no policy of aggression towards any nation and that Ireland had no obligation to take part or become involved in a war.
4. That it was the policy of the government to resist any attack which might be made on Irish soil.

Hempel reported this as ruling out the possibility of a war with Great Britain, unless of course Britain was the aggressor. Therefore the conclusion was that the only conditions to be taken into account were the maintenance of neutrality and an attack by a power with whom Great Britain was at war. It was unlikely that a power not at war with Great Britain would attack Ireland; in all probability, his surmise ran, such an attack would come from a power wanting to make Ireland a theatre of operations or a base for attack against Great Britain.

However, as Hempel's report of the following day indicated,

pat interpretations of following a policy of neutrality were thrown into confusion by de Valera's contribution to the debate. The Taoiseach had just retorted to yet another query from the Leader of the Opposition as to whether they would co-operate with Britain for the defence of Ireland if Ireland was attacked. The reply brought bluntly into the open the fact that the maintenance of neutrality in wartime would be a precarious business, scarcely possible to carry through: de Valera seemed to be saying that Ireland would almost inevitably be drawn into any war in which Britain was involved. Hempel reflected the confusion — which existed even in government circles, his report said — caused by this intervention but he preferred to await the official version of the speech before finally committing himself. At this stage however the Envoy maintained that there was no essential difference from his previous interpretations of this situation except that no illusions were left by de Valera about the danger of depending on Great Britain in wartime and this, Hempel held, was what had implications for Germany. The Envoy chose to append the following in English, as if he did not trust a translation of de Valera's words:

> The desire of the Irish people, and the desire of the Irish government, is to keep the nation out of war. The aim of the government policy is to maintain and preserve our neutrality in the event of war. The best way, and the only way, to secure our aim is to put ourselves in the best position possible to defend ourselves, so that no one can hope to attack us, or violate our territory with impunity. We know, of course, that should an attack come from a power other than Great Britain, Great Britain in her own interests must help us to repel it.

Hempel then noted de Valera's further observation that the Irish government had not entered into any commitments with Great Britain, and that his government was free to follow any course that Irish interests might dictate. Reporting on the defence debate was continued by Thomsen during Hempel's absence on leave towards the end of February 1939. The Minister was back at his desk by the middle of April to try to unravel the effects of a diplomatic gaffe arising out of

Hitler's celebrated reply to Roosevelt's appeal that Germany would not attack or invade the territory of a listed thirty-one nations. Germany had queried all of them except Poland, Russia, Britain and France. Roosevelt had linked Britain and Ireland and the Germans followed suit in coupling Ireland with Britain when they queried the other countries as to whether they felt threatened by Germany or if they had authorised Roosevelt to make his proposals. Negative replies were received. Hitler, although referring to Ireland in his reply, had omitted to consult the Dublin government separately. Hempel was agitated at this omission which he felt would offend Irish sensitivities. He need not have worried unduly. General Mulcahy, a Fine Gael deputy, got a short answer from de Valera when he attempted to raise the matter in the Dáil: Mulcahy asked what the implications were; de Valera snapped back that it was not possible for anyone to discover the implications.

Irish anger was by now directed at Craigavon's demand to extend conscription to Northern Ireland. In any case Roosevelt the Anglophile was regarded by the Dublin government as unsympathetic to Irish nationalist aspirations. The reaction of the US President to the cabled protest from six Irish-American societies to Craigavon's conscription call had been cynical though he could not ignore the electoral calculations involved.

Moreover, the Irish were a bit flattered that Hitler, albeit in riposte to Roosevelt, took notice of de Valera's speech reproaching England with subjecting Ireland to continuous aggression while claiming to be upholding democracy in Europe. In Irish eyes, remembering the Black and Tans, all the faults were by no means on one side. De Valera smugly and simplistically was of the opinion that Hitler did not really want war. He had a lot to learn. He was not put off apparently by Hitler's other reference to the incorporation into the Third Reich of Bohemia and Moravia. Hitler pronounced that just as English measures in Northern Ireland, whether they be right or wrong, were not subject to German supervision, German constituencies in like manner should not be subject to English supervision.

The Germans were not criticised for their slip. It was

Roosevelt who was weighed in the balance and found wanting: de Valera regarded his letter of appeal and remonstrance to Hitler as inept and when war broke out he felt that this partisan intervention ruled Roosevelt out as a potential arbitrator on the conflict.

In reporting the reaction to Hitler's speech, Hempel referred again to de Valera's Anglophile tendencies. He thought that public opinion was revealing de Valera's pro-British posture which his aspirations about neutrality had served to cloak: he had now to demonstrate more decisiveness than before in reiterating the 'wish' (the inverted commas are Hempel's) of his government to remain neutral. Hempel's opinion, formed after a conversation with Walshe, was that de Valera would take pains to avoid identifying with British foreign policy, but would not allow British vital interests to be compromised even if that consideration jeopardised neutrality.

He mentioned the resurgence of national feeling, and the re-emergence of the IRA who in a coming war would operate not only against Northern Ireland but also against de Valera's government. Hempel added that both in his own interests and also out of consideration for Britain de Valera had introduced the Offences against the State Bill and the Treason Bill, but that these had met with opposition even within the government party. In spite of de Valera's repeated denials of the existence of any secret deals with Britain, Hempel recorded the opinion that there was more in the Anglo-Irish Agreement of 1938 than met the eye. De Valera had cleverly exploited that Agreement to spring and win a general election, something Hempel insisted he would not have been able to accomplish a year later.

He reasoned that it was fear of an adverse reception from Irish nationalists that prompted de Valera to call off a proposed American trip. He does not seem to have considered the possibility that the trip may have been called off at American insistence, under British pressure, in order to deprive de Valera of a transatlantic anti-partition platform. Sean T. O'Kelly went to represent the Taoiseach for the opening of the Irish Pavilion at the New York World Fair. As Hempel read the position, O'Kelly was sent because his reputation for keeping alive the fighting spirit of Irish nationalism made him more acceptable than de Valera to Irish-American audiences. The nationalists suspected that de Valera's method of solving the partition problem was to obtain a US guarantee of the neutrality of a free Irish state which would serve to protect vital British interests and secure her western flanks. Walshe told Hempel that there was no truth in these rumours: de Valera would not pay a price for the return of Northern Ireland which he regarded as an integral part of his country.

Then the Envoy (in a long sentence of 174 words) illustrated a widening gulf between the British and Irish governments, instancing the removal of the king's name from Irish passports, the treatment of IRA prisoners in English courts and the anti-conscription campaign to support this view. On the other hand,[3] he concluded, de Valera did nothing to conceal his sympathy for the democracies; the Anglo-Irish remained implacably opposed to Germany; and the Catholic Church feared that a German victory would increase the danger of the suppression of Christianity and the aboliton of the traditional freedom of Western Europe.

Hempel had already reported on Sean T. O'Kelly's anti-British nationalism and on 27 May 1939 he noted conflicting voices within the Irish cabinet: Sean MacEntee, the Belfast-born Minister for Finance, sounded pro-British and saw defence policy as not merely protecting Irish freedom but also as having a function in repelling possible attacks on British interests. He then cited Sean Lemass as saying (in a by-election speech) that the only country they had a quarrel with was Great Britain; that they had no obligation to get involved and were only interested in remaining neutral. There was no reference to another Minister, Frank Aiken, who was alleged to be sympathetic to the Central European powers, but the German Minister rounded off his report by observing that Sinn Féin wanted not only neutrality in the event of war — but had demanded a campaign against Britain.

He next submitted an extract from de Valera's by-election speech verbatim, in English, as if to be sure that he had heard right and that he was repeating correctly. The sentiments expressed by de Valera on this occasion did not at all accord with Hempel's previous pro-British portrayals of him. It was a recruiting speech for the Volunteers:

> I appeal to the young people to get into the ranks and defend what has been won, and, if necessary, *be prepared to secure what has not yet been won.*

The emphasis is Hempel's. This could be interpreted in Berlin as an indication of the narrowing of whatever gap existed between de Valera and the IRA as to the aims and methods of securing freedom. The Envoy later reported Dr O'Higgins's (Fine Gael) criticism that the army did not know whom they were supposed to fight against. De Valera's answer to that was that they would fight not alone against the Axis forces but against anyone else who might attack them: government policy was to keep Ireland out of the war, though he acknowledged that this was going to be difficult if normal trading with Britain were pursued as intended. Hempel expressed doubts that de Valera's intentions to continue normal trading could be compatible with neutrality.

On 7 August 1939 he telegraphed a warning that the *Sunday Times* was trying to involve Ireland in the war by goading Germany to take precipitate action. It was quoting German papers who were saying that Ireland would be dragged into the war on the side of Germany's enemies. Be careful, the Envoy warned: British propaganda was extremely active, laying false trails to wrong-foot the Germans.

German foreign policy at this stage was to isolate Poland by diplomatic means: the largely predictable factors of logistics and weather would determine the date for the commencement of the military campaign. Towards the end of August Walshe, in a meeting with Hempel, stressed that Ireland would remain neutral unless attacked and suggested that Germany declare that she had no aggressive aims on Ireland but, on the contrary, had sympathy for Irish aims and aspirations, with particular reference to Northern Ireland. Referring to the possible dropping of bombs on Irish towns Walshe said that he could not believe the Germans would ever do such a thing: for one thing they could not be indifferent to Irish sympathy, especially in view of Irish-American influence which could be exercised against the formation of a

British-American alliance and could also deter the British from violating Irish neutrality. Ribbentrop instructed Hempel how to respond in friendly terms:

> in accordance with the friendly relations between our-selves and Ireland we are determined to refrain from any hostile action against Irish territory and to respect her integrity *provided* [my italics] that Ireland for her part maintains unimpeachable neutrality towards us in any conflict. Only if the condition should no longer obtain as a result of a decision of the government themselves or by pressures exerted on Ireland from other quarters, should we be compelled as a matter of course as far as Ireland was concerned to safeguard our interests in the sphere of warfare in such a way as the situation then arising might demand of us.

There was no direct mention of Northern Ireland but there was a reference to the wide sympathy felt in Germany for the national aspirations of the Irish people. Irish nationals were to be permitted to remain in Germany and Ireland was expected to reciprocate. An awareness of the problems involved in Ireland's geographical position was expressed. The message may have been delivered in a friendly fashion but an authoritative tone was evident. De Valera took up the challenge on ground of his own choosing: Professor Desmond Williams has written that few politicians have paid more attention to the significance of detail in the use of words.

The Taoiseach sent for Hempel and received him in the presence of Walshe. He told the Minister that he could not accept the expression 'unimpeachable' (translated as 'non-objectionable'). Ireland's dependence on Britain for trade vital to Ireland and the possibility of British intervention made it inevitable for the Irish government to show 'a certain consideration for Britain', which in similar circumstances would be shown to Germany. De Valera warned Hempel of danger points: any violation by Britain or Germany of Irish territorial waters; exploitation of the anti-British radical nationalist movement; or any hostile action against the population on the other side of the border who wanted to return to the Irish State. Hempel concluded that his general impression was one of sincere effort to keep Ireland out of the conflict. He felt that de Valera cloaked his fears of war by discussing his reasons for neutrality in his usual doctrinaire fashion which betrayed his real weakness.[4]

Next day, 1 September 1939, Germany invaded Poland. On 3 September Britain declared war on Germany. In de Valera's words there had been 'one crisis too many'. On 2 September he had introduced a bill to amend Article 28 of the constitution in order to pass emergency legislation. The Emergency, as the period of World War II was known in Ireland, had begun, although the term did not come into popular use until the formal declaration of a state of emergency by the government in the following June.

Hempel had been at his post representing the Third Reich in Dublin for just over two years. During that time he had observed the political scene with perception and monitored de Valera's unfolding blueprint for a solution to the related problems of neutrality and defence. He reported de Valera's utterances on the difficulties in dealing with those two linked problems which were complicated by the convoluted history of Anglo-Irish relations and the unresolved problem of partition which involved the IRA in an apparent identity of aim with the government.

De Valera had told the Dáil that it was very difficult to remain neutral. Hempel had reported him as saying that it was 'hardly possible' to uphold Irish neutrality in time of war. But it was Hempel's report[5] and not de Valera's actual words which stated that neutrality was probably impossible.

De Valera's advance planning for neutrality now seemed to fall into shape and place and the day before the war broke out Hempel's telegram to Berlin recorded in effect that Ireland, fearful, but firm and sincere and piloted by the 'doctrinaire' de Valera, was determined to stay out of the coming conflict.

THREE

Off the Record

The inexorable gearing for war had increased demand for intelligence at all levels in the Third Reich. The adoption of the IRA by the Abwehr brought Hempel into that net. The question he had to resolve was how far he might go in neutral Ireland where the IRA was an illegal organisation, in order to gather the information Berlin demanded. A peace-time diplomat functions in a context that can make him almost an intelligence agent. Was this the case with Hempel? First, he represented a regime which under Hitler defied the cautious criteria of professional diplomacy in implementing foreign policy. Second, the relationship between information-gathering and the intelligence process must be understood before a circumstantial link with the German Minister can be suggested. Third, the connection between military intelligence and spy-networks is clear only to the extent that military objectives are clear, and in Germany the spawning of agencies meddling in policy-making produced friction, fragmentation and a blurring of objectives. Fourth, all embassies and legations are information gatherers for their countries and there is a notoriously grey area between information gathering and spying in those circumstances. Hempel only moved to make direct contact with extremists (e.g. IRA connections) through Helmut Clissmann just before the outbreak of war. He reckoned that such surveillance was the function of other organisations like the *Auslandsorganisation* or Clissmann's own Academic Exchange organisation. His detachment may have had a 'need to know' basis, which on security grounds is established intelligence practice. Fifth, there are well founded precedents in previous German representation in Ireland for the type of information gathering in which Hempel overtly indulged. From the Irish side — and particularly from de Valera's viewpoint, steering in hitherto uncharted waters with an unproven policy of neutrality — presumed activities of German legations and other German representation presupposed a requirement for counter-intelligence.

At the beginning of this century when Graf Metternich was appointed Ambassador to London, he addressed his staff thus: 'Gentlemen, I'll make the politics: your job is to keep me informed of who breakfasts with whom and who sleeps with whom.' By the time Hempel took up his Dublin post, however, the age of the great ambassadors who were policy-makers in their own right was well over. Diplomats of the old school — Hempel was one of them — generally sought to exploit their position to promote Germany's post-Versailles revisionist aims without jeopardising the national existence. Their loyalty to the state was in turn exploited by Hitler for his own ends: though not policy-makers, the diplomats were the implementers of policy abroad, the emissaries in keeping up appearances and the suppliers of essential information. However as other people could also claim to be well-informed about conditions in other countries, the diplomat was no longer regarded as the sole source of information. He was nevertheless — and this was specifically the case with Hempel — the principal means of inter-governmental communication: that meant at surface level establishing official sources and transmitting information via normal diplomatic channels. This information would then be fed into the intelligence process. Hempel's contribution in this respect was copious but untargeted: it was directed towards his country's aims only to the extent that career diplomats of his generation were fully apprised of those aims.

A stereotyped approach to the intelligence process required that the following stages be followed: stating what the problem is; making an intelligence estimate related to the solving of that problem; collection of information and then the three stages of intelligence handling — collation, interpretation and dissemination. Hitler's ambivalent attitude towards the British during this period did not lend itself to a clear-cut determination in Berlin of the problem as far as Ireland was concerned.

On his visit to the Führer in November 1937 Halifax had intriguingly classified Germany as the bulwark of the West against Russia; he also expressed the hope that an appeased Germany would rejoin the League of Nations. The psychological battle for hearts and minds in the guise of peace-seeking had already been joined.

Information for psychological operations had to be drawn from political, religious, social and economic fields. Hempel covered these aspects diligently. Through normal diplomatic channels he reported comprehensively on Dáil debates and transmitted banal information from the newspapers. It is a cliché in intelligence work that much of the required information for processing is freely available and that selectively milked newspapers are rich sources. The Dublin legation had an important role to play in collecting this information for processing into intelligence. If the military objective of the *Wehrmacht* were to keep Ireland neutral initially, then Hempel's reportage was an important contribution to making an intelligence estimate of that situation. In that connection he strove to establish the courses open to the British and soberly listed the indications pointing to the course they were likely to adopt. There was nothing wrong with that.

To provide the calibre of information called for, however, Hempel had to fish in troubled waters. There was a requirement to report on subversive groups, principally the IRA, and at the same time officially keep his distance from them. Not only were these groups hostile to Britain, they were also openly contemptuous of the authority of the democratically elected Irish government, and their links with Nazi Germany envisaged the securing of aid with the aim of ousting de Valera and usurping the Dáil. Hempel had to maintain a fine balance to keep up appearances.

The duplication of Nazi agencies added to the disorder. Hempel did not know where he stood between them and the IRA. It is hard to credit the indulgence shown by Hitler to his assorted associates who used these organisations to advance their personal ambitions in the power struggle within the Nazi hierarchy. Rivalries and animosities took precedence over fundamental aims.

Maintenance of the aim is a principle of war. But as far as

German intelligence in Ireland was concerned that aim was neither professionally determined nor properly defined. There was no unity of command. Lack of co-ordination and confusion were the inevitable consequences.

In 1937 Admiral Canaris, the Head of German Intelligence, was supposed to have been finally given a free hand to initiate intelligence operations in England. But some other agency had apparently been operating there previously unfettered by this constraint. In March 1936 Hermann Goertz[1] a German spy, had been sentenced to four years penal servitude in England for espionage. When the restriction on Canaris was lifted an alleged strict injunction not to trouble the Irish was not revoked. But if that so-called injunction did actually exist some agencies would appear never to have heard of it. Espionage has been called the second oldest profession in the world: it rabbits away even after the armies and causes it served have been defeated. Over the years robot-like intelligence involvement had gone on in Ireland. That might explain the disregard of the injunction in favour of established precedent.

Back in 1927 Hempel's predecessor had set the headline of reporting on the strength of the Irish army and reserve and speculating about the ability of Ireland to remain neutral in the event of Britain being involved in a war (he doubted it). He also reported Dáil debates on defence, quoting the then Minister, Desmond FitzGerald, on the necessity for co-operation between British and Irish forces in the event of an attack by a third party. Full reports were also made on army organisations; establishment tables; the names of officers[2] going on courses to the US; lists of training manuals; dress regulations; appointments and promotions; and pay and pensions. A recurring preoccupation was the role of the Irish army and the question of military relations with Great Britain.

At another level in 1928 the German consulate in Dublin reported General Murphy of the Garda Siochana as alleging that he had evidence of links between a Johann Otto Egestorff and an illegal organisation and that he had letters in code which even Scotland Yard failed to decipher. Egestorff was married to a Catholic Irish woman and had difficulty in re-entering either Britain or Ireland after the First World War.

When he did get back he made a film, 'Turf instead of Coal'.[3] That concept might have sounded subversive and sinister to Scotland Yard at the time. The IRA remained in the consulate's sights and in 1929 were reported as being represented at the World Congress of the Anti-Imperialist League in Frankfurt-am-Main by Sean MacBride and Donald O'Donoghue.

As a further indication that German intelligence work in Ireland was an ongoing process with a life of its own — on the surface a pointless one — is indicated by a request initiated on 15 March 1927 from the Head Office of the overseas German Maritime Union[4] for the names of agents they could trust in Ireland.[5] They did not indicate what kind of trust they had in mind. In time, by definition, these activities would come under the wing of the *Auslandsorganisation*. The net was cast wide: the infrastructure for intelligence work was set up.

Anything related to defence was reckoned by the German representation to be worthy of note. One explanation for this could be deduced from a report of an article carried on 21 February 1935 by the Paris weekly magazine *Gringoire* to the effect that the British government was aware that the continuing wide field of negotiations between Ireland and Germany was a prelude to a military treaty in the event of war. The gist of the report was that although Ireland had no army to speak of, the country could still be an important base and strong point for Germany's aircraft and U-Boats in the event of war with Great Britain.

There were many precedents for Hempel's information gathering activity. Freiherr Geyr von Schweppenburg, the German military attaché in London (1933-7) was concerned enough during his tour of duty to visit Foynes and the mouth of the Shannon to make an appreciation of the strategic significance of Ireland's geographical location, with particular reference to the Foynes-Newfoundland air route. He had made an accurate forecast of the Second World War order of battle, aligning Italy and Japan with Germany and thereby allowing the Luftwaffe freedom to poise itself lethally at the heart of the British motherland, as he put it. His visualisation took the following shape: at the other end of the gigantic defence front, that stretched from Port Darwin in

Australia, stood the might of the Japanese fleet; German-Spanish politics sought for naval and air bases which posed a threat through the Mediterranean to the Cape, while the Mediterranean route itself would be rendered insecure for Britain by the position of Italy in a future war. The position of Ireland remained a conundrum in this strategic jig-saw. The route to the USA had the disadvantage of being flanked by Ireland: von Schweppenburg's theory was that in the coming war the USA, while remaining nominally neutral, would give *de facto* support to England and that this gave unusual importance to Foynes in the context of transatlantic traffic development. He saw British politics as being militarily motivated, using British diplomacy to clarify relationships with a view to securing this vulnerable Irish flank. In point of fact in January 1938 one of the questions put to the British chief of staff's sub-committees included a question as to whether the importance of the Irish ports was so great as to warrant military operations to regain possession and use of them. The reply indicated that this would require a campaign of Gallipoli proportions if it were carried out in the face of opposition: denying their use to the enemy was what was paramount; to this end a friendly Ireland was essential; in any case German intelligence work would only thrive in an environment unfriendly to Britain.

In pre-war Ireland information-gathering of one kind or another for the German intelligence process seems to have gone on unhampered. Right up to 1939, military geographical data on Ireland was being garnered for the Department of War's maps and survey in Berlin. All the information in question could not have been gleaned from open sources: much of it had to be purposefully acquired. The volumes produced described historical backgrounds, administrative structures, industry, transport, communications and traffic, surface forms, types of ground and vegetation, climate, weather and waters. These factors were appraised in a military context. This summarised the likely effect of terrain and resources on an invasion force. Landing beaches, obstacles, observation posts, traffic mobility, provisioning and billeting were considered. With regard to the latter the Germans had a pigs-in-the-parlour perception of Irish conditions and concluded that they would have to provide for themselves. They thought that the Wexford-Waterford area held the most promise as a landing place and a starting point for the occupation of the island, particularly on account of the fan-shaped network of communications radiating into the interior. Other suitable gateways identified were: Cork-Cobh; Shannon estuary; Galway Bay; Donegal Bay and Belfast Lough! The middle of the east coast was acceptable only where harbour facilities existed and Clew Bay was rejected.

This activity can be put into perspective by noting that between the wars Germany published data covering practically every coast in the world including Ireland. The first volume of this military account of Ireland was completed on 30 September 1940. The point is that a lot of information gathering must have gone on in open disregard of the Reich's injunction about intelligence operations in Ireland.

Who provided this information which, in spite of some stereotyped gaffes, was meticulously detailed? In 1936 there were 529 German nationals living in Ireland. In 1946 there was a decrease of 69. In the same period there was a decrease of 27 Italians out of 325 and a decrease of 49 Czechoslovaks out of 124. This could have been one source of supply for the mass of data accumulated.

Another source was the Siemens firm's involvement in the construction of the hydroelectric scheme at Ardnacrusha on the Shannon which provided full access to capacities of Irish waterways. There was also ongoing research into fields like archaeology which made available a wide range of maps and charts with readymade data for translation into intelligence. In addition the Nazi 'Strength through Joy' movement brought a flow of touring hikers who seemed to be compulsive photographers of coastal areas. Many of these 'happy wanderers' were army reservists. The work took time and involved a hard core of professionals and a legion of part-time amateur helpers. There seems to have been no shortage of German sympathisers. The IRA were pro-German: it was the corollary of being anti-British.

On 31 October 1936 Sean Russell, acting as Quartermaster-General of the IRA and special envoy to the US, wrote to the German ambassador in Washington regretting the reported refusal by the Irish Free State government of landing rights to Germany for an international air service, 'a right apparently conceded without question to England, the traditional enemy of the Irish race'. The 'puppet Irish Free State government', the letter conveyed, were doing 'their British masters' bidding but the IRA were disposed to 'make returns to her friends in Germany for valued assistance in the early days of our present phase of the fight'.

Notwithstanding these protestations of brotherhood from the IRA no comradely responses were forthcoming from the Germans. They were more concerned at that time with coming to an understanding with England. In June 1936 the Nazi paper *Volkischer Beobachter* praised de Valera for disciplining the IRA. Koester of the Dublin legation explained that the suppression of the IRA was associated with the murder near Cork of Vice-Admiral Sommerville who was distortedly supposed to be a recruiting agent for the British Navy. No sympathy for the IRA was expressed by the Germans, who took the view that they had got what was coming to them. Changing circumstances altered that kind of attitude.

By the time the IRA bombing campaign in Britain began in 1939, the prospect of a German understanding with England had greatly receded. The Sudeten crisis had soured relations already disturbed by the occupation of the Rhineland and the annexation of Austria. On 24 January 1939 the *Frankfurter Zeitung* editorialised favourably about the IRA bombing. The *Volkischer Beobachter* also changed its tune from a few years previously, pointing out that sooner or later there would be a war with Great Britain and that allies would then be needed.

The interest of the Abwehr was awakened. The files were called for and one Oscar C. Pfaus was dispatched as contact man to the IRA. Kurt Haller, former Section Leader in Abwehr II's Office I in West Berlin, confirmed the opinion of Pfaus that up to that point the Abwehr were in the dark about Ireland and the IRA: he said that neither the Espionage Division nor the Sabotage Division had previously troubled themselves over Ireland, and that in fact contact with the IRA had been strictly forbidden. Only one man at that time,

a Major Voss (cover name Director Magnus), represented
Abwehr II. He was supposed to be a specialist for all dis-
contented minority groups ranging from the Flemish and
Bretons to the people of South Tyrol and the Irish! There
were links, however, with the *Deutsche Fichtebund,* the
pseudo-cultural organisation nominally founded to honour
the great German philosopher Fichte, but in reality set up in
1914 by Heinrich Kessemeyer as a vehicle for the dissemination of pan-German propaganda. Pfaus was an active member in the US. The only other possible excuse for his recruitment was that the Abwehr[6] was then in the throes of
reorganisation and rapid pre-war expansion. The Sabotage
Division which concerned itself with Ireland was now under
the comparatively new appointment, Lt Col. Lahausen,
whose job included such special operations as inciting minor-
ities to open rebellion. Part of the Irish side of this task was
alloted to Pfaus.

The Pfaus encounters in Ireland with the IRA moved with
the pace of a Chicago gang-land movie. He made contact
with them through the offices of none other than the Blueshirt leader, Gen. Eoin O'Duffy, and his adjutant, Captain
Liam Walsh.[7] Pretty young Joy Paine — referred to pejoratively by Colonel Dan Bryan[8] as a flapper, and by Enno
Stephan[9] as a patriot with *Fichtebund* interests — helped
to make the contact. To sustain the movie analogy, she proceeded to fall madly in love with Pfaus.

In February 1939 Pfaus invited Sean Russell, Chief of
Staff of the IRA, to send their agent to Germany where he
would be instructed in the procurement of small arms and
hand grenades. Jim O'Donovan was nominated. He became
the chief Abwehr agent in Ireland and was known as "V.
Held". O'Donovan, an M.Sc., had given up teaching at
Clongowes to become an employee of the Electricity Supply
Board. He had been a leading member of the IRA in the
early twenties and had returned at Russell's request to train
young IRA men in explosive and sabotage materials for the
bombing campaign in England. He was the instigator of the
'S' Plan — the Sabotage Plan. A torn pound note, one half
to the Abwehr and the other to be produced by the IRA
emissary to Germany on arrival, was to provide the means

of identification and recognition. O'Donovan visited Germany in February, April and finally on 23 August 1939. In May he checked the route to France of the Breton courier, Paul Moyse. The August trip nearly shattered the liaison when an officious German customs officer had Mrs Moty O'Donovan, who was accompanying her husband on the trip, strip-searched as a result of discovering an undeclared packet of cigarettes! O'Donovan consequently became very critical of things German for a time. However, there had been confirmation of the IRA decision to collaborate with Germany; plans in the event of a war between Germany and England were considered, links between agents were discussed and possibilities were weighed up about sending the IRA weapons for the fight against Northern Ireland. But the three meetings omitted to arrange a secret code for future wireless traffic. Haller thought out three English words containing as many letters as possible but incorporating a minor error for security purposes viz. HOUSE OF PARLIAMENTS. It was 1 September 1939 — the twelfth hour. Paul Moyse was hurriedly dispatched on the courier route to London and there delivered to the IRA contact the code, instructions for transmissions, co-operation etc. and a large sum of money. During this time Jim O'Donovan had no personal contact with Hempel. Later on he did visit the German Minister's house but in his own words he beat a hasty retreat when the policeman on duty there ('G' men he called them in the movie slang of the day) asked him his business.

General Eoin O'Duffy, on the other hand, was a frequent visitor to Hempel's. This may explain why he was the first person Pfaus tried to get in touch with in Dublin. It is typical of the confused muddling in the Abwehr with regard to Irish affairs, that, having given Pfaus the task of liaising with IRA headquarters in Dublin, they put him in contact with O'Duffy, a sworn enemy of the IRA, to help him accomplish that nebulous mission.

Before Pfaus was recruited, the Abwehr, because of either confusion or incompetence or for some other reason, had rejected a ready-made source of information available in this area, Helmut Clissmann. Clissmann's association with Ireland went back to 1930, when — then a member of the left-wing

Young Prussian League — he made a trip to Dublin as a student; in 1933 he returned first as an exchange student and later to do a doctoral thesis on 'The Wild Geese in Germany' for Frankfurt University. Before he came back to Dublin in 1936 he attended a lecture there entitled 'Celtic Leaders from Vercingetorix (55 B.C.) to de Valera'. Official attitudes towards him remained cool. Departmental apprehension was conveyed to the German legation that Clissmann's activities in the German Academic Exchange Service (he established branches in Dublin, Cork and Galway) were regarded as a front for a form of espionage activities.

There had been tension between Clissmann and the *Auslandsorganisation*, probably on account of his having been a member of the left-wing group; but on the occasion of his being accused of being a 'spy' there had been a closing of ranks. As was customary in correspondence of the time even Clissmann's application for permission to get married ended with the ejaculation 'Heil Hitler'. That was a public protestation of party loyalty: a password.

In the summer of 1938 Clissmann got a tip-off from his prominent republican friends of developments in the IRA. He promptly made his way to Germany to inform the Abwehr, an action that would appear to confirm earlier official misgivings. In what seems to be an unlikely story, credible only at a certain level of German bureaucracy, Captain Marwede, alias Dr Pfalzgraf of Abwehr II turned him away on the grounds that it was forbidden to become involved in Irish questions. This attitude of Pfalzgraf does not easily fit in with Carolle Carter's allegation that the Abwehr made its first contact with the IRA in 1937 through a Breton, Mill Arden, who was married to an Irishwoman:[10] or that another contact with the IRA had been established through Eivars and McCutcheon, two ex-Trinity College students who were supposed to be sympathetic to Nazi activities and who went to Germany to study. There is no indication that Clissmann's previous membership of a left-wing organisation had anything to do with his being rebuffed: inter-agency rivalries may have held the clue to it. This is another example of the lack of communication between the overlapping intelligence organisations. When the IRA bombing began it did not occur to Abwehr II that Clissmann was the ideal man to establish contact with the IRA. Nor — before they turned to Pfaus — do they seem to have considered recruiting a contact man from the ranks of the *Auslandsorganisation*.

Although Hempel remained the principal means of intergovernmental communication, the *Auslandsorganisation* also had official status to communicate directly. Its members drawn from the German colony in Ireland kept in touch with the IRA. The members were extremely well insinuated into the Irish commercial scene. Wolfgang Hahn (economic adviser to the Dublin group of *A.O.*) was a consulting engineer in 69 Fitzwilliam Square. Karl Krause (on the staff of the commander of the local *A.O.*) was representative of the AEG in Dublin. Franz (Frederick) Winkelmann (reputed to be Gauleiter designate for Ireland) was director of the Irish Glass Bottle Manufacturers Ltd; Oswald Müller-Dubrow (deputy leader of the local *A.O.* group and chairman of the German Association in Dublin) was a director of Siemens-Schuckert Ltd (Ireland). The other director was also an *A.O.* member Henri Broekhoven, a Dutchman who later turned anti-Nazi. And of course the leader of the organisation, Dr Adolf Mahr, was handily placed as curator of the National Museum! Another leading member was Colonel Fritz Brase, director of the Irish Army School of Music who had been made a professor by Hitler. The army authorities gave him a choice: leave the army or leave the *Auslandsorganisation*. He formally chose to leave the latter. The War Organisation (*Kriegsorganisation; K.O.*) assumed that if an intelligence service was to function in wartime it should be acquired in peacetime and camouflaged as a commercial undertaking or found some suitable niche in existing German official overseas missions.

Perhaps Hempel was aware of the extent of this penetration by the *Auslandsorganisation* or perhaps, in deference to their mission to maintain contact with subversive organisations, he had not himself cultivated relations with extreme nationalist opinion. It was true that Hempel moved in what he termed 'radical nationalist' circles but these, whether they liked it or not, were now, to the contempt of the IRA, incorporated in the establishment: Hempel referred to them as representing 'responsible radical opinion'. His interest in art for instance brought him into close contact with Dr L. S. Gogan, a '1916 man' and Dr Adolf Mahr's subordinate in the National Museum.

Hempel was, however, prompted to feel that something more was required, and that 'extreme nationalist opinion' should be cultivated. This meant the IRA. He sent for Clissmann and gave him the task of bridging the gap. Hempel obviously knew about him: Peadar O'Donnell in the left-wing paper *The Worker* had pilloried Clissmann as an alleged spy.

Not alone had Clissmann contacts with prominent IRA men, particularly Frank Ryan, but he also had contacts with the *A.O.* in London.[11] Herr Bene, 'State Group Leader for Great Britain and Ireland' had come under scathing criticism from another left-wing paper, the *Irish Workers' Voice*, for his propaganda stunts in Ireland. If left-wing criticism was anything to go by, Clissmann should have by now purged his 'Young Prussian League' associations in Nazi eyes. Time was short but Clissmann introduced Hempel to Sean MacBride 'and a few others' (Clissmann's phrase). Hempel thereafter regularly consulted with MacBride and he and Frau Hempel regularly visited the MacBrides in Roebuck. MacBride had the formidable task of constantly counselling Hempel: his golden rule for him was not to appear to be on the wrong side of the law at any time.

Clissmann went back to Germany when war broke out and in spite of Hempel's assurances that he would be back he did not return until it was over. He maintained that he was called up because of official bungling. Another story is that when his name did not appear on the list of Germans to be sent home from Ireland after 1 September 1939, the British, aware of the extreme company he kept, had influenced the Irish government to add his name to the list and he was asked to leave. Nowadays when there is some idea of the extent of the British infiltration and permeation of the German intelligence services – even Canaris himself is suspect – it is not fantastic to conceive a link between the two incidents. Clissmann was accompanied by forty-two key members of the colony – scientists, academics and administrators: this move was later regretted in Berlin as it was felt that they could have done more to help the German cause if they had remained in Ireland.

In fact, there were no possibilities for using them in any practical way in the early days of the war. Moreover, some of Bewley's theories were shared in high places in Ireland and Britain. He was convinced that National Socialism, whatever might be its defects, should be upheld by the western powers as the strongest, perhaps the only, force which could prevent the spread of a communist empire over half of Europe. That, he said, did not imply an unquestioning acceptance of all the practices of Hitler's regime. Lord Halifax had indicated an inclination towards the same line of thinking. Bewley saw an active role for Ireland in this context. Among the diplomats of the old school in Germany, however, he found no sympathy for meddling in Ireland. They regarded Ireland as a similar disturbing element in the British Empire as Alsace-Lorraine had been in the first German Reich.

Although those old school diplomats no longer ruled the roost in the corridors of power in Berlin, one of their members, Hempel, did influence opinion there, although not exactly in the way he intended. His roundabout style of reporting was interpreted in Berlin as saying what they wanted to hear. When Hempel referred respectfully to radical nationalist opinion, it was taken as a euphemistic reference to the IRA. They took Hempel's reports to substantiate their view that the difference between de Valera and the IRA lay mainly in methods. They recorded that the government hoped to attain its objectives by legal political means while the IRA tried to achieve success by terrorist means, but noted that most members of the present government had formerly belonged to the IRA. They concluded that by reason of its militant attitude towards England the IRA was the natural ally of Germany. Some of de Valera's rhetoric, reported verbatim by Hempel, blurred dividing lines even further and reinforced their convictions. The Abwehr was acknowledged to have secret connections with the IRA, which were undoubtedly impeded by the outbreak of war. It laid down at that stage, without analysing the mission, that the interest of the Abwehr was confined to promoting acts of sabotage.

Hempel later spelt out firmer opinions about IRA capabilities or the lack of them. But by then it was too late to affect preconceptions in some quarters that were later to result in the injection of a bizarre assortment of agents. In that sense the circumlocutory envoy had made a rod for his own back.

The chief Abwehr agent, Jim O'Donovan, was also contributing scrappy information at the time but the key feed to the intelligence process before the war was Hempel's reporting. His denigration of de Valera's pro-Britishness was taken to reflect the Taoiseach's wiliness and ability to ride two horses at the same time in order to achieve his undying aim of ending partition. The praise for Sean T. O'Kelly's fighting-cock nationalism substantiated the notions that the IRA represented the true soul of Ireland about which the government were forced by protocol and prudence to be circumspect.

Hempel had not succeeded in scotching absurd ideas of the value of German intervention in Irish affairs. His task was a difficult one at best. He was a conventional career diplomat representing, in a small strategically located country, a ruthless Nazi government which was at war with that country's closely related neighbour and 'ancient enemy'. German interpositions complicated the situation for him in the area of intelligence operations. These operations demanded dissembling of one kind and another over and above normal diplomatic requirements. A 'phoney' dimension was inevitable before the shooting war cleared the air in 1940.

FOUR

The Phoney War-Irish Style

The phoney war was an extension of phoney diplomacy. From the collapse of Poland in September 1939 until the opening of Hitler's *blitzkrieg* the following spring – the so-called 'phoney war' period – Ireland was a happy hunting ground for the double-talk on which the phoney diplomacy thrives. For a start the arrangement with the British crown for the accreditation of foreign diplomats to Eire was put out by the Irish side to be purely a constitutional contrivance in which words were not intended to mean what they said. Bewley jeered that de Valera had found this way out to convince Ireland of his independence and Britain of his loyalty because he could not afford to defy his British patrons or jeopardise his standing at Geneva. He ridiculed the Irish constitutional position wherein the Irish government could neither sign a treaty nor appoint an ambassador except through the medium of the king. In foreign eyes, King George VI was still head of the Irish state. Bewley thought it ludicrous for the Irish government to treat these reserved powers as a mere formality, to regard His Majesty as a mere 'rubber stamp' useful for registering the decision of a native government.

De Valera was not affected by Bewley's sneers. He knew what he was about. He was maintaining his aim of fashioning a form of external association which he had first put forward in 1921. This seemed to involve recourse to double-talk and even double-think. Bewley's gibe was that such tactics were no bother to one as devious as de Valera. However, Ireland was not alone in resorting to semantics: more than ever before diplomatic speech became a language on its own. The cynical pre-war peace feelers can be put into perspective by recalling that Hitler, as far back as 3 April 1939, had fixed 1 September as the date for launching an attack on Poland.[1]

The Polish campaign was a case of horses versus tanks and presented no obstacle to Hitler, intent on a quick military victory to further his *Lebensraum* policy. He obviously anticipated the inertia of Britain and France in failing to engage him while he was allowed a free hand in Poland. The phoney war, in essence, was the time when those who had declared war on Hitler did not fight.

The French army, then reckoned to be the strongest in the world, with no more than twenty-six German divisions facing them, sheltered shamefully behind their steel and concrete while a valiant Polish army was being exterminated. British bombers dropped leaflets, not bombs, over Germany while Poland was being ruthlessly overrun. They carefully calculated that if they had dropped bombs, they were ill-prepared to counter any retaliation: the thousand bomber raids of Air Marshal Albert ('Bomber') Harris on Köln, Hamburg and finally Dresden were not possible at that time. The Poles did not figure largely in these calculations.

In neutral Eire on the day Poland was invaded, a solitary sentry with a fixed bayonet was posted symbolically at the Northern-line Amiens Street station: 'as a purely precautionary measure'. A formal army statment was issued to reassure the Irish public. There was no panic: just a faint tremor of excitement at the prospect of routine moulds being broken.

Britain declared war on Germany on 3 September 1939 and the following day de Valera called a press conference at which he spoke of the German Envoy's visit to him a few days previously. Hempel had conveyed to the Taoiseach that Germany would, *under certain conditions*, respect Ireland's neutrality. De Valera had stressed that the aim of the Irish government was to preserve Irish neutrality. To accomplish this aim a National Emergency was declared. The Offences against the State Act was applied. The Special Criminal Court was set up. Powers of requisition were extended to authorised officers.

Shortly after the outbreak of war, Hempel, for the first time, found himself with a British counterpart in Dublin. Heretofore, disagreement about title had proved to be a barrier to British diplomatic representation in Eire. The title High Commissioner had too many imperial connotations to be acceptable in Ireland while the British baulked at the appointment of an ambassador or minister as they felt that such action would be tantamount to recognising Irish independence. De Valera's prepositional dexterity — substituting 'to' for 'in' — made possible the acceptance of a title for the proposed post: 'United Kingdom Representative *to* Eire'. Sir John Maffey's appointment to the post was approved on 22 September 1939. Chamberlain thanked de Valera for solving the title problem: de Valera sympathised with Chamberlain in his anxieties.

From the beginning Maffey made it plain that his job was to represent Britain's interests: where British and Irish interests coincided well and good, but he would always put his own country's interests first. That position was appreciated by the Irish side. Part of Maffey's problem was that he was not as well versed as he would have liked to have been on the complex convoluted nature of the history of Anglo-Irish relations. On 1 November 1939 he made a plea to Machty of the Foreign Office for background information on partition, explaining that he found himself drawn into difficult conversations on the subject. This led to an interesting shuttle of memos. In his first reply Machty gently hinted that the history and documentation of this subject was immense. He pointed out that there had been efforts to promote relations between North and South but that a press interview given by de Valera a couple of days previously charging the UK with maintaining partition by subsidising Northern Ireland and with gerry-'mandering and unfair treatment of the minority was one factor that suspended that line of advance. Before much progress had been made in promoting North-South relations de Valera's interview brought the partition issue out into the open as a political question and brought the predictable rejoinders from Northern Ireland. The other impeding factor he listed was the current IRA campaign.

Files were forwarded to Maffey and his interest was quickened when he came across a proposal for a solution on federal lines. Machty however poured cold water on that option: he did not rule it out but said it would raise considerable difficulty. Maffey recorded that he found the following note, found in the files, interesting and important:

Ulster 6 Counties
Though it may sometimes be proper to die in the last ditch there is no sense in living there. The word 'surrender' in the Orange slogan is deplorable as implying defeat and consequently suppressing reason.

Possible basis

(1)	No secession from Commonwealth (not bound to help; pledged not to hinder)	South gives
(2)	Ulster joins Irish parliament and relinquishes Westminster (with local vetoes on police, compulsory Gaelic etc.)	Ulster gives
(3)	The King is recognised as Head of Commonwealth (with Irish Royal Standard)	South gives
(4)	Elected President retained	Ulster gives
(5)	New National Anthem	both give
(6)	Abolition of '12th July' and 'Wear an Easter lily' slogans	both give
(7)	Armed Forces as in Dominions	Ulster gives and gains
(8)	Proportional Representation	
(9)	Free Trade with England (provided existing factories built up in South protected by preferential quotas if efficient)	
(10)	Finance on British Legion lines (money raised in the South retained there after agreed proportion deducted for Central Affairs to obviate cry of exploiting industrial North for idle South. England might have to help with a loan to offset 33% drop in South's Revenue in the abolition of Tariffs which were started for protection but are now the biggest item in Revenue).	

Do they (i.e. the Loyalists) consider the larger loyalty implied in value to Commonwealth of a settled Ireland? The interests of many and especially those of Southern Unionists have had to be sacrificed to the intransigence of the extreme Orange wing — a small majority at that.

No ready-made viable solution emerged from the files to enlighten the new UK Representative in Eire. A peevish letter from Markingley to Maffey on 13 December said he knew what contrariness the 'denizens' of that land were capable of and castigated de Valera for his speech which he held played right into Craigavon's hands. There was a wistful reference to an article by Frank MacDermot, 'The War and Irish Unity', published in the *Political Quarterly* calling for reconciliation by men of good will.

Men of good will were thin on the ground. Conciliatory exploring had been slowed down by the renewed IRA campaign: de Valera's fresh anti-partition broadside brought it to a stop. The Taoiseach's intervention set back the process then in train to reach an accommodation on the partition problem. Britain retained the bases in Northern Ireland. This outcome, by removing the compulsion by Britain to secure her west flank, made neutrality for Eire a more feasible proposition. Reunification was relegated for the duration, except for the rhetoric. De Valera was spared having to balance reunification against the abandonment of neutrality. Some feel that the word 'Machiavellian' is over-used in references to de Valera: it persists in suggesting itself in this context. He knew what Britain had to have: some bases; they existed in Ulster. He knew what he wanted: to spare his country from war. Pretexts had to be found to accommodate needs and put a face on the reconciliation of imperatives.

Sovereignty and independence were recurring themes in de Valera's speeches and he incorporated his concepts of them into the 1937 constitution. This constitution envisaged a unitary state which none the less had made expedient provision for the special place of the Catholic Church. He realised that the Unionists, to whom even diluted home rule was anathema, would find this arrangement equally abhorrent.

To leave the door open for them to come in peacefully, of their own free will, he piously made provision for the creation or recognition by law of subordinate legislatures and for the powers and functions of these legislatures. He used the word 'federal' loosely in this context so as not to abort opening dialogue. De Valera, who never mishandled words, left the term 'local autonomy or local powers' open to federal, con-federal or quasi-federal interpretations.[2] He was prepared to wring the last drop from semantics and dictionaries to unite the peoples of the island by consent and agreement although a formula which would have retained the British monarch as head of state in Northern Ireland would have stretched his ingenuity.

The External Relations Act abundantly demonstrated his skill in interpreting sovereignty when it suited: but there were limits. By 1939 pragmatic neutrality concerns had been substituted for deified concepts of sovereignty and de Valera clearly signalled his preference. The lofty declamations pro-nounced that sovereignty would not be bartered for reunific-ation: they were both God-given rights and were not for sale. In practice it meant that the price of relinquishing neutrality for the removal of partition would not be paid. Absolute twenty-six-county neutrality was preferred to a thirty-two-county unitary state with strings attached. That was the bleak reality.

Abruptly after the declaration of war de Valera showed his hand. An aide-mémoire dated 12 September 1939 prohibiting the use of Irish territorial waters and air space was presented by Dulanty, the Irish High Commissioner in London, to a perturbed Anthony Eden, the British Foreign Secretary. It was also submitted to Hempel and referred by him to Berlin. They accepted it subject to Irish neutrality being *'einwand frei'* ('unobjectionable'). This response gave de Valera an opportunity to stress the compulsion of having 'a certain con-sideration for Britain'.

This consideration did not extend to avoiding treading on their toes by the publication of the *aide-mémoire*. Joe Walshe — the *eminence grise* of neutrality policy — felt that the less put on paper about the subject the better. He had in mind the British genius for muddling through which was happier without written restrictions. De Valera had other ideas. He by-passed Walshe and gave the task directly to Michael Rynne, Walshe's subordinate, who had a purely legal job in External Affairs. It was composed overnight and the Taoiseach complimented him on the composition saying that he could not have done better himself. Walshe remained aggrieved but de Valera, apart from his own pedantic inclinations, took into account that a formal written document would commend itself to the German mentality. It was intended to serve both as a palliative and a protection. He did not realise that the Nazis would treat it simply as a piece of paper if it suited them. They did not share the characteristic German deference to written rules and regulations. The British, he felt, were worldly-wise enough to look out for themselves and anyway their interests and Irish interests largely coincided.

He underestimated British annoyance at the document. They were quite obsessed about publication and asked the Irish specifically not to publish it. Years later, however, Dr Michael Rynne clearly recalled that it had appeared in an edition of Deak and Jessup's *Neutrality Laws, Regulations and Treaties*. He remembered ordering a copy of that particular edition for the library of the Department and was quite specific about its appearance and even its price ('dark-greyish, cream coloured' paper cover, about two and a half inches thick and costing $13 to be airmailed from the United States). Not only that, Dr Rynne had earlier checked the galley proofs of the book. No copy of this edition of Deak and Jessup can now be found: neither the German archives nor the Library of Congress can find one. The edition in the Library of Congress is an earlier one and contains no documents dated later than 1 October 1938.[3] Dr Rynne remarked jocosely to the present author that the disappearance of the aide-mémoire amounted to a 'mini-Watergate'. There is a humorous exaggeration in that description but it is, none the less, a cause for suspicion that such an important document has disappeared totally, especially when one remembers how many people — not least Walshe and Maffey — had an interest in its suppression.

Once the terms of the aide-mémoire were known, Maffey set about making its restrictions less embarrassing for the

British government. Widespread knowledge of the restrictions would hamper loose interpretations. Hempel's concern was to see that the Irish government complied with the letter of the document in such a manner as to make it possible for the Third Reich to respect neutrality. He could not have guessed the extent to which it would be bent in Britain's favour. The phoney war pretences facilitated this bending although anomalies inevitably arose which sometimes stretched even the elasticity of Anglo-Irish considerations.

The attempt to appoint Dr Kiernan as the new Minister to Germany to replace Bewley was a case in point. The First Secretary, William Warnock, had been promoted *chargé d'affaires* to act as representative until a new appointment was made: as it happened he carried on alone until relieved by Cornelius Cremin in 1944. When Kiernan was nominated, Hempel cleared him to Berlin, describing him as being kind, careful, reticent, a good worker, an M.A., an ex-income tax inspector, an ex-director of Radio Éireann, versed in economic questions, with an interest in Celtic Studies. Kiernan's wife, the ballad-singer Delia Murphy, did not equally impress him: he classed her as being of humble origins from the West of Ireland. Maybe her rendering of earthy ballads offended the fastidious Minister.

Kiernan's departure was delayed and on 25 September 1939 Warnock explained to the German Foreign Ministry the difficulties in sending Kiernan abroad in wartime with a wife and five children. Hempel spotted that constitutional snags were rearing their head, and on 16 October he expressed his doubts that the king would sign Kiernan's accreditation. He still continued to press Berlin for material to give to the Irish government for the briefing of Kiernan in the event of the latter receiving accreditation. In considering the alternative of either de Valera or President Hyde signing the accreditation, the Envoy concluded that protocol insisted that it would require Hyde's signature before the Führer could receive Kiernan: de Valera's signature could only confer the status of ministerial accreditation on the Irish representative. He did not believe that either de Valera or Hyde could or would sign, as this would disturb the Commonwealth link. It became obvious to him that although the Irish government kept up a pretence of wanting full accreditation for Kiernan, de Valera had no intention of disturbing an arrangement of which he was the architect. The case was still not resolved by the following March and Hempel reported that the constitutional impediment to accreditation was now compounded by political considerations as a consequence of the conviction and hanging of IRA prisoners in Birmingham. Anthony Eden had had a word with de Valera over the difficulties arising from asking the king to sign credentials addressed to Hitler; the Taoiseach did not push to resolve the anomoly, feeling it unwise to pursue the matter. That position — not surprisingly — was not conveyed formally to Hempel, but he got the message. He fulminated openly about the disparity in representation: a Minister as against a young secretary acting as Irish Representative. Quietly he conveyed that it might be just as well to let the matter drop as Warnock seemed to be doing a good job and anyway he now remarked, in contrast to his previous glowing report, that Kiernan did not seem to have anything special to recommend him. He was learning fast that some neutrality tunes had to be played by ear.

His pre-war reports reflected de Valera's evolving conceptions of neutrality and his thinking out loud on the difficulties of maintaining it. He featured the Taoiseach's Dáil speech of 23 February 1939 which declared that neutrality was not only the most difficult but also the most costly of all the courses to implement; because whoever adopted a neutral stand had to be prepared to defend himself against the possibility of an attack from either side. The reservations he relayed about Ireland's capability of remaining neutral in the circumstances of contiguity to and trade with Britain brought a steely edge to German tones.

Their conditions and expectations were stiffly presented to de Valera by Ribbentrop through Hempel. If Ireland strayed from the path of neutrality 'as a result of a decision by the government themselves or by pressure exerted on Ireland from other quarters' the Germans would safeguard their interests 'in the sphere of warfare' in accordance with the demands of the situation. There was plain speaking on both sides. On 1 September Hempel took great care with the wording of a simultaneous press release by the two governments indicating where they stood in this matter. Both de Valera and Ribbentrop were satisfied with it.

One query did arise. Warnock was puzzled about the means used to communicate to Hempel German willingness to respect neutrality. He was punctiliously observing the letter of the law in giving official notification of Irish neutrality to Berlin. He innocently put the question to Woermann who lamely answered that he did not know exactly, mentioning the possibility of the American route then being resorted to. Warnock had tumbled to the existence of another route but neither he nor the Irish authorities realised then that a secret transmitter (later to cause much controversy and jeopardise neutrality) was located at the legation. Such matters were not taken seriously during the phoney war: diplomatic immunity and protocol conventions still dictated the play.

All the preliminary playacting however could not conceal the true face behind the phoney war mask. Although flying an Irish flag, the *Inver Liffey* was sunk in September 1939 by a German U-Boat. This action upset Hempel and he asked Berlin for an explanation. Before he received a reply, to his surprise, de Valera had minimised the incident. The ship, the Taoiseach said, was carrying contraband to a country at war and so ran the risk of being sunk. As he saw it, the U-Boat commander had done nothing out of the way; other combatants would do the same. Hempel warned the Foreign Ministry not to try to make too much capital out of this in the German press and radio. He then went on to give details of the sailing of American steamers *St John* and *Arcadia* and in the same breath sought details of the wiring and operating a condenser for his secret transmitter.

He felt that Irish neutrality should work as a favourable factor in the U-Boat campaign but, on the other hand, he did not feel that the sinking of the passenger ship *Athenia*[4] was a matter of pride. The irony was that Hempel himself was the most likely source of information that led to the sinking of another ship, the *Iroquois*, and Walshe conveyed the Irish government's embarrassment to him at an American report citing neutral Ireland as the source of the information which led to the sinking. Hempel protested over-much about the innocence of his press attaché, Petersen, in this affair, mentioning in passing his own 'careful telegram'. Woermann eventually had to tell the Envoy to keep quiet and let the matter rest, especially as Hempel had now — in a frantic effort to divert suspicion away from himself — also pointed the finger at a possible IRA involvement. This would have added to the Irish government's embarrassment and not helped the image they wished to project of a country well able to maintain strict neutrality.

In spite of the sinkings Germany wished to be seen to be respecting Irish neutrality, while ensuring that no unfair advantage accrued to Britain. Hempel busied himself reporting the possibilities of re-export of goods from Ireland to Britain when neutral ships had been allowed through with certain goods for Ireland. In this comprehensive economic report the German Minister stressed that a long war would be detrimental to Irish economic life and that the British were using the opportunity of economic difficulties to put pressure on Ireland. They also sought to make political capital out of Irish economic dependence. He indicated that a continuing Irish interest in imports from Germany would be welcome but that payment would present problems as would the danger of British connections and the mechanics of export: an Italian connection might be a solution and the Envoy left it to Berlin to examine as to whether Irish cattle and trade could be procured in such a way. He told of getting an undertaking from Boland to put a stop to re-export and in return he extracted from Woermann an assurance that German naval forces had been instructed to observe Irish neutrality strictly. These were significant contributions from the Third Reich's representative towards preserving the externals of neutrality. He was a restraining influence.

He had already rebuked the German radio for its English language broadcast to the effect that the Dublin blackout was favouring the British. In his account of an angry Dáil reaction to that broadcast Hempel used an interesting word — *bagatellisierend* — to describe de Valera's answer playing down the affair. Walshe had told Hempel confidentially that the blackout was implemented solely at the behest of the Irish Minister for Defence and that it was directed primarily against possible eventual British flying intentions but he emphasised that lifting the blackout would adversely affect the position of other neutrals. Hempel warned the Foreign Ministry that, in view of the strenuous efforts of the Irish government to maintain neutrality, such defamatory remarks as had been broadcast must cease. The Envoy seemed to be making up his own mind on issues and taking a stronger line with his Berlin base as befitted his status as the man on the spot. The influence and prompting of the firm but flexible leadership adroitly exercised by the Irish side was having its effect.

He confirmed in early October that Irish neutrality was being strictly observed, had wide popular support and should be supported by Germany. The warning notes he sounded were an index to the mistaken attitudes that he was seeking to counter. Caution, he admonished, should be exercised in submarine warfare; special treatment was required in the application of the blocade to Ireland; interference in Irish internal conflicts should be avoided. He made the point that leading British statesmen and officials — including Eden — did not have any significant objections to Irish neutrality; but that other influential groups did object and that resulted in a fear on the part of the Irish of British demands for harbours and airports if the war situation worsened. Irish neutrality, he continued, was being very closely watched in the USA and any abandonment of American neutrality would constitute a direct threat to Irish neutrality. Coupled with the repetition that Germany should continue to support Irish neutrality he recommended that they should also support Irish independence on a broad national basis. He felt that the Irish question in press and radio should be handled on a purely factual basis and that any attempts to exploit stories directly for propaganda against England should be avoided as they could only be counter-productive. He stressed that Ireland rejected belonging to the British Empire and recognised only a loose connection with it for foreign policy purposes. He acknowledged, however, that while the Irish reserved the right to criticise the British to their hearts' content they would not listen to a foreigner going too far with such criticism. He repeated again his advice against any interposition in Irish affairs. He specifically opposed giving German aid to the IRA.

He did not invoke principle and his counsel relating to the preservation of neutrality was pragmatic and down to earth. On that point Frau Hempel's caustic comment was that with opponents like Veesenmayer it was crucial to be practical if Germany's best interests were to be served especially as far as madcap schemes involving the IRA were concerned. The Envoy baldly stated that interference now could rob the IRA of all chances of future success by giving Britain a pretext to intervene, 'and Irish neutrality as well as the possibility of a future utilisation of the Irish cause for German interests' would be prematurely destroyed. This situation, the German Minister continued, would probably change if Irish neutrality were to be violated or if Britain were weakened sufficiently to make the prospects of regaining Northern Ireland more favourable: then there would be a prospect of a broad national rising supported by the Irish overseas and this would force the Germans to make a decision to promise Ireland support and the return of Northern Ireland at the conclusion of peace. Hempel passed on the rumour that hope for such an outcome had been expressed by Dáil deputies (but not by de Valera, he hastened to add). His firm opinion was that the time was not ripe for such involvement. He made clear that the IRA was not strong enough for significant action against Britain and was also probably lacking in a leader of any stature. This, however, did not deter him from mentioning at the end of November 1939 that the IRA had informed him that in the event of British action against the legation, they would defend them and take them to safety. He added, as an afterthought apparently, that the government would also, probably, be willing to do the same!

German propaganda reflected German attitudes. Hempel commented that the German broadcasts in English were listened to everywhere, and were the best of propaganda though he had reservations about the efficacy of the sharp personal attacks on Churchill, which he felt achieved the opposite of the intended effect, especially in Britain. On the other hand, as far as Ireland was concerned, he reported that the Irish-speaking broadcasts worked brilliantly and both the government and Irish speakers were well pleased with this first international recognition of the Irish language. This was the line to go on, he urged: tone down on the propaganda, stick to culture and the importance of German know-how and skills to revive old Irish cultural traditions; stress German-Irish relations. He paid tribute to the Irish used in the broadcast but suggested avoiding using the word 'Gaelic': use the word 'Irish' instead, he advised. He was also against sending certain types of material through the post, as this would militate against his increasingly successful measures against British propaganda. His representations were apparently one factor in having the virulently anti-German English papers banned from the Irish market.

His good work and homilies however did not deter Ribbentrop, in early 1940, from appointing Veesenmayer, the *coup d'etat* specialist, to foment an Irish rebellion. All the initiatives for this move came from the Foreign Ministry at the same time as it was orchestrating the so-called peace feelers.

The peace initiatives epitomised the phoney diplomacy of the 'phoney war'. Hempel's name was associated with the peace feelers. The German Minister's initial assessment of Maffey noted him as a possible player in Italian-prompted peace overtures, which followed the overrunning of Poland. The reason Hempel gave for this was that the new British Representative in Ireland — who, he said, had been partly educated in Germany and was former Under-Secretary of State for the Colonies and Governor-General of the Sudan — had been the author of reports on the Abyssinian conflict which were favourable to Italy. Having said that, he immediately (and characteristically) hedged his speculations on Maffey's usefulness: He telegraphed:

> The first impression is good; thus there is hope of useful mediation, *but on the other hand* [my italics] there is concern on the part of nationalist circles. The government is hoping that he will be appointed Minister which would signify the recognition sought by Ireland of her special position with reference to the Commonwealth.

He had already conveyed on 3 October 1939 that Chamberlain and an influential section of the cabinet would welcome peace if British prestige could be preserved in the process. In spite of his persistent obsession with the dangers of British provocation, Hempel had connections with British bishops regarding peace initiatives, though Frau Hempel held that she never heard of any such thing. Officially the only peace terms acknowledged by the Germans were those announced in Hitler's Reichstag speech on 6 October 1939, and Woermann had lugubriously commented on Chamberlain's decision for war after the Führer's hand of peace had been brutally rejected. Hempel took pains to point out that he was following the party line in any movement towards peace feelers. Referring to de Valera's probing to try to help Chamberlain's efforts against Churchill and the other hawks in the British cabinet, he priggishly wrote that he had strictly adhered to the directives of telegraphic instruction No. 185 of 24 October 1939.

The peace initiative that literally hit the front page and embarrassed Hempel was the bizarre business of Lord Tavistock, to whom Hempel referred as a crank. The 51-year-old Tavistock, who was a former active adherent of communism and an expert on social credit, was later attracted to nazism and fascism. He was also interested in the Anglican Pacifist Fellowship and accused the British government of having started the war. In March 1940 he published a leaflet setting out alleged German peace terms which he said he had obtained from the German legation in Dublin through an Irish friend. The friend he alleged was one Craig (or Greig) of Belfast who had a German wife. Tavistock (later the Duke of Bedford) held that he was led to believe by the Dublin legation that the German government was prepared to allow Czechoslovakia full independence provided she remained neutral; similarly in the case of Poland, provided an outlet to the sea with necessary rail communications and the use of the Vistula was granted to Germany; the Germans, he reported, were interested in an international disarmament pact and were ready to join a reformed League of Nations; they were prepared to hold a plebiscite in Austria and undertook to co-operate with an international body to find a national home for the Jews; but they wanted the return of their former colonies.

Hempel vehemently denied that any such information was given but the impression remained that there was no smoke without fire. (There was no fire, Frau Hempel insisted.) One way or another his circumspection in refusing to see Tavistock himself but in passing him on to Thomsen was justified. Had the German Minister given Tavistock an interview he could have been compromised. Tavistock had passed information on to Lord Halifax who, while showing little interest and describing Tavistock's action as irregular, did little to deter his unorthodox fellow peer and in the end gave him permission to visit Dublin to check if the terms were authentic. Tavistock's version then was that about that time, the Germans, having been snubbed in their peace overtures just after the outbreak of the war, were becoming evasive and were not prepared to give official sanction to these new approaches.

If that version were correct it illustrated one more aspect of the phoney war because the Germans, while posturing as the injured peacemakers, were at the same time increasing military activity behind the scenes along the Reich frontiers with Belgium, Luxembourg and the Netherlands; they were in fact forming up for the coming Blitzkrieg in May 1940. And, as the Political Department admitted the previous February, the Abwehr had secret connections with the IRA to forge an alliance against England. Also, Hitler, in outlining a five-point programme[5] in an interview to the American government representative Sumner Welles, stated that they were ready for a long war.

Tavistock for his part felt that he was not getting an adequate response to his peace feelers and John McGovern MP, who had been associated with him in this enterprise, suggesting telling the whole story to the press. The resultant political storm was an embarrassment to Halifax, as a member of the government who could not disclaim knowledge of the affair, and to Hempel whose cautious approach in the first instance now served to extricate him. Hempel was pleased with the way the *Irish Press* handled his rebuttal of the business.

As well as McGovern, George Lansbury, Labour MP for Bow and Bromley, and the Most Rev. William Temple, Archbishop of York, had been involved in peace overtures; the German historian, Martin,[6] traces the Hempel connection. The links were thought to be with an English peace party, to which the Archbishop of York belonged and which included Lords Buccleuch (who was connected with the royal family), Buxton, Darnley, Farringdon and Holden and the spokesman, the Labour MP Dick Stokes. Chamberlain, Halifax, Simon, Hoare, Londonderry and Astor are mentioned; even the Duke of Windsor seems to have played a part as a Germanophile appeaser.[7]

Hempel quoted the Irish High Commissioner in London around Christmas 1939 indicating increasing optimism for peace tendencies among the British cabinet but *on the other hand*, this typical Hempel report went on, increasing Finnish resistance had stimulated an inclination to carry on the war against Germany. It was hard to pin Hempel down to unequivocal assertions.

There does not seem to be a report from Hempel of the interview that a 65-year-old woman, Mrs Hungerford of the United Arts Club in Fitzwilliam Street, Dublin, alleged that she had with him. According to herself, it had to do with the putting out of peace feelers. She later sought to contact Maffey to tell him about it. Her gist was that Hitler did not really want to dominate the world; he just wanted equal rights with Britain and France; that he was in fact pro-British. Mrs Hungerford, an Englishwoman, said that Hempel felt that Maffey was the one person who could give those views widespread publicity but he could not see how *he* could visit him to discuss the matter. The editor of the *Evening Mail*, Anderson, felt, she said, that the views of the German Minister were sincere. She did not think that any good would come of seeing the editor of the *Irish Times*, who in her opinion was bitterly anti-German as a result of having been interned in Germany in the previous war. Maffey, although he found the feelers interesting, doubted Hempel's sincerity. In his view the German Minister could make contact informally, if he really wanted to, through one of his colleagues, say the Italian representative. He took no action.

That was the end of it, but Hempel was not disheartened and he continued to foster the phoney peace facade. He renewed his counsel for caution in the application of the blockade to Ireland and in submarine warfare and reissued warnings about getting mixed-up with the IRA. He coolly read what seemed to be British policy towards Ireland and reflected it, as he saw it, soberly and with balance.

His handling of the field of communications did not make a similar superficial contribution to the preservation of neutrality. He had no qualms about using the secret transmitter. He saw to its servicing and arranged frequencies. His job was to communicate and he was not going to be stopped by academic consideration of neutrality. (Anyway, as Frau Hempel was quick to point out, the British also had a secret transmitter in Rumania.) Hempel then busied himself to make sure that he had something worthwhile to communicate.

He was a veritable sleuth-hound, snooping after firms like McGee and Beck and Scott to uncover breaches of neutrality. Frau Hempel again bridled at the suggestion of snooping. Her husband, she retorted, constantly received unsolicited material pushed stealthily through their letter-box at home. She could never make out how they got in: far from snooping, in her view her husband was merely acting on information received.

He suspected a re-export ploy when a cargo of crude oil had to be refused in Cork because there was no refinery there. He had also heard that timber was being re-exported to Harland and Wolff and to the Ulster Timbucktoo Company who were acting for a Swedish Pulp Company in Maidenhead, London. He pressed the Irish government for clarification of regulations and for explanations and occasionally embarrassed them. Boland kept reassuring him on those points and Hempel in turn put in a word in support of Irish interests. He requested, in the event of a tightening of the blocade, that a protected route should be found for the relatively small imports of goods from countries other than Britain. Anglo-Irish trade, he pointed out, had but a minimum effect in compromising the neutrality position. His aim was to avoid driving Ireland into British hands. He was ambivalent at times about driving her into the hands of the IRA, especially if that organisation ever began to show signs of becoming a popular movement.

His report on the IRA's successful raid on the Irish army's armoury at the Magazine Fort in the Phoenix Park, Dublin at Christmas 1939 developed into an analysis of de Valera's strengths and weakenesses. De Valera, he said, was being criticised for his pacifist attitude towards Northern Ireland but he took the Taoiseach's statement that Northern Ireland would not be a bargaining counter for a cattle deal as applying also to a deal relating to the ports. De Valera had conveyed to him — perhaps deliberately — that his intention was to let the Northern Ireland question lie for the time being. But Hempel wondered whether the 'national movement' would permit such a course of action. He did not see the opposition, whom he classified as more pro-British and anti-IRA than Fianna Fáil, as an alternative government, but he predicted an increase in tension between the government and the 'nationalists'. His repeated blurring of nationalist and IRA in that report could possibly be attributable to the initial impact of the raid. It seemed to have been successful, for they seemed to have got away with it. It would appear as a result of the raid as if the IRA were truly a force to be reckoned with. Hempel hinted at Irish army collaboration, but did not substantiate his hint.

He never seemed to be able to make up his mind about the Irish army. The previous October he observed sceptically that it was supposedly ready to defend neutrality in all directions in spite of the presence of pro-British elements. The following May he swung to his other view that it was quite likely permeated with elements, especially among the Volunteer Force, in close contact with the IRA. He made these remarks in the context of commenting that the Irish government would only make concessions on the ports if the British resorted to force. In that case he thought they might put up armed resistance but *on the other hand*, considering the small size of the Defence Forces, they might not.

He had wide scope for speculation during the phoney war and his reports covered a wide range of subjects. In addition to policy matters he found time to report on difficulties with Petersen,[8] whom he had taken on as press attaché at the outbreak of the war and to whom he paid 500 marks per month. This newspaperman had a flair for getting himself into scrapes. Boland thought he was an ass — so did Francis Stuart. But Petersen's wife's opinion was that he was the only one at the legation who was not a Nazi. Hempel damned him with faint praise and put his shortcomings down to youth and political inexperience abroad and said that he was doing a good job as a press liaison officer. He saw no way of getting rid of him by repatriation and asked what form of rebuke he should administer.

He recounted his own problems in trying to get back to Berlin for a conference with Woermann. The prospect of enlisting Irish co-operation in the matter of securing safe conduct through Britain was sounded out and the precedent of the facilitation of German diplomats stranded in Europe at the outbreak of the war to return to their posts in South America were cited. No such facilitation was forthcoming from the cagey Irish side. Warnock pointed out the obstacles to travelling to Germany in wartime but for a while Hempel stubbornly stuck to his views of rights based on diplomatic practices and precedents. His demand was not as incomprehensible as it might appear.

The United States and Italy were still neutral and lines of communications were open to both of those countries. In that context the aspiration of Hempel and Woermann to have a conference in Berlin which involved Hempel travelling through enemy territory does not sound so unreal; especially if it is considered in conjunction with the following aide memoire issued on 27 December 1939 concerning reciprocal arrangements for diplomats and their families:

> The American *chargé d'affaires* in Berlin has been authorised by the British government to maintain its present practice respecting the treatment of German diplomats and consular officers as defined in the aide memoire of December 25, 1939 so long as the German authorities act in the same manner towards similar categories of British subjects.

The phoney *Sitzkrieg* in the West was quite a gentlemanly affair in the beginning. The officers did not have their swords sharpened — which was the first thing they did in August 1914 — but it would seem that time-honoured procedures on laws and usages of war might be followed. If that were so, Hempel would have been in his element; de Valera too would have been at home with formulated procedures.

The Irish side did not mediate to get the German Minister a British guarantee of a safe passage: they had to take their posture on neutrality into consideration. It is interesting to speculate how the War Office — also hidebound prisoners of practice and procedure — would have reacted to such a formal request from, in their eyes, an errant Eire. In any event Hempel never travelled, though he cherished the illusion up to May 1940, contemplating routes through Switzerland.

The sinking of cargo ships was a portent that the war might not continue to be waged in a droll gentlemanly fashion. There were also old reports that Hempel purported to have got from a reliable Irish 'nationalist' that a British offensive was planned in Belgium and the Caucasus and later in Norway. Britain obviously did not have such capabilities and, in view of what transpired later, this piece of disinformation was probably Abwehr inspired. Two channels of communication between Ireland and the Third Reich were available to them: Hempel to the Foreign Office and the IRA to the Abwehr.

The Germans were not the only ones concerned with disinformation and the creation and projection of images. A series of *Daily Telegraph* articles reprinted in the *Irish Press* had prompted Walshe to suggest to Hempel that the Germans, as a counter, supply a series of articles favourable to Germany which could also be published in the *Irish Press*, the government organ. The idea was, as far as possible, to keep both sides happy. Irish attitudes towards the belligerents during the phoney war were accommodating. They were not going to get too excited about anything. This was tempered by a realisation that, in spite of antipathies, there was a sneaking regard for the British.

At the end of October 1939, for example, Maffey received a letter from a Lieutenant Mason of the Royal Navy from Arbour Hill prison where he had been lodged by the Irish authorities on suspicion of spying for the British. He admitted that he had entered Ireland on behalf of the British government to obtain information about German submarines. As he was about to leave he was arrested as a suspected republican anarchist or a German! The letter went on to say that he eventually disclosed his identity and was assured that if he could prove it he could leave; but under interrogation which he said must have confused him he let slip that he was an officer of the RNVR. He was promptly lodged in prison though no charges were preferred. He was very distressed and feared the worst. He did not know Maffey, but claimed that they had many friends in common in the Sudan. He had also written to Lord Powerscourt admitting that he was operating on behalf of the British government but that the execution of the mission was left to himself and that it was on his own initiative that he had set foot on Irish soil. 'I assumed', he wrote, 'for the purpose, the personality of an Irish tradesman on holiday, with a bicycle and an Irish accent and a vile assortment of ready-made clothes . . . I was foolish enough to reveal that I am the holder of a commission in the RNVR — a bad blunder. Possibly the German consul had a hand in this. Since last May I have been underlined in Hitler's black list.' With his Irish tradesman's rig-out and accent it is perhaps little wonder that he was picked up! Anyway, he was released and it all ended cosily. Walshe wrote about the affair to G. D. Craig in the office of the British representative in tones of easy familiarity which underlined the relaxed relationship between the two sides. Maffey was thanked by Godfrey of Naval Intelligence for his assistance in getting Mason released.

Neither the theatrical British agents — nor their German counterparts — would get any marks for mastering the art of disguise. Attitudes were at that point softened accordingly. In 1939 and early 1940 it seemed to be nothing to worry about really: a bit of a laugh, all part of the phoney war. The Irish consideration for Britain almost went without saying: between the lines it was being taken for granted. The 'Paddies' had a high profile, helping the war effort in the fields, in the factories and above all in large numbers in the fighting forces.

The way John Betjeman of Maffey's staff related to Eire's *salon* society was symptomatic. He represented the acceptable face of espionage: he was a marvellous verbaliser, a lush and a bit of an eccentric, qualities which immediately endeared him to the natives. He was condescending about what he termed 'Irish gush', although he kept that to himself until he was back in Britain. Betjeman was Ireland's favourite spy, and his activities in this field could be laughed off. No one took them seriously.

Another case involving Brendan Behan illustrates this easy-going attitude between the British and the Irish. The Department of External Affairs read in the papers that Behan had been sentenced to three years borstal detention. This surprised them because they had refused him a permit to travel to Britain: they asked the Foreign Office to check what travel documents he had produced to gain entry. It turned out he had landed in Liverpool at the beginning of December 1939 using a travel permit (M.37315). This permit had been issued to a Peter Russell but Behan had substituted his own photograph for Russell's and altered the dates. There was no great fuss made about it on either side of the Irish sea.

The Irish attitude towards Germany, on the other hand, was no joke though they tried to seem fair and show their understanding that there was a war on. Hempel reported in October 1939 that the attitude of the Irish government towards him was formal but definitely friendly. Misgivings over the conquest of Poland remained but in December 1939 he reported that many Christmas gifts had been sent to German POWs in England. It could not and did not last.

Nineteen forty brought a change in attitudes. De Valera had held his tongue on the occupation of Denmark and Norway. Those countries were comparatively far away and Britain was in between to act as a protective buffer. The invasion of the Low Countries was much closer home: de Valera felt that he could no longer remain silent. He stated publicly:

> Today two small nations are fighting for their lives and I think I would be unworthy of this small nation, if on an occasion like this, I did not utter our protest against a cruel wrong which has been done them.

The phoney war was over. German armies overran France which had previously been judged the strongest military power on the continent. Only a reeling Britain stood between Hitler's Reich and unfettered hegemony over Central and

Western Europe with the further promise of *Lebensraum* in either the colonies or elsewhere. Hitler still envisaged a partnership with Britain on the basis of partitioning the world, with Britain as the strongest sea power and Germany the supreme land power. But as there was no reliable sign of British willingness to play ball, the Führer was constrained on 21 May 1940 to dicsuss the problem of a landing in Britain with Admiral Raeder.

History and geography had dictated that the Ireland factor be taken into account in considering a landing in Britain. The joke was over: the Great Bore War; *der Sitzkreig; la Drôle de Guerre* was ended. But what the threat of the German invasion clarified on the one hand for Great Britain and Ireland was clouded on the other hand by political obscurantism and racial prejudice.

FIVE

The Fogs of War

O_n 12 April 1939 de Valera sent a personal handwritten letter to Chamberlain to say that a free united Ireland would have every interest in wishing Britain to be strong, but when Britain's strength appeared to be used to maintain division on the island, no such considerations could have any force. In Hempel's analysis this unresolved partition grievance suggested a factor to be manipulated in the Reich's favour. In his eyes if Britain became sufficiently weakened some attempt might be made to regain the North. After the debacle at Dunkirk at the end of May 1940 only the English Channel prevented Britain from being overrun. She was weakened to a degree the German Minister could never have dreamed of when he made his prognosis for an attack on the North. De Valera did not find the Envoy's conduct irreproachable during this period. In the Taoiseach's opinion when the tide of war flowed in Germany's favour Hempel could be inflexible.[1]

In June 1940 the German people were in a state of euphoria. It would be unnatural for Hempel not to be similarly infected. Canaris was an exception in divining that the phenomenal military success, which brought German armies to the French Atlantic coast to menace the British Isles directly, concealed the Führer's military naivety and his fundamental ignorance of strategy.

With the fall of France the Third Reich was at the height of its power. To many, Germany appeared invincible. De Valera was no exception. It took courage on his part to condemn the German invasion of Belgium and Holland. There were, however, limits to which a small nation like Eire with a low grade military capability could push such a protest. The

Germans were very angry with de Valera over this speech and remarks made. The Envoy anticipated his government's instructions and had already protested on his own initiative.

As befitted their relative combat power the Irish government made muted responses to the protests and these were taken by the German side as apologies for de Valera's unfriendly speech. The German records say that both Boland and Warnock expressed themselves in an apologetic manner. The Irish version disclaimed this and held that they were merely pouring oil on troubled waters: they made it plain however that they did not want their actions misinterpreted as defeatism. They had signalled that they would resist aggression.

On 10 May 1940 Hempel reported a significant response by the Minister for Defence in the Dáil in reply to a question asking if there were an agreement with Britain in the event of Ireland being attacked: the cryptic reply then was that in such circumstances the Danish example would *not* be followed.[2] Nevertheless in the wake of the overwhelming *blitzkrieg* the Irish tone was conciliatory. Boland mollified Hempel to an extent tantamount to apologising, remarking (according to Hempel) that the people 'over here' did not really know what the Germans had to put up with from those Dutch agents, and from other Allied machinations. Warnock's mien, according to Woermann, the Director of the Political Department in Berlin, was correspondingly meek. He said that Warnock had already been informed by his government and expressed himself in a similarly apologetic manner as the deputy of the Irish Minister had done to their Minister in Dublin.

Warnock's task was difficult, especially if it is taken into account that his predecessor, Bewley, had now assumed the guise of an ultra-patriot and was still in the wings in Italy prompting the German government on Irish affairs. None the less, considering the Irish government's avowed policy of neutrality, some of Warnock's alleged remarks read rather oddly. Having made the point that Ireland wished to remain neutral towards all powers, the Irish representative in Berlin added an anti-British implication of his own. Speaking personally, he explained that Ireland in the last war against England had struck too early but this time, he implied, that mistake would not be repeated. Warnock was a Protestant from the Ringsend area of Dublin, a graduate of Trinity College and an enthusiast for the Irish language; he had been a teacher before joining the diplomatic service. Any expression of such extreme views, at variance with his government's declared policy, would nevertheless have been out of character in a career diplomat. It is unlikely that he had been misunderstood; Warnock spoke fluent German. There was no misunderstanding, however, the note of menace in the German retort: that in view of the German successes the question was whether Ireland's anti-British strike might not come too late.

Warnock does not deny that, in the circumstances, he may have made some such remarks as were attributed to him by Woermann, who later repeated his conviction that the Irish representative was decidedly anti-British. He recalled that he may have made the 1916 remarks off the cuff, as he was getting his coat, or that they may have been prompted. The point he has since stressed was that he was not specifically instructed to make remarks of that kind though he had been instructed by Boland to calm things down. That reflected the prevailing healthy respect for the intimidating German military might of the time. It was sensibly recognised that the Third Reich was not to be trifled with.

But as Hempel quietly reported on 23 May 1940 another attitude was also current. Feeling in Ireland for Germany, except among extreme elements, had materially deteriorated since the invasion of Belgium and the Netherlands especially in Church circles, influenced as they were by the Pope's attitude. The Envoy's opinion was that any German intervention in Ireland before a British attack would be counterproductive and he saw no imminence of such an attack. The British, in his opinion, would attack only in an emergency to avoid being beaten to the punch by Germany. He acknowledged that any German assistance, especially if accompanied by a proclamation of a German aim to liberate Northern Ireland, would probably give a powerful boost to the anti-English nationalist movement. On the other hand he doubted that a move by them on Northern Ireland would best serve German interests.

He speculated perceptively on the possible consequences

of invasion: a German intervention, he judged, would meet with strong resistance; the Irish army would obey orders although it contained IRA elements, particularly among the Volunteer Force, who in possible collaboration with the nationalist population might have been happier waging a form of guerilla warfare against an English attack. In the face of a German invasion, de Valera, supported automatically by the British, would, Hempel thought, proceed ruthlessly against the IRA, exploit the situation, involve the USA and press for a return of Northern Ireland. The Envoy's report went on to speculate as to how this danger of possible Irish involvement in the war might be used to pressurise Britain to take a decisive step to settle the Northern Ireland question and he even thought it conceivable — without elucidating — that the French government could be interested in such a move: nothing was certain, the situation was unstable.

As the German Minister saw it, de Valera was the only leader of any stature who could keep extreme nationalist elements under any sort of control, while at the same time maintaining friendly understanding with England, even if that meant risking the threat of becoming involved in the war. On balance he did not see any voluntary political concessions being made which would violate neutrality and he felt that de Valera would stick to this approach even if England were defeated. He suggested that such an eventuality would not prevent the Irish leader from continuing to exploit Britain's weakness and, by working as he had done for a long time in the USA, to secure the return of Northern Ireland. The German Minister saw this outcome as strengthening the Taoiseach's position and possibly redounding to Britain's advantage in the USA, which he suspected of having a hand in the game. A bridge across the Atlantic was an important factor in planning contingency counter-attacks. American good will was vital to Britain.

Up to mid May 1940 Hempel's continuous estimate on the various aspects and outcomes attendant on an invasion of Ireland had the comparatively calm detached air of a scenario for a staff college exercise: a certain remoteness was discernible. Suddenly on 24 May his reports beame more agitated and shrill. He was abruptly forced to realise that the invasion

about which he had theorised and pontificated could become
a reality: a reality which directly implicated him. The subject was no longer an academic exercise for detached dis-
sertation.

Alarmed, he reported what details he had of the arrest of
an Irishman named Held because of his contacts with a
German who called himself Brandy, but whose real name, it
turned out later, was Dr Hermann Goertz. Goertz was a
lodger in Held's house and in his room a police raid discovered plans of Irish ports and defence layouts, transmitters,
$20,000, a secret code, a parachute, insignia of the German
Luftwaffe, German First World War decorations, a military
cap and a black tie of German origin. Hempel complained
that he had already warned the Foreign Ministry about Held
on account of his association with Hamilton, who, he held,
was a provocateur for the British whose aim it was to destroy
Irish neutrality and close the German legation. As usual he
had grounds for his apprehensions about Held and Hamilton.
Held was the illegitimate son of a German father and an Irish
mother; separated from his American wife, he lived in
Templeogue, Dublin with his mistress, the wife of a British
Royal Air Force man. John Hamilton Cannon was an ex-
British soldier with an address in Ranelagh, Dublin. In
October 1939 he had complained to Scotland Yard that both
Held and the German Minister endeavoured to persuade him
to act as a spy. He had previously sued Held unsuccessfully
in the Dublin courts for the return of papers relating to what
he claimed was his invention of a safety device to prevent
aircraft from crashing! Held's defence was that he had passed
the papers on to the German Minister. Hamilton alleged that
he refused Hempel's pressures to act as a spy and that the
German Minister in turn got his own back by making an
'abominable' report about him to the Irish Minister for Justice.
He then wrote to the Home Office claiming that he was being
persecuted by Hempel, insisting to them that he had valuable
information which 'would avert a catastrophe'.

Scotland Yard's recorded reaction was that Hamilton had a
'bee in his bonnet' because he attributed losing his case against
Held to machinations by Hempel and the Irish authorities.
That was the reason they felt that he was continuously pester-

ing them with his claim to be in possession of inside information concerning activities against Britain by the German Minister in Eire. In their opinion Hamilton was chancing his arm and they concluded that the information existed only in his imagination.

He got a similar unsympathetic hearing from the British office in Dublin. He had written upbraiding Maffey with being remiss in not being alert to the information collection activities of Hempel and the Italians. They found the letter long-winded and Maffey wrote across it: 'This is a tripe-merchant. Ignore.' The unfolding events, however, dictated that such matters be taken seriously.

Hempel's report indicated that de Valera's government were showing signs of panic over the Goertz incident. He convinced himself that the whole thing was a frame-up, an act of vengeance against himself and Held and that the supposed Brandy was in fact a British agent. Hempel expressed himself strongly on this subject, saying he would speak to Boland about this renewed provocation by the British and would express the firm expectation of a satisfactory attitude on the part of the Irish government. His attitude posed queries as to either his lack of information or to his histrionic capacity: the likelihood is that he was unaware of the details behind the Held affair. It was Nazi policy not to tell diplomats more than they needed to know. According to Frau Hempel, at the funeral of Wenzel, a member of the legation staff, someone whispered the news to Hempel of the Abwehr agent's arrival: it came, she said, as a complete surprise to him; that was the first he had heard of it.

Hempel's *spiel* was that the credulous pro-German Held was taken in by a planted British agent called Brandy, who disappeared after leaving the incriminating material in Held's house. However a further remark in the same report saying that 'the English also knew about W.D.' would suggest that the German representative was not entirely the innocent abroad that he pretended to be. The initials W.D. referred to a certain Weber-Drohl, concerning whom the Minister had been negotiating. He was an Abwehr agent whose mission was the strengthening of German intelligence relations with the IRA. He had been apprehended by the Irish authorities. Hempel seemed to know all about him.

The arrest of Mrs Iseult Stuart on suspicion of harbouring Goertz upset the Envoy's pretexts of English intrigues. The finger pointed unmistakably at the Germans, thereby seriously threatening to compromise Hempel's personal position, since he had friendly relations with the Stuarts. Mrs Stuart lived in Laragh in Wicklow, a place frequented by the Hempels for weekends. She was the wife of Francis Stuart, lecturer in Berlin University, who had been helped by Hempel to return to Germany. The Hempels were very fond of Iseult Stuart: according to Frau Hempel, they were not so intimate with Francis. (See Chapter 7.)

The Irish government took a very serious view of what they saw as a German move at a high level to support subversive activity as a possible prelude to invasion. It was a delicate situation and Hempel complained to Berlin that an article by a Herr Pockhammer in an Essen newspaper did not help relations: the article he said was indiscreet and disturbing. He mentioned that all political parties supported the government and he referred to the 'influential' Bishop of Galway as being 'anti-German'. He was worried about the consequences for the legation and commented on the unsparing publication of the details of the case. He feared that the inevitable exploitation of the affair in England and America would critically undermine his position. He was particularly worried about the possible discovery of compromising statements in Stuart's letters home from Germany. Frau Hempel stressed that the main reason for her husband's worries was apprehension that these people would endanger his mission to keep Ireland neutral and out of the clutches of the Allies.

Hempel's ill-considered accusations in attempting to dissociate himself from the Held business did not enhance his credibility. His gratuitous raking up of the attempted suicide of a real Edith Brandy because she had been spurned by her English lover had no relevance to the situation. Once more, as previously in the case of the sinking of the *Iroquois*, it was time for Berlin to correct their Dublin Minister who was again seen to be protesting too much. Woermann told him straight that Brandy was the German agent, Dr Hermann Goertz, entrusted with special missions directed exclusively against England and for this purpose he was to make use of personal connections with the Irish. He explained that Goertz was expressly forbidden to initiate any activity against the Irish government though he acknowledged that subversive plans against the Irish government had frequently been submitted by certain Irish personalities (he did not name them) but had been rejected. Woermann was yet another who failed fully to grasp de Valera's determination that Ireland was not to be used in any circumstances as a base for operations against Britain. The blame for the existence of this blind spot on the part of the German Political Department which recurs again and again can hardly be apportioned to Hempel. Other sources (Clissmann, Stuart, Bewley or the IRA) are more likely to have been responsible for inducing this frame of mind, although de Valera's occasional rhetorical flourishes undoubtedly contributed to it.

Hempel's assessments of government attitudes were more realistic. He had pointed out specifically and repeatedly that de Valera would never allow Ireland to be used for an attack of any kind against Britain; and for all his own hedging and euphemisms about 'radical nationalists' he had stated unequivocally enough, and often enough, that the IRA lacked leadership and military capability; that they were not ready; that the time was not yet. It would appear that his advice had not been heeded by the powers that be in Berlin.

The Irish government was genuinely alarmed — to the point of panic at times — by this blundering from Berlin. One of Hempel's main tasks was to dispel their fears of a German invasion of Ireland and in order to understand the seriousness of this task the grounds for Irish fears must be examined: the ever-present distrust of Britain was now matched with a growing distrust of Germany.

Goertz had a general sabotage mission which required that Irish connections be developed. Such a course could only lead to a confrontation with the Irish government. Otherwise both the government and their policy of neutrality would be compromised. The contrast with another neutral country at this time, the USA, was instructive. The German High Command had agreed that no orders of any kind for sabotage in America would be given, although, for 'compelling military reasons', the procurement of intelligence from that country could not be dispensed with.

The worried Irish government did not know at this point that 'Plan Kathleen' discovered in Held's house, proposing a German landing in Northern Ireland in the vicinity of Derry assisted by the IRA in Co. Leitrim, was an IRA and not a German concept. Nor could they be aware that the Germans regarded it, for what it was, as a piece of logistical nonsense, the work of military novices. The abiding aspects of the matter were that the Germans accepted that the Irish were willing to take up arms to coerce Northern Ireland; and that they were prepared to capitalise on this willingness. This touched on de Valera's main fears: if Germany overestimated the strength of the IRA, they might be tempted to use them against Britain; if Britain were determined to occupy Irish bases these IRA links with Germany presented them with a readymade plausible pretext for doing so. There had been plenty of cause for concern but now the Held case produced the hard evidence to prove that the fears were by no means fantastic or groundless. It could happen and it looked as if the Germans were scheming to make it happen. Speaking in Cork on 25 May 1940, de Valera said that the IRA were providing incidents which could have been readily availed of as an excuse for invasion by some who found neutrality inconvenient.

It was not unexpected therefore that Britain would renew proposals (through Malcolm MacDonald) for 'Eire to enter the war on the side of the United Kingdom and her allies forthwith'. De Valera refused to bargain about partition as he regarded any offer as illusory. On the surface the proposals brought by MacDonald met with a lack of success. Meaningful contacts at official levels had, however, been made and maintained. A British army officer, Lt Col. Dudley Clarke, had been given the mission of persuading the Irish government to allow General Huddleston, GOC Northern Ireland, to send a mobile column across the border to help the Irish oppose any German attack that might occur. This initial attempt at Anglo-Irish co-operation against a possible German threat was conducted in farcical circumstances. Clarke, Joe Walshe and Colonel Liam Archer of Irish army intelligence scurried through the bowels of Government Buildings in order to throw any possible 'pursuers' off the scent. From there they made their way to the Shelbourne Hotel through which they sidled before rushing off to Baldonnel Aerodrome in a fast car. While observing the airfield through binoculars, they noted with alarm that somebody else seemed to be observing *them*, so they doubled back to town in the fast car, wormed their way once more through the underground passages of Government Buildings and at last attained the sanctuary of the front lounge in the Shelbourne. There they communicated out of the corners of their mouths around the edges of newspapers which they held firmly in front of their faces.

Varied, sometimes fanciful opinions were publicly expressed which indexed British pressures. Sir Charles Tegart had reported to the British cabinet that Eire was crawling with German agents and that 2,000 German troops could capture the whole country. Chamberlain, in a change before death from dove to hawk which embarrassed even Churchill, told the British cabinet that the IRA was strong enough to overrun the Eire defence forces. (Lord 'Haw-Haw' had broadcast that the Irish army could not beat the tinkers out of Galway.) The Marchioness of Londonderry pressed for an adequate defence for the whole of Ireland and the application of some form of conscription. The Duke of Abercorn felt invasion was almost certain and suggested that neutrality at sea be ignored and the coast of Ireland mined. Cardinal McRory thought that even if de Valera declared for 'them' the people might not follow him. In a letter to Churchill, Lord Rotherham said that the German fifth column in Ireland, 'starting with the German Minister', was enormous and that the Germans had promised the Irish a united Ireland. A landing in the West or South of Ireland would meet with little resistance, he said, and the Germans already knew every nook and cranny through the Shannon hydroelectric project: a footing in Ireland would put key factories in the West of England within range, he concluded. Lord Londonderry, writing from Park Lane, saw nothing to stop a German landing in the South of Ireland and attacked Chamberlain's concessions. Ernest Bevin's solution was to recommend a united Ireland and a joint defence council.

The advent of Churchill to replace Chamberlain on 10 May

1940 had renewed Irish apprehensions about Britain's intentions. Hempel duly forwarded the official text of some of Churchill's subsequent bellicose sentiments. In a previous report on 2 February 1940 Hempel listed Churchill, Hanley and Anderson as being foremost amongst the warmonger clique in the British cabinet, adding that Anderson was an ex 'Black and Tan'.[3] He branded Maffey as a mouthpiece of British propaganda and reported the complaint of the Department of External Affairs to the British representative about British propaganda which was geared, he stated, to provoking Germany into striking the first blow. The report added that, according to Irish-American sources, Britain had already given commitments to Ireland based on such an eventuality. He urged counter-propaganda especially against stories originating in Zurich that Germany was intent on fabricating a pretext to invade Ireland. He regretted that the German radio had not featured de Valera's assertion of Ireland's determination to remain neutral. Hempel was remarkably well informed, particularly on Anglo-Irish unity moves and the part played in these moves by the new American Minister to Ireland, David Gray.

It is less likely that he appreciated the rapport generated by the intelligence links then established between the British and Irish secret services; and these links endured throughout the war, notwithstanding political exploitation, Churchill's fulminations and de Valera's polemics. The Irish side later began to fear that Britain would use informations which they had promptly, diligently, and dutifully furnished to prove that neutrality was not being maintained. Colonel Dan Bryan's *modus operandi* was an essential lubricant in facilitating the working of this relationship between the intelligence services.

It was natural that the Irish government should remain apprehensive and suspicious of both the British and the Germans. Hempel's task of reassuring them for the German side was not made easier by the fact that he apparently had not been fully informed about the Goertz sabotage mission. Another impediment to their reassurance was the chronic mentality of the Political Department in Berlin. They persisted in the belief that it would be acceptable to the Irish government if Goertz did not direct his activities specifically against them but used his Irish connections to operate only against Britain.

Between 4 and 8 June 1940 the bewildered German Minister rattled off a flurry of telegrams seeking guidance on the Held-Stuart case. On 15 June Woermann instructed him to get in touch with the Irish government 'in a confidential way' and to point out that since Britain was the major common foe of both countries, Germany counted on the greatest possible understanding from Ireland despite her neutrality. Again a note of menace can be detected in this message, but an incentive was also to be conveyed: the outcome of the war would be of decisive importance for the Irish nation and the final realisation of its national demands. But the German Minister was also detailed to warn the government and the press to treat the Held affair with care.

The stance taken by the Irish government seemed (as still befitted a small weak nation dealing with a rampant military superpower) to be deliberately meek and unprovocative. Walshe, who had become convinced that Germany would soon win the war, accommodated Hempel by saying agreeable things to him. In a blatant effort to placate the German, Walshe hinted that he had not ruled out the involvement of an English agent in the Held case. Hempel, now aware of his gaffe over Brandy, should have winced at this hypocritical attempt to exonerate the Germans. It would be extraordinary if Walshe really believed what Hempel reported that he said in this connection. Hempel reported that the conversation, in which Walshe expressed great admiration for the German achievements, went off in a very friendly way. Hempel brushed aside the Irish fears of a German landing being linked specifically to the Held affair but declined Walshe's request to guarantee that the Germans would not make a landing in Ireland. He took the stand that such a declaration was impossible in the present military situation and he added that *'in the case of any collision between Irish interests and German measures complete and realistically wise understanding on the part of Ireland was to be expected'*. For some reason this seemed to relax Walshe who responded philosophically that they understood the German position: war was war, and in the vigorous prosecution of the war against Britain difficulties were to be expected. Walshe then remarked (and it is difficult to assess whether this was just 'talk' as reported by Hempel or whether it had a basis in realities) that the Irish government was more worried about a possible British attack than about a German invasion. According to Hempel's report, he followed this with a switch of emphasis. He made the point that, as a result of the latest measures to increase the army and its equipment, de Valera had 90 per cent of the people behind him.

In a change of line, Walshe then questioned the Führer's forlorn hopes of seeking a separate peace with Britain. He hoped that Hitler's declaration that he had no intention of destroying the British Empire did not imply the abandonment of Ireland. It was now Hempel's turn to demur and to reassure: the outcome of the war, he insisted, was important for the final realisation of Irish national demands. This especially interested Walshe and ensured for the Envoy a summons to meet de Valera. From the way Walshe and Warnock were talking it was possible on occasions to take the impression that the best hopes for the realisation of national demands lay in a German victory.

De Valera met Hempel on 16 June 1940. In the presence of Walshe a lengthy conversation was held in 'a forthright and pleasant manner'. Hempel distanced himself from the Held case but made his point about German concern for careful handling of publicity associated with that matter. Walshe supported him. De Valera listened with interest but laid stress on his continued policy of observing strict neutrality. Then he deviated from the point about England which Walshe had previously made. At the beginning of the war, Hempel reported the Taoiseach as saying, fear of British intervention had been their biggest worry. But so far, though this could change, the British had respected Irish neutrality. The government's main anxiety now concerned possible German intentions of using Ireland as a base for attacks on Britain by exploiting the 'weak minority which has been working against the government policy'. This seemed to be different to what Walshe had told Hempel about the government being more worried about a possible British invasion than a German one. The Envoy's opinion was that this anxiety

on the part of the government had been aggravated by alarm-
ist reports from the Irish in America. He also thought that
the recent efforts of pro-British groups in Northern Ireland,
who in his opinion were seeking co-ordination in defence
measures in order to undermine Irish neutrality, had no prospect of success. He did not comment that de Valera's reaction
to the proposals in question was negative, nor did he specify
who these groups in Northern Ireland were. But the reference
is obviously to Malcolm MacDonald's co-operation mission.
He did report that Craigavon had rejected all advances for a
rapprochement with Eire, an indication, he felt, of the
waning of the Roosevelt influence, assumed to have been
moderately exercised to catch the Irish-American vote in the
forthcoming November election. The Envoy now surmised
that, from their position of strength, possible German action
for the return of Northern Ireland would find 'ready acceptance in non-radical nationalist circles, among others, allegedly,
the influential far-seeing Cardinal McRory'.

On the other hand, he continued, the defence forces of
Northern Ireland had been substantially strengthened by,
among other things, recruitment to the UDF. He commented
on recruiting in the Irish army which had received 50,000
applications, many from old freedom fighters. In spite of
reports of growing pro-German feeling in the army, Hempel's
impression was that the Held case had turned the Irish people
against the Germans: the primary fear was now of a German
invasion and radical nationalism seemed to be losing public
esteem. He deduced that de Valera manipulated the Held case
so as to be better armed against the British and to gain political advantage at home against the largely anti-German
Cosgrave opposition. But once again he was in no doubt that
de Valera would not allow Ireland to become a point of
departure for an attack against Britain, underlining that it
was only by giving such an undertaking that de Valera had
succeeded in obtaining the return of the ports. He also stated
that the minimal external connection with the British Empire
provided for in the constitution was merely intended to
facilitate the future return of Northern Ireland to the Irish
state, and except for the strong economic dependence on
Britain, Ireland made no other distinction as between Britain

and Germany: if it came to an invasion Ireland would become a battlefield, with either British assistance to fight the Germans or German assistance to fight the British, depending on who was the first to attack. The Irish wallowed righteously in this unrealistic approach towards designating the enemy, though Hempel expressed his view that there was a growing realisation of the weakness of the democracies which their blandishments could not conceal.

Although the government's main fear was of a German invasion, other threats also concerned them. Gerald Boland, the Minister for Justice, had told Hempel that British pressure for the abandonment of Irish neutrality, accompanied by the bait of future concessions in respect of Northern Ireland, had been vehemently rejected by de Valera. Hempel thought that de Valera had also exploited this situation to augment further the strength of the army, units of which by 1941 had become the 2nd (Spearhead) Division under Major-General Hugo MacNeill and were alleged to be confronting a massed British force (estimated by Hempel as between 100,000 and 300,000) along the Border. Looking both ways at the same time for different enemies was a tense exercise for the defenders of Irish neutrality. The Germans made a move to reduce this tension.

On 26 June Ernst von Weizächer, the State Secretary at the Foreign Ministry in Berlin, instructed Hempel that in order to avoid misunderstandings he could intimate, without stressing the point, that the measures against England mentioned in Instruction No. 190 were not intended to include the landing of German troops in Ireland. Hempel now hoped that his conversations with de Valera and Walshe had had a calming effect after the panic caused by the Held incident: he expected a continuance of their understanding neutral attitude.

He was soon to find out the limits of this understanding and, incidentally, the very real independence of the Irish judiciary. On 27 June Held was sentenced to 5 years imprisonment for giving aid and support to persons unknown in receiving instructions for collection of information, particularly such as would affect the security of the state, and for possession of a radio transmitter. On 2 July, following a two day trial Mrs Iseult Stuart was acquitted. The understanding shown to Mrs Stuart probably had more to do with her mother, Madame Maud Gonne MacBride (widow of a patriot executed after the 1916 Rising) than with any representation made by the German Minister. There was no wish to create another martyr who might serve as a focus for subversion. But in Held's case, despite Hempel's or the government's wishes, the law took its course independently.

Hempel's self-assurance was again evaporating. He complained that although he had done everything within the limitations imposed on him to minimise suspicion of an impending German attack, the Irish government, still apprehensive from the Held and Stuart affairs, refused to be reassured. He thought that a factor in this was pressure on de Valera by the British and Americans who in his opinion were playing a dangerous game on the question of Northern Ireland. De Valera, the German representative reported, did not intend to yield to this pressure. He cited his Italian colleague to support this contention. There was no indication at this point of the tensions which existed between the German and Italian representatives. The Italian, Berardis, was instrumental in relaying de Valera's wish to elicit a reassurance from the Axis powers that there was no intention of an attack on Ireland. Hempel's attitude had been that such a statement, which involved references to strategic dispositions, could hardly be expected. He did feel however that something should be done to restore de Valera's confidence and to strengthen his position against British pressure, in order to bolster Irish determination to maintain neutrality. The strong influence, in his opinion, that Walshe and Boland were exercising on de Valera to offset British pressures had convinced him of the need for such a gesture. He gave more credit to Walshe and Boland for being determined to remain neutral than he did to de Valera. He recommended that a German statement or declaration be made indicating continuing respect for Irish neutrality and the absence of any intention to sponsor fifth column activities in preparation for the future use of Ireland as a military base against England. Hempel's report that the declaration of mid June 1940 fell short of reassuring the Irish government had the effect of eliciting a frank response from Woermann that German policy was primarily concerned with the prevention of any *rapprochement* between Ireland and Britain. He suggested that Hempel, off his own bat, could renew previous assurances of German intent to respect Irish neturality: the Envoy could repeat the contents of Telegram No. 72 of 31 August 1939 but it was not to be given out as a fresh declaration. Woermann in addition told Warnock that they all knew how Germany felt about Ireland and that in any case assurances had already been given.

Still wary of de Valera's ability to manipulate words to suit his purposes, Hempel said that there should be no ambiguity and that de Valera should be given a statement in a strictly guarded form to avoid possible misuse. He referred, without specifying, to the rapid course of developments and requested instructions on matters relating to Northern Ireland.

Woermann's reply confirmed Hempel's misgivings about the Political Department's lack of political acumen as far as Ireland was concerned. It put the fears of the Irish government down to a misconception that the German plans were for a landing in the Irish Free State, whereas Plan Kathleen had specified Northern Ireland. This was supposed to clear the matter up! It is also symptomatic of a lack of full comprehension that they felt it necessary to warn against taking reprisals for the sentencing of Held, on the grounds that he was an Irish citizen and that German interest in the case should not be overtly demonstrated! Hempel could not be blamed if he became confused by these instructions.

On 11 July Ribbentrop intervened again to give him guidance: the Envoy was to emphasise in all conversations Germany's primary interest in the preservation of Irish neutrality: *as long as Ireland remained neutral Germany would respect her neutrality*. The Foreign Minister's telegram was terse and curt: he declared that suspicions that Germany intended to use Ireland as a base against England through a so-called fifth column were utterly unreasonable; they were in the realm of fancy and had no basis in fact. Such a fifth column, he held, did not exist and he continued:

If the British government in dealing with the Irish government makes use of the idea of a union of Northern Ireland with Southern Ireland it is evident that this is only a sham, which is only engaged in for the purpose of manoeuvring Ireland out of her neutrality and drawing her into the war. The question of how Germany would act in case of establishment of the unity of Ireland is therefore wrongly posed and purposeless.

These statements did not carry conviction when viewed against the background of German agents being landed in Ireland by sea and air. One reason for Ribbentrop's condescending treatment may have been Hempel's report of the impression said to exist in the Irish Department of External Affairs that peace on reasonably tolerable terms would be welcomed by the appeasing element in Conservative circles, represented by Chamberlain, Halifax, Simon, Hoare, the Astors, Londonderry, high officialdom, the 'City' and the *Times*. The middle class and the lower classes were depressed and longed for a speedy peace, he said, but the Conservative 'ultras' who looked to Churchill were in favour of going on with the war. The British, Hempel retailed, had written off their lost position in Europe.

The report indicated Hempel's inconsistent attitude to Roosevelt. He concluded by stating that if Roosevelt were to declare for peace he could influence American public opinion in a favourable direction. Such an eventuality was however rendered unlikely by Roosevelt's anti-Axis speech of 19 July which had encouraged resistance to the totalitarian powers. Hempel referred to this speech but did not fully evaluate it when he considered Roosevelt as a possible appeaser or peacemaker. The point was that Roosevelt may have had the opportunity to declare for peace, but was obviously not that way inclined: he regarded the Nazis as gangsters to be confronted and opposed.

By the end of July the German representative's opinion was that Roosevelt was out of favour with the Irish government and that his possible re-election would increase the danger for Ireland. In Hempel's view the re-election of Roosevelt would lessen British and American inhibitions about coercing Ireland, as considerations for the Irish-American vote could then be set aside for the time being. Though Roosevelt had declined Churchill's request to send a US squadron to Irish ports he had been prepared to use any means possible — even the Pope — to pressurise the Irish into relinquishing neutrality. American opinion was worried that there would not be effective resistance in Ireland to a German invasion but, *on the other hand*, if the British had to seize the ports for their survival it might alienate Irish-American opinion. In any event, as Roosevelt told Gray, though Irish independence was very close to the American heart there could be no question as between invasion by Germany and protection by England.

There were compelling reasons, therefore, for Hempel to analyse the American scene and the effect of political developments there on future German policy towards Ireland. He was sure that regard for American public opinion had so far deterred the British from attacking. Walshe intimated to the German Minister that discreet closer co-operation between Irish, German and Italian elements in the United States could exert a powerful influence without compromising the Dublin government. Walshe and Boland, Hempel reported, were putting their hopes in a German interest in a fully independent Ireland: they were suspicious of British retaliation even if the British were defeated. The Envoy recommended that an undertaking be given — in a manner which would avoid the Irish being compromised by Britain and subject to reservations based on the example of Czechoslovakia in the First World War — that Germany would not abandon Ireland. In this lay an indication that for many the war was deemed to be as good as won by Germany.

The greatest danger of Ireland being compromised arose from Admiral Ritter's closely knit estimate as to whether Ireland should be excluded or included in a blockade of England. In the end the Führer wished to make an exception in some form for Ireland. Otherwise, he said, instead of being separated from England, Ireland would be forced into her arms. A special secret arrangement with the Irish government was proposed. Ribbentrop's telegram (to be deciphered personally by Hempel) outlined that the German forces would not attack ships under the Irish flag *provided* these ships were especially marked and reported by the Irish government, *if* these ships and their cargoes were promptly reported by telegraph, *if* they obeyed the instructions of the German forces and *if* they had on board only goods which the Irish government guaranteed would remain in Ireland. The tone was peremtory.

Walshe pointed out the problems of entering into an agreement with Germany and played for time without rejecting outright the German offer. He patiently explained to Hempel the complications of Irish overseas trade being mainly with England and in British ships. The government was also concerned to avoid giving the British grounds for a charge of unneutral behaviour. A decision was deferred by diplomatically suggesting that the proposal be discussed through the Irish *chargé d'affaires* in Berlin.

The following aide-mémoire from Warnock to the German Foreign Ministry provided tangible reasons for not rejecting the German offer out of hand:

> The Irish legation has the honour to state that its government has been informed that the following five steamships, the entire cargoes of which comprised grain for exclusive consumption in Eire were sunk by unidentified submarines at times and in positions indicated hereunder:
> 1. *Violando N. T. Mulanvis* Greek at 10.15 a.m. on June 10th
> 2. *Adamandious Georgandis* Greek at 17.15 GMT on June 19th
> 3. *Petsamo* Finnish at 11.45 a.m. on July 10th
> 4. *Kzetis A* Greek at 3.20 p.m. on July 14th
> 5. *Nafitkus* Greek at 9.30 p.m. on July 15th
> The Irish legation has been instructed by its government to bring the foregoing to the attention of the German Foreign Office. The legation would be grateful if the Foreign Office would be good enough to have enquiries made and to furnish the legation with any information at the disposal of the German government as to the circumstances of the sinking of these vessels.

Hempel's counsel that consideration be given to Irish ship-

ping when it was not in English ports was being consistently
ignored. He had protested after the sinking of the *Munster*
and the *Kerry Head* which had been plainly marked and
flying the Irish flag. The protest did not have the desired
effect.

Boland's complaint to Hempel about the sinkings was
diluted by his concession that there may have been some
grounds for the sinking of the *City of Limerick*, as she
seemed to have had a cargo for Liverpool. That giveaway
would hardly have pleased the British: it did not deter the
Germans.

German mines were sown in Irish waters: German planes
trespassed Irish air space and the Irish government made
meek protests until they dropped bombs on Campile Creamery (Co. Wexford) causing casualties. Hempel apologised; but
for some reason he did not want Warnock to know that he
had asked permission to do so. Warnock was cynical about
the special treatment Germany was supposed to be giving to
Ireland. Hempel put it all down to British provocation designed to embroil Ireland in the war against Germany. He
reported that the British had not consulted the Irish when
they mined the St George's Channel to within seven miles of
the Irish coast at Dungarvan but that the Irish would only
protest when Irish interests were directly affected; though
they did not want their territorial waters used for British
shipping traffic. He observed sourly that there had been a
closing of ranks, consolidating Mr de Valera's position, when
it seemed as if the danger were coming from Germany but
maintained that the declaration to respect Irish neutrality
had a calming effect and that events were now working in
Germany's favour. His *'agent provocateur'* excuse no longer
held water though Walshe agreeably continued to hint at
such activities when he had an axe to grind and wished to
remain on the right side of the mighty Germans who were
pausing prior to devouring Britain, or so they thought.

On 16 July Hitler had issued his Directive No. 16 for the
controversial 'Operation Sealion'. In support of this operation, a deceptive diversion towards Ireland was conceived.
In August two IRA leaders — Sean Russell and Frank Ryan
— left Germany by U-Boat to land in Ireland. Hempel had

opposed the coming of Russell to Ireland; nevertheless he was given a part to play in the operation. A flower-pot was to be placed in the window of the legation as a signal for Russell that the invasion of Britain was under way.

It was apparently imagined that a series of uprisings would detonate throughout Ireland to synchronise with the landings on Britain. This would toll the death-knell of neutrality, signal the outbreak of civil war and bring British intervention in Eire. Contingency planning (musing might be a better word) went on in Berlin to cater for some such development.

On 9 September a Foreign Ministry official radioed Hempel looking for essential elements of military information, if they could be covertly obtained without the source being compromised. Was there conscription in Ireland? How was mobilisation effected? How many able-bodied men of military age were there? What was the war organisation, equipment and strength of the Irish army? What was known about dispositions, employment of troops and defences? The report complimented Hempel on his very valuable reports on the effects of air raids on England and indicated that the greatest detail possible of the effects of the bombings on the civilian population was desirable.

Hempel's estimate for the total strength of the Irish army was 659,000. He mentioned Ireland's successful tradition in waging guerilla warfare against England. He did not hold out prospects of facile victories if invasion were to be attempted, though he did make reference to the shortage of equipment in the Irish army, navy and air corps. Taken together with Warnock's reports, the recommendation could be read as advising against German military intervention. When Warnock was giving a resumé of the military situation in the North of Ireland to Woermann he emphasised the assignment of the dreaded Special Constables to operate against parachutists. He hoped he would discourage any tendency to intervene. He made a special point of conveying the pleasure of the Irish government at German assurances on the Canaris injunction against the further insertion of agents. He further allayed German fears that an Anglo-Irish deal on Northern Ireland would change Eire's stand on neutrality, poo-poohing all such reports as mere press speculation.

Hempel and Warnock may have given the Germans second thoughts about invading the British Isles but they were not the deciding factors. As always, it was the realities of combat which decided events. The great German air offensive, Operation Eagle, started on 15 August 1940 with the aim of achieving air superiority, an essential pre-requisite to the launching of an invasion. It was repulsed. After a reverse in a decisive air battle on 17 September the Führer made the momentous decision to postpone Operation Sealion. The Battle of Britain, imperceptibly at first, indicated a turning of the tide. It diminished the danger of a German military diversion in Ireland. But it did not remove the menace to neutrality of German meddling in Irish affairs.

Hempel's report on the military forces in Ireland left the door open for such meddling. He gave 8,000 as the figure for the cadre regular army nucleus with 4,000 reservists and 17,000 volunteers. As a result of the 'call to arms' in June 1940 he added 180,000. He did not put figures on the Local Security Force and the Local Defence Force but he arrived at a total estimated figure of 659,000. He did not translate this figure into units or into combat power terms but he gave enough information to tantalise the planners in Berlin who were contemplating intervention if not invasion. On account of its policing character, he distinguished the Local Security Force (Group 'A') from the combat Local Defence Force (Group 'B'). He concluded his report by suggesting that military opinion be consulted to assess the military potential of these forces. He requested a military adviser. This gambit was basically an exercise in passing the buck but it turned out to have more dangerous implications than the Envoy intended.

SIX

A Rethink for the Reich

Hitler's thoughts turned to Hempel when towards the end of 1940 he mused that possession of Ireland could have the effect of ending the war. The importance of Ireland as a base for attacks on the north-western ports of England was obvious. Ribbentrop took his cue accordingly.

Hitler had accepted that from the naval point of view 'Sealion' could not be launched before mid-September. Admiral Raeder had emphasised the requirement for air superiority over the crossing area. Goering's air offensive did not succeed in accomplishing that mission.

He had assured Hitler that the Luftwaffe could neutralise the Royal Navy as well as drive the RAF out of the sky. He had also undertaken to provide the fire cover for a landing which was outside the range of artillery located on the Flanders coastline. The theories of the Italian air strategist, General Douhet, over-rating the capabilities of air power, had yet to be disproved. But wars had been won before on military heresies and the German air offensive had caused more damage and disruption than was generally admitted. If the attacks had been better co-ordinated and concentrated on major industrial centres, the effects would have been even more serious. Goering dissipated that opportunity by changing to a new policy of night bombing, opening on the night of 14 November with an attack on Coventry.

Air power had not provided a short-cut to solve the problem of invasion. 'Sealion' was effectively abandoned in October but because it was not definitely postponed until the spring of 1941 the possibility of an Irish diversion or feint remained a practical consideration up until then.

The failure to achieve air superiority in the Battle of Britain showed up more than anything else the German high command's incapacity to conduct a combined amphibious operation. Their concept of such an operation was limited to large scale river crossings. Legend persists that 'live Jerries' did attempt a commando type raid on British shores but that the RAF poured petrol on the sea and set it alight with tracer bullets burning them out of it. The Germans may have attempted a reconaissance-in-force. That would have been the height of their amphibious capability. Their training was woefully inadequate and their assembly arrangements were clumsy to say the least. Their landing barges were cumbersome tubs dependent on calm seas to function. They also handicapped themselves by allowing inter-service rivalries to run riot. Furthermore, they deferred slavishly to Hitler who did not know his own mind from one day to the next about invading England. One of his impulses — to defeat Britain by a quick knock-out blow from air power alone — had manifestly failed. All this underlined the limitations imposed by time, space and relative combat power on any possible adventure in Ireland.

Part of the trouble arose from Hitler's ambivalence about Britain and his fixation about *Lebensraum* in Russia. The German estimate for an invasion of Britain did not flow from a logical process of military thought. Ireland was inseparable to the concept but the estimate lacked either the coherence or co-ordination to take full account of it. Even when Hitler himself had spoken, it could not be taken as representing settled policy. The command structure was unstable. This posed problems for Hempel, de Valera and Britain alike. None of them could ever be certain where they stood.

One effect of all the unpredictability was to bring home to the British and Irish authorities how much they had in common. Their mutual interests led to some faltering steps in co-operation being taken, but the burden of historical distrust could not be dispelled. The North was an eternal bugbear. South of the border the memory of the Black-and-Tans was still green. Straightforward defence considerations were blurred. Moreover, Whitehall had had the jitters, and had entertained some outrageously wildcat schemes. For example,

Montgomery was told to prepare plans for the seizure of Cork and Queenstown (Cobh). The only division which was fully equipped and fit to fight in battle at a time when Britain was almost defenceless was being earmarked to fight the Irish!

Montgomery recalled that he had fought the 'Southern Irish' once before in 1921 and 1922. After he had passed out of the staff college in 1920 he was sent as brigade major to the 17th Infantry Brigade in Cork to a war which he found to be far worse than the First World War. He recorded that it developed into a murder campaign in which the soldiers more than held their own, but only at the price of lowering 'their standards of decency and chivalry'. It looked to him as if the renewed contest, 'might be quite a party — with only one division'. The plan came to nothing and is still gathering dust in the 'war babies' cupboard in the War Office. Montgomery's energies were sensibly channelled to countering the expected German invasion of the South of England.

In the latter half of 1940 Hitler tossed out the following operations to be planned simultaneously: defence of the Finnish nickel mines; protection of Rumanian oil fields; bolstering the Italians in North Africa; seizure of the Azores, Canary and Cape Verde Islands; the occupation of Greece; an attack against the Soviet Union and an invasion of England. Nothing seemed impossible to the Führer.

The dice had rolled luckily for him from his prewar *coups* of reoccupying the Rhineland, annexing Austria and absorbing the Sudetenland from Czechoslovakia. On the field of battle, under his inspiration, the Germans had defeated the Poles, the Norwegians, the Dutch, Belgians and the French: the bemused Danes had yielded without firing a shot and the mighty British had been ignominiously forced to evacuate the continent. In the face of these victories the supine German army commanders were stunned into silence and submission. Grand strategy had never been a strong point of the German high command but deferring so abjectly to Hitler's untutored intuition was a disaster for the Third Reich.

The concept of invading England had not matured at either strategical or tactical levels. No plans were seriously made for it even after the crumbling of French resistance was obvious.

Hitler's admiration of the British Empire and of the necessity for its existence produced military absurdities. His aim remained to make peace with Britain on a basis that she would find compatible with her honour to accept. He had no wish to press the conflict with Britain to a decisive conclusion. He felt that Britain was bound to recognise the hopelessness of her position and compromise accordingly.

Even Churchill's rhetorical rejections failed to get through to him until 2 July when he then tardily ordered a study of the problem of overcoming Britain by invasion. It took another two weeks for him to order preparations for it.

Two plans have been distinguished for the German army's projected operation against Britain. They differ as to the size of the landing frontage, the number of divisions to be employed and the rate of reinforcement envisaged. Landings were planned for various points between Ramsgate and Bexhill and between Brighton and the Isle of Wight. Field Marshal Rundstedt's Army Group A were given these missions. Simultaneously, three divisions of Field Marshal Reichenau's 6th Army, operating under Field Marshal von Bock's Army Group B, were to embark in the Contentin Peninsula and carry out an early landing in Lyme Bay between Weymouth and Lyme Regis. The aim of this landing, apart from broadening the bases and splitting the British forces, was to threaten Bristol and seal off Cornwall, thereby securing the western flank of the operation by pushing northward to the Severn estuary.

To extend the possible frontage of the attack, further preparations for a subsidiary landing in Eire were simulated by a number of German divisions on the French coast. Von Bock ordered General Leonhard Kaupisch, commander of the 4th and 7th army corps, to draw up plans for an amphibious operation against Ireland. 'Be prepared' was the watchword. It all depended on the progress of the main attack on the southern English coast as to whether the simulation would be translated into reality or not.

Kaupisch was now able to find a use for the military geographical data on Ireland[1] so painstakingly collected in peacetime by the Berlin Department of War Maps and Survey. The Abwehr ensured that his deception plans were filtered through to the British by various clandestine means thereby increasing tensions and the danger of a British pre-emptive strike, which would have played into the Reich's hands.

The subsidiary landing planned for Ireland has received perfunctory treatment from military historians. Yet it was the one aspect of the entire operation for which a sound military case could be made. It made good tactical sense to divide British forces by diverting them to Ireland, away from the area of the main attack. In addition there existed in Ireland a prospect of local support for a cause. Liaison had been established with the IRA for that purpose. While the scale of the diversion would be affected by the logistical support available it was not dependent on it: spontaneous supportive uprisings, properly fomented, were viable, at least on paper.

By contrast the main attack was ill-conceived. When France fell the German army was totally unprepared for an under-taking of the magnitude of an invasion of England. A com-parison with the scale and meticulousness of the planning required by the Allies for the Normandy landings four years later gives some idea of how badly prepared the Germans were. The staffs had not seriously studied the problem. The troops had been given no training in amphibious warfare: the German soldier was strictly a land animal. Landing craft for the purpose had not been built and when they did attempt to assemble barges and shipping they lacked the seafaring tradition which had allowed the British to improvise with such magnificent flair at Dunkirk. The prospect of success for their hasty improvisation lay in the British having lost most of their arms and equipment in France.

Nevertheless, 'Sealion' was by no means a forlorn aspir-ation. If it had been cohesively conceived as a combined operation with each of the three services given a crucial role in a co-ordinated offensive, then the clash between the Luftwaffe and the RAF would have been on more equal terms. Concentration of force in the operational area could have made parity and even victory in the air possible. Taking a grip on a beachhead was not outside the bounds of possibil-ity. Once ashore the opposition was weak. Churchill's clarion calls notwithstanding, British morale was low. But German lack of sea power presented a problem which makeshift could not master. Hot pursuit, hard on the heels of Dunkirk, with air cover, fair weather and an airborne landing in support could possibly have brought off the establishment of a foothold in the British Isles. After the Fall of France German soldiers and civilians alike were possessed of a confident elan, while defeatism[2] was widespread in the British cabinet: the British army had been badly defeated in the field. The momentum of the blitzkrieg had proved to be irresistible; almost all the equipment of the British Expeditionary Force had been abandoned and the heroic saga of the evacuation of that Force from Dunkirk could not conceal the magnitude of the military defeat.

The captured equipment gave Ribbentrop ideas for translating the Führer's reflections about Ireland into action. He instructed Hempel to offer some of it to de Valera. Hitler, however, was now reverting to his *Stufenplan* and concluding that a military solution in the East would be a better way than invasion to force Britain either into rapid surrender or to support the Reich as its junior partner.

The Führer's concepts at this stage were grandiloquent and global. How much or how little thought went into his soliloquising remark that Ireland in German hands would spell the end for England can only be surmised. He voiced no objection to Ribbentrop's proposals: the Reich's representative in Dublin should find out de Valera's attitude to the offer of assistance in the form of captured English arms and ammunition which could be transported to him aboard separate ships. The Führer agreed with the assessment of Admrial Raeder at a conference on 31 December 1940 attended by Keitel and Jodl, that the despatch of an expeditionary force and the occupation of the island of Ireland was impossible in the face of superior enemy naval power, unfavourable geographic conditions and the problems of supply and reinforcement. Hitler's main concern now was his central war aim – pursued since 1925 – of overrunning Russia. After the frustrations of 'Sealion' he became more and more convinced that the defeat of Russia would serve him also against Britain: thus he would kill two birds with the one stone. These considerations – unlike those of General Jodl – were not based entirely on calculated strategy: Hitler still hankered to have Britain on his side. General Halder supported him: as he saw it, the smashing of Russia would shatter Britain. Germany would then, in his opinion, be master of Europe and the Balkans; therefore the destruction of Russia must be made part of the struggle to subdue the British Isles. He did not separate Ireland in this context. The big danger for Ireland lay in feints or diversions taking on a life of their own which would have compelled British intervention. That would have been closer to Ribbentrop's way of looking at things.

To him, since Great Britain was first and foremost Germany's main enemy, the main attack should be concentrated against her to destroy her. He had frequently expressed disdain for the Irish but he felt he could use them as a means of getting at Britain through her back door. That was what he had in mind when he recruited Veesenmayer to stir up rebellion in Ireland. Then he persisted in pressurising Hempel to persuade de Valera into accepting military assistance. His motives were muddled. The offer of arms assistance to resist a British attack is clear enough. But in the absence of that attack Ribbentrop had only vague unformulated expectations of initiatives.

He told the Führer that he was convinced the Irish would fight to the last round and the last man against a British attack and that this action would arouse tremendous anti-British reverberations in America. In the sounding out of de Valera he suggested that Hempel's opening gambit might be to express his concern about the fate of the legation so that prudent alternative preparations could be made and to enquire innocently whether de Valera considered an English attack on Ireland probable. It is not evident what further role Ribbentrop envisaged for Hempel. He seemed to want him to have the best of both worlds. He did not wish him to be involved in direct dealings with the IRA: the clean front image was to remain untarnished. At a different operational level he enjoined him to keep the secret transmitter intact for future use.

It was left to Veesenmayer to try to sort out what exactly Ribbentrop had in mind for fomenting an Irish rebellion. The *coup d'état* specialist's reputation rested on his proven ability to get things done. But first he had to find out what was to be done. That was his difficulty in analysing his mission to foment rebellion in Ireland. He was not at all clear about Ribbentrop's intentions.

Ribbentrop's fancies hopped from fomenting an IRA *coup* against de Valera to backing a rising by the nationalists in Northern Ireland. There was no telling which of these courses he favoured. His main aim was to get at Britain through Ireland by hook or by crook. The Irish and their boring causes were incidental and expendable.

Using Ireland as a base to get at Britain was precisely what de Valera was determined to prevent. He declined to be cornered by Hempel's loaded questions and an infuriated Veesenmayer blamed the Envoy for being no match for the wily Irish politician. Ribbentrop could not see how de Valera, if his rhetoric meant anything, could refuse such a tempting offer of arms and equipment. He blamed Hempel for not presenting the package properly and harassed him to keep pestering de Valera with the offer.

Prior to this badgering, Hempel had managed to reassure and calm the Irish government after their near panic arising out of the Held affair.[3] The real weight attaching to those reasurrances on German intentions to invade Ireland can be measured by considering that plans to transport Sean Russell and Frank Ryan to Ireland were in train at that time and that on 12 August 1940 an operation order for a landing in Ireland was issued.[4]

This order specified landing areas in the Waterford-Wexford area and outlined the extent of the bridgehead: Gorey-Mount Leinster-Thomastown-Clonmel-Dungarvan, in order to advance against the line of Dublin-Kildare and the high ground west of 'Mountmeldick' [sic], followed by the seizure of bridgeheads on the north banks of the intervening rivers and canals. If it is granted that this constituted part of a grand plan of deception then the extent of deception intended has to be examined.

On a tactical level was it intended as a secondary attack to support a main attack on the South of England? Was it purely an exercise? Wat it a feint attack? Did deception go as far as simulating a landing? Hempel's political reports to the effect that in Ireland the unexpected always happens now came back to haunt him. There was the specific precedent of the 1916 Rising where, from unlikely beginnings, a revolution took place. A spark was all that was needed, seemed to be the thinking in the German high command, whose agent Goertz was loose in Ireland at the time, making, by all accounts, significant contacts at official and unofficial levels. Where did Ribbentrop's cynical importunings fit in?

On a strategic level, there remains the larger question as to whether 'Sealion' was, from start to finish, a gigantic deception plan to conceal the Führer's preconceived ideas of conquering Russia in pursuit of *Lebensraum* and of a European hegemony, which, when achieved, should automatically bring the British to their knees. In any case the hard modifying facts around mid-September 1940 were the failure of the Luftwaffe in the Battle of Britain and the bad weather conditions prevailing at the time. According to the Halder diary, the chief of staff of the army was convinced from 1 July to 12 October 1940 that Hitler intended to invade the British Isles, if necessary and if the chances of success appeared to justify the risks. The German soldiers sang '*Wir fahren gegen England*' 'We will march against England' and the staffs were actively engaged in drawing up logistical tables. It seems incontestable that Hitler did, at least for some weeks, seriously consider invading southern England. The Germans achieved a significant degree of readiness for that purpose.

This invasion was bound to affect Eire, if only to put to the test de Valera's proclaimed certain consideration for Britain. The British chiefs of staff had advised Churchill that the invasion must of necessity include Ireland. This raised for Britain the historical preoccupation with flank protection. Who would make the first move? Was there a case for pre-emption?

The question of a possible German invasion of Ireland remains controversial. One point of view is that it received passing consideration but was neither named nor planned. The existence of the order for *Operation Grün* proves otherwise. It was considered, it was named, but however impractically, it was planned. The Irish government had grounds for their concern. Insistently they voiced their worries about

German intentions to Hempel who in turn, acting as the official means of communication between the two governments, tried to reassure them. The fact remains that if subterranean German plans had surfaced, Hempel would have, in effect, been lulling the Irish side into a sense of false security. It is unlikely that the German representative was fully aware of all such covert plans: it is equally improbable that he was oblivious to all that was afoot. There was always that flowerpot in the legation window.

There is enough evidence to assume that if the plans for 'Sealion' had been implemented, force would have been used to capitalise on the 'Ireland factor'. By the autumn of 1940, however, with 'Sealion' in abeyance, German rethinking on Ireland was coming around to the idea of persuading the Irish government to accept German aid in the form of arms to be used against anticipated British aggression. Hempel had stated that a British attack would be resisted by de Valera who, he pointed out, no longer accepted that Northern Ireland could be used as a bargaining counter to persuade them to depart from their policy of neutrality. The Germans estimated that a pre-emptive British attack was the one sure way of bringing Eire into a common front with them.

On 25 November 1940, Kramarz telegraphed Hempel from Berlin that the German Naval Department had picked up and decoded a British message telling their troops that all orders would issue from the 'Irish Commander' and that they were not to fire except on his orders. This brought home the real dilemma of Ireland, in pursuit of preserving a pragmatic neutrality, choosing to face both ways at once. This was the difficulty de Valera had never attempted to conceal. He insisted that:

> Neutrality if you are sincere about it means you will have to fight for your life against one side or the other — whichever attacks you. Neutrality is not a cowardly policy if you really mean to defend yourself if attacked. Other nations have not gone crusading until they were attacked.

He did not pretend that his policy was immutable and he stressed its non-doctrinaire nature. But there were parameters and it is significant that when at the end of October 1940

Hempel was reporting a mood prevailing among members of the Irish government to reach an accommodation with the new order under the Axis he had to underline de Valera's reservations about any such proposal. The impetus for these proposals seemed to have come from Walshe and Boland, apparently convinced as they were at that time of the inevitability of a German victory. They were very civil to Hempel.

In tune with this mood, protests by the Irish government were subdued. Hempel got a hearing when on 21 October he replied to representations being made about the bombing of the steamer *Edenvale*: that incidents like that were to be expected in a war zone. Walshe's protests about German overflying were calmly made with a plea for an understanding of his and Warnock's position in lodging protests against widespread German violations of Irish airspace. When the Germans bombed Campile Creamery, Co. Wexford, however, the Irish protests were more vigorous. After the bombing, a Cartaucherie Francaise mortar shell was found nearby. The Irish implied that the Germans were using captured French ammunition. But to the intense embarrassment of the Department of External Affairs, it was then discovered that shells of this type had been supplied by the French firm of Stokes Brandt to the Irish army: the shell at the centre of the controversy had in fact been lost by the army while on field exercises near Campile. This refuted the implication that the Germans were using captured French ammunition but it did not alter the fact of German air violations from Carrigan Head to Donegal to Carnsaw, Co. Wexford and again from Clonakilty to Donegal where the steamer *Bannthorn* was attacked. These German aircraft flew in over the coasts of Waterford and Wexford and inland over Tullow and Baltinglass. The Irish side did not turn a blind eye but kept their tongues under control.

Churchill's utterances on 5 November reinforced their circumspection towards the Germans: it was difficult to be certain at this stage who would be a future enemy, who maybe a future ally. Consideration of an invasion threat from one side had to be constantly set off against the possibility of a previous invasion by the other side. An increasing threat from one side served to heighten the danger of a pre-emptive strike by the other side. Here was the dilemma of a neutral relying on the use of force to defend its neutrality against all comers.

In reconsidering the invasion threat there was a grim paradox and judging from their attitudes, neither Walshe nor Warnock seem to have been fully alive to it. If, as 1940 went on, the Irish government seemed to become more apprehensive of the British threat than of the German one, that did not mean that the German threat had disappeared. On the contrary, the tendency of the Berlin Political Department to oversimplify and to overestimate the British threat — even to the extent of seeming to wish it or will it — had the effect of increasing the assumptions and expectations of the Germans that they would automatically be called upon to render assistance. Hempel gave the impression that Walshe was eating out of his hand. In making his apologetic protest to Hempel about the sinking of the *Kerry Head* by the Germans, for instance, Walshe managed to hint once more at possible British provocation. Warnock's protest too was made in a very friendly manner. His message was that they did not want to make trouble but that the British press were playing the matter up as proof that Ireland could not defend herself. Warnock could not be more accommodating, but it would be inept in the circumstances of relative combat power as between Ireland and Germany to imply criticism. The fact remained, however, that at this point Warnock took pains to distance himself from any implied criticism of German actions, specifically repudiating allegations of intimidating motives behind the Campile creamery bombing. In addition, Hempel reported a thawing in the attitude of Church circles towards Germany, under the influence of Cardinal McRory who, according to Hempel, had pro-Axis sympathies. He later explained that the Cardinal was an exception amongst the clergy in this respect. He thought that de Valera's position had been strengthened, remarking that the Taoiseach was well able to handle the IRA. All in all, the climate could be construed as coming good for German intervention.

Ribbentrop now saw Roosevelt as the only real obstacle to his plans to destroy Britain. He was annoyed by what he called Roosevelt's 'foreign policy exhibitionism' which branded the Nazis as revolutionaries who should be resisted and not appeased. This led to a hardening of German attitudes. On 6 August 1940 Ribbentrop instructed Hempel to make the Irish government aware of the existence of a war zone in the waters around Great Britain and to inform them that the Germans would not be responsible for damage done to persons or ships in those waters. The Envoy was again to add that Irish ships would not be attacked if they followed German instructions to the letter. Two months later, Ribbentrop appointed Admiral Ritter to handle all activities dealing with economic warfare and foreign policy. This appointment and Roosevelt's open stance added new elements to Hempel's considerations. On 7 November he reported conversations he had had with Walshe about Churchill's anti-Irish speech delivered appropriately enough on Guy Fawkes day (5 November). A few hours before Roosevelt had been re-elected with a small majority, as anticipated. When Hempel remarked that it looked as if Britain had now, as a result of that election, shed her fear of unfavourable backlash in America to threats to Ireland, Walshe's reply was that although Roosevelt was undoubtedly pro-British he was still strongly dependent on the Irish-American vote as a result of the large vote that Wilkie had received. Hempel's 'radical-nationalist circles' welcomed the wave of anti-British sentiment in Ireland following Churchill's hostile rhetoric. According to the German Minister, Churchill's declamations and the predictable treatment of the subject in the British press caused understandable anxiety in Ireland.

The German high command estimated that de Valera's firm stand against Churchill's verbal onslaughts inclined the IRA to lend him support and that while the illegal organisation was kept under strict surveillance, it was less harassed then heretofore. Nevertheless Hempel reported that the Irish government remained apprehensive and feared that the IRA would obtain substantial quantities of arms and ammunition from Germany. The high command estimated that the Irish government further feared that the IRA-German connection would give the British the pretext they required for invasion and that in those circumstances, Ireland would first seek American aid and, failing there, would turn to Germany for assistance; that the German blockade was beginning to bite, thus alienating the Irish middle classes from Germany; that the population was distrustful of all elements with British connections. Their conclusion coincided with Hempel's own opinion that consideration of an enormous American reaction would, in the final analysis, deter a British invasion.

He expressed the view that the disadvantage for Britain of attempting to take the ports outweighed any obvious advantage that their possession might bring: they were strongly fortified, he said, and vulnerable to German air attacks from the French coast. In addition, the cost of a war with Ireland had to be counted not to mention the repercussions in the United States. The indications were, the Envoy went on, that Britain would continue to put on the pressure to extract concessions, but Walshe had told him that de Valera would simply refuse to yield.

He reported de Valera's speech protesting full understanding for England, referring to partition as the stumbling block to friendly relations between their two countries, and denying that U-boats would be succoured or advantaged in any way in Irish harbours. He reported in English and German de Valera's clinching call to defend neutrality: *if we must die for this then we will die for it.*[5] The Envoy added that this statement brought applause from all sides except from the Germanophobe opposition deputy, James Dillon. That phrase became a slogan and a secret weapon: potential enemies had no doubt but that de Valera meant it: his Emergency army accepted it without question.

Hempel telegraphed that he was expecting de Valera to lunch on 14 November and he looked for guidance from Berlin on how to handle the Irish leader. He enquired in what form he might indicate to de Valera Germany's willingness to render effective assistance to Ireland in the event of a British attack. The German State Secretary replied that it was in order for Hempel to tell de Valera that determined resistance against any British attempts to violate Irish neutrality would result in Ireland being 'in a front' with Germany. One possible Ribbentrop-Veesenmayer scenario seemed to be falling into place.

Ribbentrop renewed his offer of arms. He would not take 'NO' for an answer; unlike his Envoy, he did not have to deal face-to-face with de Valera. He instructed Hempel to continue to discuss the matter of assistance in the form of arms with influential persons in Ireland, preferably with de Valera; but not exclusively with him; he could deal elsewhere if necessary. He also again directed him as to how he might approach the matter: he was to proceed cautiously, not pretending that he was acting on instructions, but deferentially to ask de Valera if it were appropriate for him to enquire from Berlin how Germany viewed the possibility of assistance for Ireland if the British attacked. In Ribbentrop's prompting the German Minister was to answer his own question there and then: in that position the Third Reich would be ready, willing and able to give Ireland vigorous support. Hempel was then instructed to develop the theme further. He was reminded again by Ribbentrop to give the impression of speaking only for himself, to discuss the 'how' and the 'where' of the operation and by what ships German aid might best be sent. In this message the Foreign Minister also answered a previous query of Hempel's as to what the legation should do if the Irish government and Department of External Affairs left Dublin in the event of a British attack. Whatever happens, Ribbentrop replied, the radio transmitter and other material were to be kept intact, ready to use, as they would be crucial in the event of German operations being initiated.

Hempel's reporting contributed to convincing Ribbentrop, already previously disposed in this direction, that offering arms to Ireland was the best course of action. The Envoy only reported the facts as he saw them: his conclusions from a conversation on 11 November with Gerry Boland, the Irish Minister for Justice, that in the event of a British attack a request for help addressed to Germany was actually under consideration, almost certainly represented the surface situation in uncertain oscillating circumstances. Be that as it may, he was to find the Taoiseach evasive. He informed Ribbentrop that a calmer atmosphere seemed to prevail in Dublin and that de Valera was extremely circumspect in avoiding anything that might be taken by Britain as a departure from strict neutrality. He said that he was given no opportunity for any substantial conversation with de Valera and that he tried to broach the matter at his next meeting with Walshe. Walshe also sidestepped and changed the subject to discuss the anxiety many were expressing that Germany would sacrifice Ireland to Britain at the conclusion of the peace. Walshe pointed out to Hempel that he, of course, did not agree with that widely held sentiment. He accepted that Ireland was important strategically and he did not rule out Britain's thirst for revenge for Ireland's neutrality, which Hempel described as a 'deep sore in her side'. Walshe again instanced, said Hempel, a British desire to retain control of the Atlantic in order to ensure a bridge to Canada and the US in the contingency of an eventual counter-attack having to be mounted from that area.

His report of these conversations gave the impression that the British also thought that defeat was inevitable and, for that reason, and since Roosevelt's re-election — they did not attach as much importance to American reaction to interference in Ireland as they had previously done. The German Minister acknowledged the strategic importance of Berehaven, Swilly and Foynes but advised caution about prevailing rumours, as he felt that these could have been circulated by British counter-espionage to induce the Germans to make the first move and so put them in the wrong as far as the Irish were concerned. In spite of British moves the Irish were still reluctant to accept German assistance.

Ribbentrop was not deterred. He returned to Hempel to bring the matter up again with de Valera, offering *free of charge* a considerable quantity of arms identical to the weapons in use in the Irish army. Hempel had indicated that the British attack would take the form of a simultaneous thrust from Northern Ireland together with landings at unfortified ports on the east and south-east coasts of Ireland. This, he said, would create the conditions in which the Irish army would prefer to operate: they would then await the German assistance, which they anticipated would start with early effective action by the Luftwaffe. The lessons of the Battle of Britain had not yet sunk in. Hempel thought the Irish would hold their own at first, despite a lack of sufficient heavy weapons.

The serious deficiencies in arms and equipment in the Irish army made it difficult to refuse the German offer. The US

eventually shipped a derisory consignment of obsolete Spring-
field rifles and .300 ammunition to equip the Local Defence
Force. It was barely better than nothing. In the spring of
1941 Frank Aiken confirmed what General Michael J. Costello
had found out in 1938: the pro-British Roosevelt administration was hostile to the delivery of arms to neutral Ireland.
A clue to the persistence of this attitude is found in Hempel's
report of insistent assertions in IRA circles that the Germans
would attack Northern Ireland in the spring of 1941 and then
support the IRA to overthrow the 'Free State' government.
British and American intelligence coupled these rumours with
what they regarded as de Valera's ambivalences. They could
never be sure what use he might make of the arms. It was not
beyond the bounds of possibility in their view that he could
use them against the British.

De Valera continued to make it clear that only a physical
attack could dislodge Ireland from its policy of neutrality
and that not even the return of Northern Ireland could
change the situation. He was adamant that such an attack
would be opposed by force of arms. The compulsion to procure arms at almost any price was pressing. The small neutral
country was beset externally by superpowers and internally
by subversives. The need for arms was so great that a view
prevailed that it did not matter where they came from so
long as they ended up in the hands of the Irish army.

General Hugo MacNeill, then on the General Staff (his
2nd Division had not yet been formed), was pressing in his
official capacity for arms and equipment to bring the army
to a state of combat readiness. At another level his liaisons
with Goertz and Thomsen were likely to have had a bearing
on Ribbentrop's obsession. As Ribbentrop saw it, once de
Valera's doctrinaire objections to accepting the arms offer
had been overcome, the rest would follow. De Valera did not
voice any lofty objections. He even dryly jested with Hempel
to the effect that the German high command knew its own
business best about contingency planning. His one voiced objection was that they would not get away with the gun-
running; they would be found out, he contended, and Ireland's
neutrality policy would thus be jeopardised. He saw no chance
of having the arms shipped to Ireland unnoticed and for that

reason he told the German Minister that he felt that Ireland's hazardous situation did not allow the taking of any risks.

The limits of the risks de Valera was prepared to take were more definitely demonstrated when he refused Hempel permission to bring in extra staff for the legation in a Luftwaffe plane. Legend has it that the plane got as far as hovering over Shannon: but it never landed. Just as de Valera had indicated his willingness to co-operate with Britain to the limit that such co-operation could not be seen to jeopardise the Irish stand, so too he was prepared to listen to the Germans up to a point. That point was well short of the distance he was prepared to go with Britain although in the popular perception of the day Germany was invincible. De Valera regarded the defeat of the Luftwaffe in the Battle of Britain as a miracle: he could not believe it. Therefore it was neither diplomatic nor expedient to reject out of hand either the previous German offer of an agreement affecting Irish shipping or the present offer to provide arms. The tactic adopted was to play for time. That tactic was less easy to adopt when the demand to augment the legation staff was pressurised by Ribbentrop and personalised by Hempel.

When questions of a military nature had been posed to Hempel previously from Berlin, he answered that certain aspects of the questions could be handled more comprehensively by a military man. In a conversation between General Warlimont and Ambassador Ritter, discussing the extent to which help might be given to Ireland, reference was also made to increasing the legation staff by an official or officer experienced in military reconaissance. General Jodl too wanted the legation strengthened, and this move seemed to be in line with discussions the legation was having with a high ranking Irish Army Officer, code named in Hempel's reports as 'L'.[6] He is alleged to have envisaged close co-operation with the Germans in common active service against the British. Hempel felt that he was on strong ground not only in offering the weapons but in pressing the case for augmentation of staff.

He made the point that as great latitude was allowed to the Allies in the way of having military and naval attachés at their embassies, so similar consideration should be shown to the Germans. He instanced to Weizächer that the British had a naval attaché who probably also had disguised staff; the French had a naval attaché who had been accredited to London before the fall of France; and the Americans had a military and air attaché who, he held, were intended to be used to put pressure on de Valera. Why not grant a like facility to the Germans, he queried.

Like many rules devised during the war de Valera was well aware that this arrangement favoured the Allies but he evaded Ribbentrop and Hempel in Euclidian fashion. Having lectured Hempel on Ireland's daring to remain neutral at all, he insisted that the German officials proposed to be transferred from America to the Dublin legation must use ordinary means of transportation: Pan-American passenger line to Lisbon and then to England by British plane; which was impossible. The solution to this problem lay in the absence of any solution.

Ribbentrop fired testy telegraphs at the legation expressing annoyance with the Irish. Hempel's advice had been to get in the military advisor under the guise of a replacement for the deceased legation secretary, Wenzel, but confronted with the Taoiseach's *reductio ad absurdum* he had reluctantly agreed, to this impossible proposition of de Valera's, so there was nothing more that could be done unless the Germans wished to force the issue to the point of confrontation. Ribbentrop, with a bad grace, gave up the idea of strengthening the legation staff for the time being. He had to climb down from the position he had taken up on Christmas Day 1940 of instructing Hempel to inform the 'Eireann' authorities that Germany and not Eire would decide the strength of the legation staff. On 29 December he told Hempel not to press further with the matter.

He was not however going to give up so easily his pet project for the delivery of arms, and again he curtly directed Hempel to discuss with de Valera ways and means of German assistance in the event of a British attack. Hempel found de Valera, who was having trouble with his eyes at the time, increasingly non-committal. To further weaken the prospects of success for that project Admiral Ritter also recorded his reservations.

Hempel continued to try to promote the idea. On 7 December 1940 he had formally suggested that it might help discussions if Germany showed interest in the continued existence of an independent Ireland. *On the other hand*, he hedged at once, any German commitment to a United Ireland would be premature. Ribbentrop's frustration was increasing.

In exasperation with what he viewed as the Irish government's shilly-shallying, he briefed Hempel to emphasise to de Valera that Ireland could assert her national demands and remain fully independent only if Britain were vanquished. Germany, he pointed out, subscribed to Irish aspirations and that, in the final analysis, put them both in the same camp. But it was no use: de Valera would not budge.

Hempel's explanation for the Taoiseach's polite but firm refusal of the beguiling German arms offer was that Irish-American activity had given him some immunity from a British attack. He had also managed to buy time and get more breathing space by ensuring that one division of the Irish army at least would get some semblance of proper equipment. That was not enough to restrain the impatient Ribbentrop from prompting Hempel to express 'mild doubts' about the Irish will to resist when it seemed that they would do nothing practically, outside of theorising, to prepare their defences.

Despite all this, the captured British weapons were held ready to transport from 13 April 1941. They were of sufficient quantity to make an Irish divisional commander's mouth water, particularly as the attitude of Churchill and Roosevelt dampened prospects of getting meaningful supplies from Allied quarters. The cargo prepared for shipment consisted of 46 field guns; 550 machine guns; 10,000 rifles and 1,000 anti-tank grenade throwers – all with necessary and appropriate ammunition.

In German eyes Roosevelt's resistance to supplying arms to the Irish government was regarded as a bonus especially when, according to a German reporter (12 March 1941), the American League for the Unity and Independence of Ireland had sent a telegram to de Valera from Chicago stating that it was silly, unfair, illogical and unchristian to request that Ireland would take a course of action that would directly involve it in war while it own territorial integrity was being

violated and while it was denied the right to secure equipment of the kind needed for its own self-defence. In
Ribbentrop's reading the scene was set for the use of captured British weapons by the Irish against the British; and,
most important, it would seem that Irish-American acquiescence, or at least lack of opposition, to such a scheme could
be anticipated. It did not work out that way: there was no
getting around de Valera who had to maintain a very fine
balance between the belligerents.

An analysis of events and utterances up to mid-1941
showed that there was a threat of invasion from both sides.
Contact had been established between the British and Irish
secret services but that did not eliminate the British threat:
if anything it increased it. The crunch point, however, was
that de Valera was greatly disturbed by the physical mani-
festations of German violations of neutrality. There was also
the tangible evidence given in open court of IRA liaisons with
the German high command and there was the insertion of
agents who had missions of sabotage and subversion.

The German breaches went beyond undue pressures to
augment legation staffs or persistently compromising offers
of arms assistance; and far beyond Petersen's drunken indiscretions. Hempel reported that British and American propaganda were turning to good account the dropping of
bombs on Drogheda, Terenure, the Curragh, Enniskerry,
Wexford, the South Circular Road in Dublin and on different
places on the east coast. The bomb dropped in Wexford had
caused considerable damage and casualties and consequently
grave disquiet. He relayed an American radio report that the
Irish government had threatened to expel him and, added
that he had to complain about an *Irish Times* leading article
attributing the Oylegate (Co. Wexford) bombing to the
Germans. He repeated that he had made a stiff protest to
Walshe warning him to be careful about such imputations.
Walshe took the rebuke quietly, according to the German
Minister, pointing out the adverse effect the bombings were
having on Irish public opinion and the capital such actions
was providing for British and American propagandists.

Ribbentrop continued to puzzle and smoulder at the incomprehensible attitude of the Irish, not alone to the offer of

arms but particularly to their obtuseness when it came to a question of reinforcing the legation staff. He could not reconcile this resistance with what he took to be offical connivance which allowed Goertz to remain at large, moving, it seemed, at will. There were recurring protests from the Irish government to Hempel about violations of airspace and attacks on Irish shipping but Ribbentrop did not attach great importance to this. Dillon asked questions in the Dáil about the bombing of Irish ships and the machine-gunning of crews. No-one, he was informed, took Dillon seriously. He did not take increasing Allied pressures into full account.

'The Great White Father', as the German reports refer to Roosevelt, had, according to Hempel, advised de Valera not to insist on the incorporation of the six counties during the war: the message, he said, was to wait until the war was over, when US support would be forthcoming to achieve a united Ireland. There was of course a price: leading US political personalities like Cudahy, Wilkie, Donovan, followed by Prime Minister Menzies of Australia, beat a path to de Valera to try to persuade him to modify his stand on neutrality. The Taoiseach dared not compromise by an indiscretion with the Germans. Maffey found it necessary to put Eire's neutrality in perspective. He rebuked London with the following memo:

In the general resentment against Eire it seems to be forgotten that up to a point they have been friendly and helpful. Hateful as their neutrality is, it has been a neutrality friendly to our cause. I need not give in detail what we have got and are getting in the way of intelligence reports, coded weather reports, prompt reports of submarine movements, free use of Lough Foyle and to the air over Donegal shore and territorial waters. What I must stress is that I am constantly asked to put proposals to the Eire government which could not be put in an unfriendly manner. If we could say: 'Eire can go to the devil, we don't want the ports, we don't want anything', my task would be easy. To-day I have on my table a proposal from the Admiralty for installing boom defences in the Shannon Estuary, a scheme from the Ministry for a corridor of considerable extent over Eire territory and territorial waters enabling

the full development of Lough Erne as a flying base, plans
for the extensive use of Foynes on the Shannon Estuary
replacing Poole to some extent and developing a Lisbon-
West African or American link based in Foynes and not
only that — for the American traffic to be based on the
aerodromes of Rhinanna and Collinstown. I am happy
to say that I have made some headway on better air
space — good reasons for hoping that my appeal on the
subject of the full use of an air corridor to the west of
Lough Erne will be conceded. . . . I feel that to-day, whatever the morrow may bring forth, the Eire government is
willing and anxious to help in any way that does not
expose the country to danger. This may not be very
heroic, but there is no mandate here for heroics.

That did not mollify all those engaged in the day-to-day
mechanics of the war at a tactical as distinct from a strategic
level, particularly those embroiled in the Battle of the
Atlantic. That was a constant factor impelling the threat of
a British attack to secure the Atlantic ports. Maffey had
considerable success in securing the concession for the RAF
to use the so-called 'Donegal Corridor' between Rathlin
O'Beirne island in the North and Inishmurray in the South to
facilitate the flying boat base in Lough Erne. For the RAF to
have to detour north around Malin Head would have been a
great disadvantage to them. This facility made a significant
contribution to winning the Battle of the Atlantic and defeating the Germans. If that concession did not altogether placate
the British it did serve to restrain them. Maffey's contention
was that essentially Irish neutrality was operating to their
advantage and his message was to lay off harassing de Valera.
   Churchill reacted negatively to Maffey: he had no time at
all for de Valera. He concurred with the RAF plan to drench
Ireland with poison-gas if the Germans invaded there. The
British chiefs of staff were assuming that Germany would use
gas bombs and chemical weapons in 'Sealion' and that they
would have to reply in kind. A requirement was outlined, in
the event of the Germans setting up a bridgehead in Ireland,
of spraying their landing sites and axes of advance with
poison gases including mustard gas which would have caused

incapacitating blistering and inflamation of the lungs and respiratory tract. There was also a phosgene gas which would kill by choking. It would not separate Irish from German, and no thought seems to have been given as to the possible effects on the Irish civilian population, north or south. This could hardly have been termed assistance to repel the German invasion. A bomber squadron at Feltwell in Suffolk was equipped with gas spray containers for the contingency. Bases in Beribrook (Lincolnshire), Old Sarum (Salisbury) and Grangemouth (Scotland) were also alerted that no gas bombs or spray containers had been laid down in Northern Ireland and should it be necessary to employ gas against an enemy force invading Eire, this work would be undertaken by bomber squadrons based in England.[7]

There was no implication that it would be necessary for the Germans to make the first move with chemical weapons before Britain would resort to these counter measures. It showed how seriously the German danger of an invasion of Ireland was taken by the British. It was also an indication of how sceptical many of them remained regarding the value of de Valera's considerations, which seemed to some of them to be worthless in a life-or-death situation such as the summer of 1940 was for mainland Britain.

The threat of a German invasion served to hold the rhetoric of doctrinaire neutrality up to the cold light of stark reality. The Germans were seriously in the ruthless business of war. For the British war *was* a business to be waged without sentiment: they had a lot of practice at it. For both belligerents Ireland was merely a factor in their struggle for survival and supremacy. Both would violate neutrality if the compulsions of that struggle dictated it. Britain would probably require a legalistic or a moralistic pretext for doing so, but there was no guarantee of this. In any case they would have found no problem in turning out one: their survival was, for them, a compelling justification. The only pretext the Germans required was the prospect of a military victory: for them the end justified the means. Both sides continued to monitor the other's each and every move on Ireland.

In May 1941 Woermann quoted the Irish ambassador in Washington as telling the Italian ambassador there that

Roosevelt had sought in vain a declaration that England would not attack Ireland. Cordell Hull was very definite in his views that, from a German point of view, nothing could be better than a British invasion of Ireland, under any pretext, or in any form. The *New Yorker* magazine supported him.

The big difference between the two belligerents however was that there were actual German attacks on what Irish nationalists of all persuasions claimed to be their territory. The first German air raid on Belfast on 8 April 1941 killed 13 people and injured 81. During the Easter holidays, one week later, an estimated 100 German aircraft again pounded the city. At least 700 lives were lost and 1,511 people injured. De Valera dispatched fire brigades from Dublin, Dun Laoghaire, Drogheda and Dundalk to succour stricken Belfast. The niceties of neutrality did not deter him at a time like that. On 5 and 6 May two further raids caused extensive incendiary damage. These raids on Belfast shattered the illusion fondly held by the Irish government that the Germans had been respecting the integrity of the thirty-two counties in refraining from bombing Northern Ireland. On 18 May Cardinal McRory approached Hempel to have Armagh spared from being bombed. The German Minister strongly supported the Cardinal's request. Armagh was of no military significance, he said; there was only a divisional headquarters and a few hundred soldiers there; there were no munitions or aircraft factories or large industry there. The Cardinal, Hempel continued, was a personal friend of his: he was very anti-British and a strong supporter of Irish neutrality and independence as well as having good relations with the Italians.

Joe Walshe put in a word with the Envoy to spare Derry, making the case that shirt-making was the only industry there. Hempel added that four hundred nationalists were interned in Crumlin Road, Belfast inferring that this was also a target to be avoided. Joe Walshe may have done the British and Derry a greater turn than he realised. Derry was a vital naval base, crucial to the winning of the Battle of the Atlantic, and the location of the critically important anti-submarine warfare school. Inexplicably the Germans failed to bomb it. It looks as if Joe Walshe deserved the credit for that.

South of the border, too, the war seemed to be getting nearer and nearer. Hempel reported that several German aircraft pursued by two RAF plans were over Dublin on 25 May 1941 and that Irish anti-aircraft guns fired on them. His subsequent accounts cover the North Strand bombing in Dublin on 31 May 1941. He reported houses destroyed, 17 to 20 people dead and 150 wounded in that raid. The Envoy's 'radical nationalist' friends tried to persuade him that the bombing was another example of British provocation.

The evidence of German involvement produced to the Envoy could not be denied. Warnock's protest said that a light blue coloured plastic material generally cylindrical in shape and bearing the inscription *'hier nicht anheben'* had been found in each bombed area. It was also reported that the bombs dropped in Malin, Co. Donegal on 5 May also had German markings (DL 284). Hempel's report to Berlin conceded the position indicated by the evidence and he recommended the keeping of a low profile by the German radio in particular. He emphasised that the efforts to pin blame for the January bombings on the British had met with little success.

Kramarz replied that Liverpool had been the target that night and, while it was improbable that Dublin had been mistaken for Liverpool, they did not rule that out. He remarked that the bombing would not have happened at all if Dublin had not been blacked out — reviving a complaint that the black-out was favouring the British. Hempel's response was to advise the Foreign Ministry to either accept responsibility as in Campile in 1940 (though he pointed out that reparations would be high) or to use the opportunity specifically to declare intentions. He said that the German success in the airborne invasion of Crete had reawakened Irish apprehensions.

The Irish protest was accompanied by a demand for full compensation and reparation. The incident, however, did not fully divert the government's mind from anxieties about the British. Walshe continued to humour Hempel with the theory that by bending a guiding beam the British may have directed the bombers over Dublin.

The British, it was true, had discovered a method of deflecting the beams guiding the German bombers so that they jettisoned their bomb loads over open countryside,[8] but this method hardly had the precision to deflect the plane to a specific target such as Dublin. The Germans discountenanced this capability but Dr Gogan, a German sympathiser, went one better: his version was that the British dropped the bombs from a reconstructed German plane!

When bombs were dropped again on Arklow on 1 June the British repeated the accusation that the Irish were incapable of defending themselves. Hempel admitted on 2 June that German aircraft regularly followed routes along the east and south-east coasts. Anglo-Irish relations were further strained by the proposal to introduce conscription in Northern Ireland. The fact remained, however, that it was German actions rather than British motions which were outraging the government and the people. Hempel's account of his summons to de Valera, who expressed the strongest misgivings of German intentions to respect neutrality, leaves no doubt as to the strength of feeling and perplexity caused by the German transgressions. Walshe, according to the Envoy, took it more cooly; though Hempel crankily observed that, while Walshe did not appear to be all that disturbed by British incursions into Irish airspace, he was demanding strict German compliance with the letter of the law. In his honest opinion the Irish anti-aircraft fire was ordered only to appease the British and that it was because of this fire that the Germans had dropped their bombs.

The Germans in Berlin responded with some condescension, if not arrogance. They did not seem to be unduly worried by the protests. The SS *Kyleclare* was attacked by a Junkers 88 aircraft off Brownstown Head, Co. Waterford in spite of the fact that the ship bore conspicious 'Eire' neutrality markings that it would not be possible for Hempel to plead mistaken identity. General von Waldau added a subsequent snide remark, supporting the contention that the North Strand bombings would not have happened if German advice against the blacking out of Dublin had been acted on. It may have been this superior attitude of the Germans that prompted Warnock to add orally to his written protest that in spite of enemy propaganda no one believed that the Germans had done the bombing on purpose! Walshe's representations had been reported by Hempel as being friendly.

Ribbentrop intervened to outline to Hempel the form of the reply he was to make to the Irish protest: it was to be non-committal but conciliatory and a press release was to be agreed. Concerning the request to lift the blackout Warnock explained to Woermann that the problem here was that this would give rise to a request from the British for an intensification of the black-out.

Hempel agreed a press release with the Irish government in which the Germans expressed their sincere regret and in view of the friendly relations existing between the two countries were prepared to give compensation for the deplorable loss of life and injury to persons and property. Strictest instructions were to be issued to prevent recurrence. Nevertheless on 26 July 1941 Hempel had to report that yet another bomb had been dropped: this time in the vicinity of Dundalk by a plane returning from an air raid on Belfast. Fragments of the bomb picked up were found to bear an imprint of the German eagle.

Hempel nevertheless still persisted with his hints about British and US machinations and provocations. He still, he said, did not rule out a British attack on Ireland and felt that the danger of such an attack would increase with the entry of the US into the war. He referred in the same breath to the problem of conscription in Northern Ireland and the foundering of Frank Aiken's arms purchasing mission in the US. It is possible then to read some significance into the Envoy's report that de Valera was pleased with the German reply to the Irish protest, especially when the same report refers to Walshe's accommodating attitude and also when the German Minister seemed to have been given a hearing from both de Valera and Walshe to the German point of view on the black-out problem.

Then the Envoy reported more specifically on Aiken's return from the US and the failure of that mission, with the exception that the Irish politician had got support from Irish-Americans for the neutrality position.

A report from Berlin on 29 May had done little to elucidate or explain the previous bombings. If viewed in a psychological warfare context it would be possible to see them as a strong-arm tactic to persuade the Irish to fall in with German schemes. But that would presume a defined aim and a degree of co-ordination which did not exist in the Third Reich. It would, however, be consistent enough with Ribbentrop's petulance and his growing impatience with the lowly rated Irish. Error is a more likely reason.

On the other hand, Ribbentrop did instruct Veesenmayer to put wireless and money at the disposal of the IRA and plans were hatched accordingly for a suitable landing to be made by seaplane in an inland Irish lake in Sligo. Clissmann was to provide political and military liaison. Frank Ryan's job was to harmonise the warring factions of the IRA and to sweeten and hoodwink de Valera. Ribbentrop was completely fed up trying to persuade the slippery Irish government to accept German arms to repel an anticipated British attack. He now took the line that perhaps the IRA would put them to better use.

But far greater schemes were afoot which impeded the implementation of such a proposal. In Directive No. 21 dated 18 December 1940 Hitler decreed that the German armed forces must be prepared, even before the end of the war against Britain, to overthrow Soviet Russia in a rapid campaign (Operation 'Barbarossa'). On 22 June 1941 he turned his forces against Russia.

The German generals continued to regard an invasion of the British Isles as the surest way to defeat England and when Hitler turned east they were haunted by the fundamental error of leaving an undefeated resurgent enemy in their rear. But they lacked the courage of their convictions, and they made no attempt to convince the Führer of their military logic.

De Valera had been let off the hook. As Bernard Shaw put it he had been 'triumphantly saved by the folly of the Führer in making for Moscow instead of for Galway'. But the British threat remained: the weakening of one threat was balanced by a strengthening of the other. De Valera never knew whence a blow might come. Ribbentrop's mission to Veesenmayer to foment rebellion in Ireland still stood. The British foreign intelligence agency, M16, offensively exercised surveillance on the German legation in Dublin. Their information was that the legation was making efforts to use the IRA to mount attacks on the North. That development could precipitate British intervention of an explosive nature.

SEVEN

Unconventional Operations

It was comparatively straightforward to estimate the possibilities and consequences of a conventional German invasion of Ireland. Terrain, weather, time and space, reinforcements and combat power were relatively tangible factors. The political problem of partition blurred but did not blot out the fact that in the event of a German attack British aid would be at once forthcoming: de Valera publicly acknowledged this. Contingency concepts envisaged British assistance of up to corps strength, concentrating initially in the River Boyne area. No one except Churchill and some of his more manic warlords dreamt for a moment that such assistance might take the form of indiscriminately drenching the Irish countryside with poison gas.

The implications of a deliberate British invasion were more difficult to assess. This assessment was bedevilled by the clumsy intrusion of ham-fisted Reich agents. The Germans had a genius for conducting tactical warfare: their conduct of unconventional operations was less surefooted.

The insertion of German agents in Eire embarrassed the Irish government. They were uncovered with ridiculous ease and their presence inspired some sinister attitudinising on the Allied side. They lost no opportunity to profess their scepticism and to deride Eire's capability to defend herself against a German attack. The madcap capers of the amateur agents played into the hands of the anti-Irish cliques who made the most of the incidents to discomfort de Valera. They provided manna for the Fleet Street 'Paddy bashers'.

The British had rejected a proposal from South African Premier Smuts in June 1940 that the Irish ports should be seized at once even in the face of Irish opposition. They saw to it, however, that the Irish were never able to rule out that threat absolutely. This approach kept relationships in a nervous state and encouraged underground activities.

The British were psychologically disposed to oppose Irish neutrality. They were not deterred by the knowledge that a belligerent who refused to recognise a state as neutral violated international law. Academic points of law counted for little when the fight for survival was on. The presence of the German legation in Dublin gave them material enough to vilify the Irish government's neutral stand. Their stance was provocative.

There are varying opinions as to the extent to which British provocation was practised. With Hempel it became an obsession. (Colonel Dan Bryan, the head of Irish intelligence, pooh-poohed the idea.) The suspicion of provocation aggravated Hempel and sharpened his requirement for reliable intelligence. All the information needed was not now simply to be read in the papers, or in the unsolicited documents which Frau Hempel claimed were surreptitiously stuffed through the German Minister's letter-box in Dun Laoghaire. The perennial dilemma for any diplomat is knowing where to draw the line between information gathering and spying. Hempel represented one of the major belligerents in a neutral country which was traditionally hostile to the other belligerent.

The Third Reich kept drawing the anachronistic conclusion that Ireland and Germany had a common enemy in England. 'England's difficulty is Ireland's opportunity' was the traditional recurring Irish slogan for dealing with Britain, the ancient enemy! Mahr used that theme in his Berlin radio propaganda programmes. He exhorted Irishmen to fight for freedom, to break the yoke of the British Empire. De Valera, however, was not governed by such simplistic slogans and while Hempel recognised this, his superiors failed to do so.

The British propaganda machine wilfully contributed to the confusion. Although they knew full well how de Valera had faced up to the IRA challenge to his authority they chose to make capital out of his anti-partition rhetoric, portraying it, when it suited them, as identifying the Irish government's aims with those of the IRA. The Abwehr connection helped dissemination of disinformation prejudical to neutrality.

An IRA Order of the Day issued on 27 May 1941 did not blame the Germans for the bombing of Belfast the previous Eastertide but read: 'already one of our cities has been laid in ruins and thousands of our people killed because against the will of the Irish people it has been made a stronghold of British power'. De Valera was later to utter similar sentiments publicly. Hempel reported that James Dillon had taunted the Taoiseach in the Dáil for not protesting against the German bombing of Belfast. De Valera struck back that such a protest should be made not to Germany but to those who dragged Northern Ireland into the war against her will. That sounded very like what the IRA were saying.

The IRA order called for a new battle to be fought on Irish soil: 'we shall regret as all people regret to be compelled to see our land suffer the ravages of war but we shall know that only final and complete victory can save it from similar ravages, decade after decade, generation after generation.' Although the IRA professed a desire to avoid civil war, this document accepted that in achieving their aim of a *coup d'état* 'in both areas' (Northern Ireland and Eire) they would be left with 'a weakened people to face the British'.

Echoes between sections of de Valera's rhetoric and the language of the IRA could not conceal — except from some wilful sections of the British and from myopic elements in the Third Reich — that de Valera and the IRA were on a collision rather than on a collusion course. The Minister for Justice, Gerry Boland, in a Dáil reply to James Dillon said that it was not clear whether the IRA intended a *coup d'état* at home or an attack on the North but that it was the government's intention to take their weapons from them and put them behind bars.

The inherent threat of the IRA to the institutions of the Irish state was evident in the fact that the illegal organisation had already established liaison with the Abwehr and had prepared a plan ('Kathleen') for a German landing in Ireland. Fortunately for the security of the state and the preservation of neutrality this liaison proved to be fitful and inefficient. Lahausen, the head of Abwehr II, complained that every undertaking proved abortive and that the IRA went off and did things on their own without a word to anyone. An entry in his diary on 11 December 1939 confirmed that relations had deteriorated to the point where U-Boat commanders would only undertake to land agents on the Irish coast if they could be assured that IRA were *not* informed beforehand as to the time and place of the landing.

The British, with good cause, were not so contemptuous of the IRA capabilities. With the exception of the bungling, through panic, in Coventry the IRA bombing campaign in England in 1939 had been carried out with alarming efficiency. Their so-called S-Plan for the campaign was so efficiently prepared that M15 thought it was the product of the Abwehr. It was in fact the brain-child of Jim O'Donovan, the ex-Clongowes science teacher. He subsequently derived amusement from the British supposition. He would not have given the Germans that much credit. Since the strip-searching by them of his wife he had no great opinion of them. There was a mentality gap as well as a language barrier between the Abwehr and the IRA but circumstances forced them to examine ways in which they could be of use to one another.

O'Donovan's plan decreed that the bombing in England should be directed at public utilities. The actual campaign impressed upon the Germans that the IRA, for all their fantasies, really meant business this time and would be a useful ally. Bombs went off in Willesden power station, Birmingham, Manchester and Alnwick. In London there were explosions in underground stations, in shops, cinemas, aqueducts, left luggage offices and Madame Tussaud's waxworks. Innocent civilians were the victims. Cinemas were also attacked in Liverpool and Coventry and Walton Gaol was bombed. Brendan Behan had a go at blowing up Hammersmith Bridge. Pillar boxes burst into flames.

The British government introduced the Prevention of Violence Bill which gave the police new powers of detention and forced Irish nationals to register as aliens. Whatever about Lahausen's mistrust, Scotland Yard and MI5 felt that the IRA were a force to be reckoned with. The House of Commons tally at the introduction of the bill to deal with terrorism was that a total of 127 terrorist offences had taken place since January 1939: fifty-seven in London; seventy in the provinces. It was a great embarrassment to de Valera and the Irish people generally, though there was a public outcry when Barnes and McCormick were hanged. The IRA in response raided a British army barracks in Ballykinlar, Co. Down and got away with two hundred rifles and a good supply of amunition. This worried the Irish government but impressed some factions in the Third Reich.

Hempel's instructions about discreet liaison with the IRA, like Goertz's were based on an approval of the proven performance of their English campaign rather than on Lahausen's experiences of trying to work with them. The Envoy approached Clissmann to do the contacting but the versatile Academic Exchange man involuntarily returned to Germany before he could set up comprehensive liaison. Hempel had no option but to turn to his second-in-command to carry on the work. Henning Thomsen had neither Clissmann's experience nor public relations talents and he was further hampered by Hempel's insistence on turning a blind eye to any covert activities that might implicate him.

The Envoy's main concern was to avoid being compromised and to keep up appearances for the legation. Much has been made from hindsight of his downgrading of the IRA. His reservations about them were based on his estimate of their capabilities. In his opinion their lack of leadership meant that they lacked the capability for any meaningful action which might be useful to German purposes. He never fully ruled out their potential: the very point he was making was that premature action could damage that potential for future operations. Together with his press attaché, Petersen, he clung to the possibility that when England's difficulties presented a national opportunity to end partition by force, the IRA would have an important role to play. The IRA offer of protection for the legation in the event of a British invasion did not offend his normally sensitive susceptibilities for proper procedures. De Valera's warning to have nothing whatsoever to do with the IRA did not seem to have weighed unduly heavily on him in that instance.

Hempel flirted with espionage while making his reservations and inhibitions in that area very clear. His relations with Francis Stuart are a case in point. Stuart wanted to return to his lecturing job in Berlin University and enlisted Hempel's aid. He told the Envoy in strict confidence that he belonged to a group of nationalist Irishmen who wished to have a representative in Germany to maintain the previous close links which had been established with the Pfaus group and the *Fichtebund* propaganda agency.

Hempel was unhappy with the activities of such agencies and complained to the Propaganda Ministry about their indiscretions. Pointing the finger at the Ministry, he said that making contacts with radical Irish nationalists should be pursued only with the utmost care. They were being watched, he warned.

Pfaus had been in correspondence with a Dr Anna Sloane in New York. Through her he contacted an American, General Mosely, and James Philip Gaffney with a view to influencing Irish-American opinion. He put Gaffney in touch with a Captain Liam D. Walsh of Drimnagh, Dublin who was General O'Duffy's right-hand man. Hempel later reported unfavourably on Walsh, the ex-army officer who had become an agent for the *Fichtebund* and had insinuated himself into employment at the Italian legation. Walsh had written to Gaffney on 22 June 1939 saying that he was very glad to learn that he was doing such good work to help smash the semitic groups in America and that he personally would like very much to help in this very necessary work. The following year, Walsh was uncovered and interned; the Italian representative, Berardis, erroneously harboured the suspicion that Hempel had planted him in his legation whereas in fact that Envoy had been strongly opposed to *Fichtebund* activities in Ireland. Someone of course had planted him there.

Hempel expressed his opinion to Berlin that the British were only allowing the *Fichtebund* to send their propaganda to subversive elements through the post in order to build up a dossier of breaches of neutrality to be used against the Irish government. Here he showed adroitness in covering his tracks: he insisted that the *Fichtebund* were not to know that it was he who had fingered them. He had already reported the rumours abroad of undercover connections between German intelligence agencies and the IRA. But all his adroitness could not avoid entanglement with Liam Walsh. In September 1940 he telegraphed that Walsh's wife was demanding regular payments from the legation now that Walsh was interned. The Abwehr obviously had uses for Walsh, though he would not have been Hempel's choice.

Francis Stuart, an Antrim Protestant, was selected because other efforts to maintain contact had foundered. Hempel vouched for him as the son-in-law of Maud Gonne MacBride. Her credentials were impeccable: she had been active in the independence movement and was also the mother of Sean MacBride who had recently been the IRA chief of staff and a friend and confidant of Hempel's. Stuart had promised him that he would keep a low profile and Hempel undertook to pay his fare to Germany *via* the US.

On 15 January 1940 he asked Köcher in the German legation in Bern to meet Stuart on arrival, to provide him with some money and look after him generally. However, after the capture of Held and the arrest of Mrs Stuart the following May, Hempel's solicitude evaporated. He was worried that Stuart might prove indiscreet. Righteously, he demanded that Berlin reprimand Stuart for not supporting his wife and family. Stuart could compromise him. His instinct was to distance himself from him; to ditch him if necessary.

Stuart for his part remained well disposed towards Hempel though, like Haller, he thought that the German diplomat was a fussy old woman devoid of daring. Still it was the introduction Hempel gave him to Weizächer, more than Abwehr contacts made through the IRA, that stood to Stuart when he needed assistance in Berlin. Before he left Ireland Sean MacBride had put him in touch with IRA chief of staff, Stephen Hayes, and Jim O'Donovan who had given him messages for the Abwehr.

Hempel was a sound man: he disliked melodrama. It was typical of his circumspection that he responded negatively to a Berlin proposal for the return of Sean Russell from New York *via* Germany to Ireland. They were convinced that it was technically possible to transport Russell by submarine and that politically it was a suitable time to do so. Hempel persuaded the Political Department that this would be an inappropriate action at an inopportune moment: the time

had not yet arrived, he stressed. Veesenmayer was disappointed and frustrated by this reaction. He had analysed that his
best chance of accomplishing his mission was to leave the
Irish to their own devices, to give them a chance to prove
themselves. He realised that the material he had for fomenting revolution had shortcomings. He knew that Russell lacked
political acumen but he preferred him to Ryan whom he
regarded as being too far to the left. But the important thing
in his estimate was that both Russell and Ryan had a rapport
with de Valera going back to the days when they were all
brothers-in-arms together in the IRA and that partition left
unfinished business about which de Valera felt strongly.
That, he felt, must count for something: he assumed that the
IRA and the government differed only as to methods in their
efforts to achieve the same national objectives.

Although he had not been consulted about Ryan's par-
ticipation, Hempel knew better than that. Ryan's role was
obscure. His inclusion in the expedition was an afterthought.
When Russell died aboard the submarine he was not sufficiently briefed to take over and carry on. Hempel knew that
Ryan was an old pal of de Valera's but he also knew that
de Valera's sentimentality for Co. Limerick and comrades
from the fight for freedom did not extend so far as to influence his actions as head of government. An awareness of
Ryan's inclusion would not have altered the German Minister's
advice to stay out altogether.

Woermann reported to Ribbentrop that Hempel had spoken
out against sending Russell to Ireland at that time: the
Envoy's point, said Woermann, was that in combat terms the
IRA was not strong enough to produce a successful outcome
to operations. It can only be speculated as to what Hempel's
reaction would have been had he formed a different opinion
of the IRA's combat-readiness.

He was apprehensive that the insertion of Russell would
result inevitably in his arrest by the Irish government and
that this would reveal the German connection, further discredit the IRA and diminish their potential to assist the
Reich. He concluded that only Britain would benefit and he
drew a parallel with the landing of Sir Roger Casement from
a German U-Boat during the First World War. But that very

parallel had been a positive factor in the estimates of the
Berlin planners: the 1916 Rising, despite its military failure,
had produced a successful revolution from what were, militarily speaking, the most unlikely beginnings. Berlin hoped for
a similar 1916 concatenation of events. So Woermann insisted
that the contact with McCarthy in New York be maintained.

McCarthy was the mystery man of this period. He was
unknown to Irish intelligence. He was the courier between
New York and Genoa, the link man between Russell, the
German consulate in Genoa, the Foreign Ministry in Berlin,
the Abwehr, Veesenmayer and thence *via* the Foreign Ministry
to Hempel. Initially the Abwehr's interest was restricted to
a demand for sabotage. Ribbentrop got bigger ideas.

McCarthy's main object was to get agreement to the smug-
gling of Russell from New York to Europe with a view to
getting German backing for the IRA leader's return to Ireland.
Hempel, as was his wont, again counselled caution. He was
suspicious when he observed that McCarthy and Russell had
the same New York address and perhaps he produced the key
to the McCarthy mystery when he queried whether McCarthy
and Russell might not in fact be one and the same person.
The intriguing query remains unanswered.

Hempel's misgivings and warnings did not stop Ribbentrop.
The drama of Russell dying in Frank Ryan's arms from a
perforated ulcer aboard a U-Boat, a hundred miles west of
Galway in mid-August 1940, is well known. This was the
time scheduled for the German feint or secondary attack on
Ireland in conjunction with 'Sealion'.

Hempel's part in the game was intended to ensnare and
embroil de Valera. He was to arrange to put a flower box in
the main window of the top floor of the legation to signal
that 'Sealion' was under way and thus give the green light to
Russell to go ahead with his schemes: that signal has passed
into folklore. Whether these putative schemes embraced a
link up with the *Operation Grün* bridgehead landing in the
Wexford area or not can only — as far as present documentation goes — be a matter for speculation.

Hempel remained sceptical. His main concern was to avoid
being compromised. True to form he took immediate steps
to cover himself. No sooner had he agreed the arrangement

than he qualified it: he would put the box there all right but it should then remain there permanently. By that device he planned to head off any possible official query that could link the flower box signal with any Russell-Ryan adventure.

He emphasised once more his desire not to be seen to be involved with underground contacts. A reliable person, he wrote, wished to be put in touch with Goertz, 'assuming he was still in the country'. He declined her request saying he had nothing to do with that business. When he advised the German high command on 23 August 1940 to be sure to listen on the 38.25 m band the following weekend he added that receipt of this intelligence should not be made known to Goertz.

It was a vain hope on Hempel's part to expect that he could continue to wash his hands of the Abwehr agent. The blitzkrieg that brought about the Fall of France was an event of enormous political as well as military consequence: old norms had been swept away. For a small neutral country avowed to take on the first invader, some contingency planning was inescapable. It is neither ludicrous nor fantastic in the climate of the times to suppose that even cabinet ministers could make some unorthodox contacts. Some such contacts allegedly involved two cabinet ministers and a senator. This suggested that some cabinet ministers were not unsympathetic to the landing of Russell. Hempel, of course, was totally opposed to Russell's mission, and had said so. This dichotomy of views between the German Minister and some members of the Irish government became the subject of a report from Hempel to Berlin. In that twilight area, it is conceivable that some overlapping could occur between customary diplomatic practice, overtly followed by Hempel, and undercover initiatives into which the Envoy was inevitably, albeit reluctantly, drawn.

Initially Hempel had to be convinced in writing that Goertz was officially commissioned for his unorthodox task. Goertz, after all, was more than a mere agent: from Hempel's point of view he was a rival representative authorised to function by no less a body than the Abwehr, acting for the German high command. His links with the IRA could undermine all Hempel stood for.

Hempel envisaged a new radical movement — not the IRA — arising in Ireland in the framework of a Europe dominated by the Axis powers. In that setting he likened de Valera to Portugal's Salazar. He put his own position, now menaced by the presence of Goertz, into that perspective.

Like the flower pot story the melodramatic meeting arranged between Hempel and Goertz at a cocktail party in the Envoy's house has captured the imagination. Goertz was instructed to arrive as a guest and to ask Hempel's maid for the w.c. They met and greeted each other politely.

Maud Gonne MacBride used to say that Hempel was 'frightened out of his wits' at the mere mention of the name of Goertz. Anything that might seem to reflect on her husband's physical courage infuriated Frau Hempel: the phrase 'frightened out of his wits' particularly maddened her. He was not frightened of Goertz, she said, but he did find him a burden. She explained that the Envoy had to see Goertz to find out what his task was, to elicit the agent's opinions of the IRA and to explain his own position and views. He was satisfied with the way the meeting had gone and the Minister had the same opinion as Goertz about the IRA. He found reassurance in the old misconception that it was all right as long as his caller had no hostile intentions against Ireland and so he was only interested in an objective way in the agent's task, which he regarded as dangerous and unpleasant. The prosaic diplomat seemed to find something vicariously appealing about the romantic agent's derring-do but he was uneasy at the implications arising. He realised that such exploits would be regarded as hostile acts by de Valera and that they could damage beyond repair his own official function as Minister Plenipotentiary for the Third Reich. Although he had grown ever more cautious with the passing of time, his agreement to meet Goertz compromised him. He did not shout 'Stop' to the agent.

In earlier days (February 1940) he was quite happy about such matters and in the case of Weber-Drohl he was almost offhand. The seriousness of such business was not so apparent during the 'phoney war' period, though he did warn of the dangers of such ventures in a country overflowing with spies. Although there were codewords and secret contacts security remained inadequate.[1] Infiltration was widespread. Weber-Drohl's chances of remaining undetected were slim. His mission had been to deliver money to the IRA, to invite them to send a representative to Germany, to present plans for landing weapons, to warn them to limit themselves to important military objectives and to avoid wasted efforts. According to an entry in Lahausen's Abwehr diary dated 27 March 1940 Hempel confirmed that Weber-Drohl had given the money to the 'Irish Friends'.[2]

Incidentally the fact that Weber-Drohl was sixty years of age and had arthritis did not inhibit him from having romantic interludes and, to add to Hempel's consular concerns, indulging in extra-marital procreation.[3] He also wrote lugubrious greener-than-green patriotic ballads. Hempel reported on 25 October 1941 that Weber-Drohl was free in Dublin but had to be supported by the legation for the previous ten days at the rate of £8 per month. Hempel's only effort to conceal his association with Weber-Drohl was to refer to him in his reports as W. D. or W^r. D. He referred by name to Francis Stuart, but he invariably used K to identify Goertz. For the other agents he simply used their initials after they had been apprehended. He distanced himself from them and reported that he had destroyed the files on Gartner, Tributh and Obed.

That trio — two South Africans and an Indian — were landed from a requisitioned French yacht, *Soizie*, on the south coast in July 1940 (Operation 'Lobster 1'). They were quickly picked up. One of them asked a bus conductor a question in Irish! That attempted masquerade was even more derisory than the adopted Irish accent of the British agent, Lieutenant Mason.

A few weeks previously another couple of agents waded ashore from U-Boats in separate sorties. Walter Simon *alias* Karl Anderson, who had a previous conviction in February 1939 in Tonbridge, was picked up almost at once. The other one, Willy Preetz *alias* Paddy Mitchell (who happened to be a brother-in-law of an Irish army officer) got a better run for his money but after three weeks transmitting from the loft of a small shop in Westland Row he too was picked up. The next landing in the following year did not fare any better.

Gunter Schutz *alias* Hans Marschner was arrested shortly after landing in Co. Wexford on 12 March 1941. An address of an important contact man, Werner B. Unland of 46 Merrion Square, was also found on him. He was also interned.

The agents were all malapropos: one of them had to be rushed away for urgent treatment for VD after his touchdown and immediate arrest. But for their tasks of reporting on weather, convoy movements and the effects of the bombing in England their equipment was adequate, and even sophisticated. Their transmitters, properly operated, were serviceable and Schutz was equipped with a microscope to read microdots and with chemical ingredients for secret writing.

Apart from Goertz who remained at large to the end of 1941, one of the most intriguing fish was as usual the one that got away. A young civil servant named Lenihan was convicted of falsifying a document and dismissed from the Customs and Excise. After serving a term of imprisonment he emigrated to the Channel Islands and after the German occupation he volunteered to spy: the Abwehr dropped him in the Dublin-Meath area on 18 July 1941. He was well connected politically but he decided to cross the border and surrender to the British. They gave him the codename 'Basket'.

The counter-espionage division of MI5 could not believe their luck in getting the perfect recruit for their double-cross system, which employed captured Germans to feed false information back to Germany under the pretext that they were still active. The Abwehr planned that Lenihan would set up a weather station in Sligo. In an effort to prepare the Irish to collaborate the British sent Lenihan's surrendered set to Dublin for examination and flew him to England. They quickly released him with the stipulation that he keep in touch. But Lenihan vanished and Joe Walshe would not hear of any collusion in using the radios in the double-cross operation.[4]

Lenihan was well educated, articulate but unpredictable. Irish intelligence lost track of him: they felt that he might have been swallowed up in the criminal underworld of wartime. Another theory was that he was siphoned back over the border and integrated into the double-cross system.

Jan van Loon, a Dutch quasi-Nazi, was another unusual

agent. He was self appointed and motivated by ideology. He jumped his ship when it put into Belfast and made his way to the legation to present to them useful sketches of British convoy formations. Fearing provocation and knowing that they were under constant surveillance the legation would have nothing to do with him. Next day he was arrested and lodged with the German agents in Mountjoy prison.

Lenihan and Goertz were the only two agents who evaded almost immediate detection. Lenihan was the only one to avoid ultimate internment. He had the advantage of local knowledge.

Enno Stephan,[5] who did the spade work in taking the lid off the spies story, missed out on Lenihan. Mrs Carter[6], who got on so well with Colonel Dan Bryan, only gives the official version: that he simply disappeared after the British slackly released him. Joe Walshe was shocked at the very idea that the British double-cross exercise from Sligo was even mooted. All the 'frostiness' between G2 and MI5 had not thawed. Walshe knew that de Valera's considerations would not go that far. On the other hand, there was no question at all but that the Germans had gone too far.

Of all the agents the Germans inserted Goertz was the one who caused the most concern. Not alone did his activities give the Allies material with which to pillory the Irish government, his presence had a destabilising influence on the home front as well. Even the agent's choice of Brandy as a *nom-de-guerre* caused cabinet ministers to wonder and to look curiously at one another. The real R. L. Brandy, a consulting engineer with a particular interest in producing ranges to burn turf, had close links with Frank Aiken and the Germanophile, P. J. Little. Aiken was Minister for Defence and Little was Minister for Posts and Telegraphs. Brandy came under suspicion from the Irish civil service as being interested in more than commercial matters and with using turf promotions as a smoke screen for espionage. Speculation arose as to why Goertz should happen on that name in particular as an alias.

Goertz's mission epitomised German unconventional operations in Ireland. The main aim was sabotage and espionage with an underlying belief that political discontent could be harnessed to Germany's military advantage. The execution

was to be left to the Irish themselves. In other words Ireland
was to be used as a base against Britain. A pious aspiration
was that no harm would come to the Irish government in the
process. In this they were at odds with their IRA allies, for
whom the Dáil was as spurious as Westminster.

Around the autumn of 1941 Hempel had become pre-
occupied with Goertz. As far as possible he monitored his
every move and his reports were veritable signposts to the
agent's inevitable capture. He made clear that Goertz's
presence was an acute diplomatic embarrassment and a
matter for immediate inter-governmental concern. A worried
Irish government was demanding explanations.

Clissmann advised Lahausen on how to reply to Woermann's
query requesting information on the Abwehr's attitude to the
position to be adopted by Hempel on the arrest of Goertz.
Hempel was to say that naturally he had heard stories about
Goertz but that he had no official information about him.
He could state categorically that Goertz had no mission
against Ireland; otherwise he, as official representative, would
have known about it! He was counselled to seek a discreet
meeting with Goertz to find out how much the agent had disclosed after his arrest. With regard to Goertz's other activities
such as chartering a military aircraft, he was to say that he
could only presume that the agent was acting on his own
initiative. Clissmann's advice unwittingly served to bolster
the basic false assumption made by the Political Department
in Berlin: that Goertz's kind of adventure was all right so
long as the agents were not acting against Ireland. This ignored
the fact that the corner stone of de Valera's policy was his
reiterated determination that Ireland would not be used as a
base for operations against Britain. An analytical sifting of
Hempel's reports would have made that abundantly clear.

The point the German Minister chose to stress in seeking
to calm the Irish government and avoid compromising himself was that Goertz had no authority whatsoever to contact
the Irish army. The oddness of this assertion did not occur to
him: if Hempel, as he professed, knew next to nothing about
the activities of Goertz or the agent's mission how could he
speak with that degree of certitude on such a delicate matter
as interference tantamount to suborning the forces of the state.

On that point Walshe kept Hempel on the defensive. When the German Minister expressed his perturbation at de Valera's friendly neutral reference to the USA in a speech on that country's entry into the war on 7 December 1941 Walshe did not reply directly but rounded on the Envoy by saying that incidents like the Goertz affair should not occur again. Eventually, however, it was the Minister for Justice, Gerry Boland, who annoyed Hempel most by making political capital out of Goertz. Boland's pejorative personalised utterances stung Goertz who felt that they had impinged on his honour as an officer. Hempel reported that Goertz had given all his codes and diaries to an Irish army officer and that neither he nor the IRA ever had any intention of interfering with the integrity and neutrality of Eire. He dismissed Gerry Boland's accusations against Goertz and the IRA as unfair and ill-informed and referred to the Minister for Justice as 'insignificant'.

The Irish government remained very concerned because Goertz provided a pretext for unfavourable propaganda against their capability to maintain neutrality. His presence was also prejudicial in the conscription crisis. After consideration, it was resolved, in spite of Hempel's objections, that publicity was the best means of countering this propaganda. The reason for this, Hempel reported, lay in de Valera's continued stress on the threat that existed from both the Germans and the Allies. He had reported the Taoiseach as complaining that the Irish people did not seem to be fully alive to the dangers threatening them *from both sides*.

He hinted that he had been given to believe that Goertz was now the main lever used by the Allies to persuade de Valera to enter the war on their side. This pressure, he reported, was the main cause of the high tension that existed in Ireland in mid-December 1941. He attributed the eventual easing of the tension in part to the assurances that he had given to the Irish side in which he had disowned Goertz. As a sign of the easing of tension, he mentioned that the Irish army generally were allowed Christmas leave that year. He also reported that he found de Valera in good humour when he visited him on New Year's Eve 1941.

The reasons for de Valera's good humour on that occasion are not very obvious. Hempel reported that a widespread covert smear campaign was being conducted by the Allies in an effort to undermine him. His consideration for Britain was not enough for some of them. On the other hand, the German Minister surmised that the British may have reluctantly become reconciled to what they saw as the intransigence of de Valera, balancing this against the advantages of the consideration shown and the possible repercussions from the Irish-Americans if they behaved otherwise and seized the ports. Joe Walshe's opinion was that the US had its hands full in the Pacific and would not risk upsetting Irish-American opinion by joining with the British in an attack on Ireland. Hempel reported a trickle of arms being delivered from Britain, particularly some badly needed anti-aircraft guns. There was, he went on, a drying up of deliveries of goods from the US to Ireland: but he did not see this as seriously endangering Irish neutrality. *On the other hand*, he did not rule out surprise moves.

For whatever reasons, Hempel felt coming into 1942 that there was an easing of tension. The ruffled Allies may have been less worried because Goertz was now locked up and therefore no longer available to illegal organisations as a direct channel of communication to the German high command. They may too have been satisfied with the co-operation forthcoming from official Irish intelligence under Colonel Dan Bryan.[7] As Germany's military fortunes waned in 1941, even the residual necessity for the Irish government to contemplate using Goertz as a liaison officer with Berlin had passed.

Bearing in mind the ongoing Battle of the Atlantic and preparations for an Allied counter-attack, the capture of Goertz significantly diminished the Axis powers' sabotage and espionage capability in Allied eyes. From de Valera's point of view (if he were fully informed) the locking up of Goertz should have meant that a source of temptation and compromise for cabinet ministers, army officers, romanticists of all descriptions, as well as subversives, was out of the way. His arrest, of course, did not seal off all espionage routes. There remained the legation's manipulation of the internees for information gathering purposes.

Hempel turned one blind eye to these activities though he collaborated nightly with Thomsen in processing the information collected for transmission. He confined direct contact with the internees to advising them not to attempt to escape. Thomsen was their man though he got on better with the NCOs than with the officers, who regarded him as an upstart with anti-officer tendencies. Herr Voigt, an ex-internee, recalled that the NCOs would tell Thomsen things that they would not tell the German Minister. Hempel's image among them was that he was one of the old school of ineffectual diplomats and the only impact he seems to have made on them was through erotic speculation on the comparative youthfulness of Frau Hempel, whom the internees thought was the Envoy's second wife; she wasn't.

An incident known as the food farce illustrated differences in mentality and approach between Hempel and Thomsen. The internees asked the latter how much money was available for their food and who paid for it. He told them that the Irish government had not yet paid for the Ardnacrusha Power Station, so they could fire away in ordering provisions. Day passes were available to the internees, and on this occasion they took full advantage of this liberal regime. The internees went on a shopping spree in Newbridge and ran up a bill of £3,000 for all sorts of delicacies which was presented to the Irish authorities. Hempel was furious at this behaviour and according to Voigt, he 'blew a gasket'. De Valera was not amused.

That however did not put a brake on Thomsen's intelligence activities. The internees provided too valuable a source of information to be neglected. They were on a loose rein. They got passes to go to Dublin; they could occasionally visit the legation; they had a free run of the pubs and they forgathered in Mrs Bridget Byrne's café in Liffey Street.

Love also inevitably found a way for these sex-starved internees, thereby increasing their circle of contacts. It is not proposed to list these liaisons here or to deduce their value as sources of information: they are mentioned merely to illustrate another worry for Hempel. The importance of the internees lay not in their romantic entanglements but in the fact that they, particularly the NCOs, were in contact with

Irish workers who were toing and froing across the Irish Sea and who were able to provide tit-bits of information which were passed to Thomsen and fed into the intelligence process. The information supplied covered items ranging from factory locations and troop concentration to accounts of the effects of Luftwaffe raids.

A large number of Irish volunteers were serving in the British forces. There were 165,000 next-of-kin Irish addresses on record. In addition, there was a very large Irish workforce (around 100,000) working in Britain in industry and agriculture. Thomsen's men made contacts easily. It was easy enough to start a seemingly innocent conversation; especially over a few drinks.

Thomsen's wife broadened the arc of contact. According to the internee Fleischmann she drank like a fish, swore like a trooper and cursed the officer class as big Junkers. That probably added to her popularity as a drinking companion. She was an architect with the then *avant garde* firm of Michael Scott and Partners and moved around freely in Irish social circles.

Combat intelligence had been defined as being in effect that knowledge of the enemy, weather and geographical features required by a commander in the planning and conduct of tactical operations. Tactical operations at this stage involved air and sea attacks and a possible land invasion of the British Isles. Hempel's contribution therefore is more relevant to a commander's area of interest than to his own area of immediate influence; a more obvious contribution lay in the bearing the Envoy's reporting had on reconnaissance: securing information about the enemy and the detection, identification and location of a target in sufficient detail to permit target analysis.

Hempel's reports incriminate him for breaching neutrality and confirm that the *Auslandsorganisation* were not in Ireland for the good of their health. The puzzle of their exodus at the outbreak of war remains. Their pre-war melting into Irish society was masterly. The trouble was that they did not have a clear-cut aim to maintain. Nazi muddle confused their mission. On 15 August 1941 Hempel reported that he had destroyed confidential documents (with the exception of

essential codes and ciphers) dating from the period immediately preceding the outbreak of war. Just before that, he
reminded, selected files had also been burned though, in his
opinion, they contained hardly any compromising material.
He also referred to the *Auslandsorganization* files which had
been deposited with him for safe keeping when the officers
of that organisation had returned to Germany. The Envoy indicated that he had only destroyed some of these files, where
he deemed that to be advisable, and he requested instructions
as to how he should dispose of the balance, including a register
which would be useful, he thought, in the event of a recon-
struction of the files being required. Perhaps if the *Auslandsorganization* had been reactivated to its pre-war capacity it
would have been less inhibited than Hempel seemed to have
been in his reported handling of an alleged offer from a
London-based American technician, B. G. Carter, who had let
the legation know that he was prepared to betray confidential
information — but for a sum not less than £25,000. Hempel
feared provocation and pointed out to Berlin that the legation
was not to be involved if the matter was pursued. Hempel
remained suspicious and it was hard to blame him. Spurious
reports came in all the time. For example, an approach, signed
by 'N', purporting to have inside information from British
army sources, sounded too pat, too good to be true; and other
reports were not borne out by subsequent events.

Some of the information supplied by the legation, as distinct from straight reportage of events, had the appearance
of replying to queries which had been professionally broken
down into essential elements of military information. If
Hempel had any misgivings about the provocative nature of
certain information, he simply said so, and transmitted it
'raw'. It was not his job to analyse and translate information
into intelligence; though a more positive contribution to interpretation en route could have been useful to Berlin's eventual
evaluation. He was on surer ground when he confined himself
to hard facts supplied by proven sources.

In a target acquisition operation he pinpointed in Luton,
the Vauxhall tank factory, the Percival Aircraft Company, an
airfield, a barracks of the Fleet Air Arm School, an Electrolux
factory, a Skefco ball-bearing factory and an anti-aircraft

location in the vicinity of an electricity plant. This was the kind of information returning Irish workers could impart to the internees who, in turn, could pass it on to Thomsen. Prior to this he reported that he had learned from a technically inexperienced informant (without verifying the source) that the British had invented a plane fuel additive, fumes from which when focused on appeared to be a different colour from the German colour which was red. He was unable to say what the British colour was. He also reported that American troops were equipped with a jeep capable of being quickly converted to an anti-aircraft mounting and noted other unorthodox developments in anti-aircraft weapons. In general these reports gave locations of underground factories; American and British troop movements — including a comment that the Missouri Regiment in Northern Ireland was composed mostly of Ku-Klux Klan members; and a report on the movement of signal personnel of the 8th (British) Army to India. A possibility of provocation could be detected again in the reported assertion of a British army engineer of sabotage of the German bombs dropped in Britain by someone inserting chewing gum between the fuse and the charge. That sounded like something calculated to cause dissension on the home front and would fit the script of a psychological operations ploy.[8] A report locating a new power station in Larne and an airfield fifteen miles from Derby contained an unusual doggy story as well as an orientation on the estimated Allied objectives. Thousands of dogs, the Envoy reported, were being trained to spring ashore in Europe to explode the minefields before the troops went in.

Another report signed by Thomsen and Koecher located aircraft factories in Manchester, Stoke-on-Trent and Stockford and nine miles from Birmingham (the latter said to be turning out six 'Stirlings' [*sic*] per week). This report also stated that American strength in Northern Ireland had reached 36,000; that discipline and training was of a very low standard; that there were a great number of damaged coastal steamers in Londonderry.

The Envoy charily reported on 15 September 1941 the endeavours of a Wilhelm Masgeik, a steel worker in

Haulbowline, to return to Germany. Captain MacGuinness of the Irish Naval Service, who gave Masgeik to understand that he possessed material relevant to a German invasion, was prepared to pilot him in a motor boat to the French coast. Hempel did not like the idea: the association with MacGuinness's supposed materials for a German invasion provided yet another compromising link. Apart from the consideration that Masgeik would be leaving a wife, two small children and a mother behind him, he felt that Masgeik's trustworthiness had to be investigated first of all. He had no faith in MacGuinness: he proved to be right.

When Schutz later escaped from Mountjoy Jail on 28 February 1942 he was put in touch with MacGuinness who also promised to take him to France. But MacGuinness was arrested on 30 March 1942 and correspondence found on him identified his efforts to get military reports to Germany *via* Petersen. Irish intelligence held their fire. A month later they picked up Schutz. Although he had received refuge from the passionately patriotic Catlin Brugha he only succeeded in remaining at large for two months. Hempel ascertained from a contact that the complaints about internment which Schutz had made to him while on the run were ill-founded. Schutz turned out to have been a bad bet for the Third Reich. He was a loser.

In his case Berlin dropped its guard about involving the legation directly. They had become obsessed with using his escape to set up an alternative channel of communication in the event of diplomatic relations being broken off. Hempel was instructed to help the escapee with money and identification papers. Although uneasy he complied with instructions. He went so far as to relay frivolous enquiries from the agent about his fiancée, Lilo Henze, in Hamburg.

Then he got word not to give Schutz the £600 originally arranged or to help him out with a new cover address. It was too late: MacGuinness had been arrested and the legation was compromised. It gave Hempel an opportunity to protest. His damning of MacGuinness as unreliable and mercenary condemned the Schutz escapade and his involvement in it. He had constantly warned the agents and the internees alike to be careful of the company they kept. He made his point about MacGuinness by referring to his gun-running exploits between 1918 and 1925 with the 'Irish Jew Briscoe'. The entire mess made him more suspicious than ever.

Bungling by the Irish authorities increased his apprehension. In accordance with an agreement they informed the British government of Schutz's escape: in breach of the same agreement they had refrained from notifying a previous escape by an internee named Konrad Neymeyer on 18 January 1942 because they did not want to let on to the British that there could be any laxity surrounding the army controlled internment camp in the Curragh. Schutz's escape from the civilian controlled Mountjoy jail a month later must have been graded differently. According to Fleischmann, the earlier escapee — whom he kept referring to as 'Niemoller', was helped to stow away on the Lisbon-bound S.S. *Lanarone* by an army officer with IRA sympathies. The ship had not been properly searched leaving port. The British were not having any more of this. At their insistence a Royal Marine service officer was installed in Dublin to oversee inspections of ships at the point of departure.

It was while looking for Schutz on the high seas off Lisbon that the British happened to recover Neymeyer. He had a job proving his proper identity and was lucky not to have been shot. He was interned in England where his efforts to effect an exchange by simulating insanity were unsuccessful. Hempel detached himself from the affair.

He did permit himself to assist the internees formally, as instructed, but kept a discreet distance and, in general, with the exception of the Schutz episode, tried to avoid embarrassing de Valera. He did not write to them or visit them, but he did send books, tobacco, and soap and arranged for Red Cross parcels to be delivered. Badgered by Goertz, he made use of the Red Cross agencies continually to reassure him that his wife and family were safe in Hamburg and that his home had escaped the bombing. He trusted no one and saw British provocation everywhere. He was particularly sensitive to approaches from the Scottish Independence Movement. He also suspected provocation — never substantiated — when in December 1942 the Sudeten German, Oscar Metze, who claimed to be acquainted with Thomsen, approached the legation with what seemed very pertinent information. He identified in detail the units of a brigade in the British army in which he was serving. The suicide later in a Co. Cork garda station of this mysterious Sudeten leaves a question mark over his role and Hempel's assessment of him. He reported that Metze's death caused consternation in Irish army headquarters.

Hempel undoubtedly had grounds for some of his suspicions. On the other hand, he had his own window into the British secret service. Again he trimmed his source: personally reliable, well versed, but of questionable accuracy and judgment was how he classed him/her. Hempel passed on the following British secret service report: in their judgment the Irish army was very good, in spite of a shortage of armament; that factor meant that a large force of, say, 100,000 men would be required for a quick occupation of Ireland. In the event of a British/American attack, the Irish defence, in anticipation of German aid, would concentrate in the South under its most capable General, M. J. Costello. In that event, the report continued, it could be assumed that German-Irish contingency planning would have provided for landing places for the Germans in Southern Ireland.

An Allied attack would change everything, but outside of that threat, the German psychological battle for Irish hearts and minds to collaborate with them failed to make any significant impact. Their broadcasts provided more mirth and material for mimicry than anything else. Their star broadcaster, Galway man and ex-Black-and-Tan, William Joyce, 'Lord Haw-Haw' (executed for treason after the war) had increasingly diminishing returns to show for his efforts. Dr Liam Gogan (Adolf Mahr's understudy in the National Museum), defending Joyce, said that British intelligence attributed phrases to Joyce, and circulated them, which Joyce never actually said. Joyce was supposed to have broadcast that the Germans must bomb the South Circular Road on account of the Jews there, and bomb Amiens Street Station because so many Irishmen went North from there to join the British Army. According to Gogan, bombs subsequently fell according to this pre-conceived British propaganda pattern. The bombs on the Curragh, he held, were not designed to hurt the Irish army but to bring them in on the side of the British. Gogan was one of Hempel's intimate associates, and these figments reflected their deluded conviction that British scheming was diabolically efficient. It was not.

There were, however, valid grounds for acknowledging that de Valera did not exaggerate when he stressed the threat from *both* sides. Some very anti-Irish growls were coming from London. One opinion voiced was that a German *coup de main* in the West or South West of Ireland would not require great strength if the resisting powers of Eire remained in their present state. Yet, although Whitehall accepted that de Valera was sincere when he said that if Britain armed Eire she would create a most powerful weapon against a German invasion and free her own forces, there was no inclination to supply the necessary armaments. It was reluctantly conceded that he had been thoroughly efficient in containing the IRA extremist and pro-German element. Yet a mood prevailed of letting de Valera stew in his own juice. Because he could not get supplies without making concessions to the British which would compromise his stand on neutrality it is said to have taken the intervention of two archbishops to dissuade de Valera from retiring.

Maffey remained bitter about the 1938 Agreement. De Valera, he said, had bluffed the British negotiators and his success has been a tragedy for both countries.[9] On 17 December 1941 he wrote: 'I had a long, friendly but fruitless talk with de Valera this morning.' Since de Valera was intractable, the alternative, Maffey said, would be to get a divided Eire into the war. Yet the British representative continued to point out that the long-range trend of the Irish neutrality policy was plainly working in the Allies' favour. Official Britain did not want to know. As far as they were concerned de Valera was anti-British and that was that. But the IRA *did* want to know. Hempel's 'radical nationalist' acquaintances were continually complaining that de Valera was far too pro-British.

From the beginning Hempel noticed that the British mission in Dublin was behaving less than conventionally, albeit with some finesse. Initially there had only been a naval attaché in the British installation (Greig),[10] but, as Hempel reported, he was quickly supplemented by a military attaché (Price) and an air attaché (Haywood), together with appropriate staffs whose true identity was concealed. The Irish government, he added, did not approve of such a large number of attachés and insisted on a declaration by the British of their proper identities. But, he continued, clumsy censorship of these declarations gave rise to rumours leading to public disquiet as to Allied intentions with regard to the ports. The British representative gave assurances, which were published in the *Daily Mail*, and Hempel's caustic comment was that he had no grounds to doubt these assurances, not least because the British attachés were of second-grade quality and no further augmentation of staff had taken place. He also reported that Greig was replaced by Bradley; Price by Woodhouse (after five weeks) and Haywood by Begg. He missed Major Cairns.

His report of de Valera's speech in Navan on 17 January 1942 had, he thought, put the record straight as to how the Taoiseach felt about the British. De Valera had reviewed economic and defence pressures; told of his frustrated efforts to secure arms; issued a strong appeal to join the army, calling on all to look danger in the eye and die confronting it; asserted that no secret agreements existed; dismissed smear rumours and lashed out at pernicious Allied propaganda. Berlin could be forgiven for concluding from their Minister's factual reporting at that period that the Irish and the Germans had a common enemy in the Allies. But the reality did not coincide with the rhetoric. This made the Envoy uneasy. It was getting more and more difficult for the German Minister to know what to believe.

For all his apprehensiveness Hempel failed adequately to assess a serious violation of the spirit of neutrality by the Irish side. Daily, under British tutelage and under British codes, the Irish Meteorological Office was uninhibitedly exporting to London precious weather reports. If there were a danger of the information falling into German hands — as for instance on occasions when the telex was out of action — they were encoded for transmission in a code supplied by the British Commonwealth Office. This was a vital contribution to the British war effort. Only de Valera could have authorised such a consideration for Britain. It seems extraordinary that Hempel did not complain about it. His agents kept him constantly informed about every bit of tittle-tattle and it is inconceivable that he could have remained ignorant of what was happening.

Such substantial concessions by the Irish government to the Allies did not satisfy the minority of southern Irishmen who, like James Dillon TD, were opposed to neutrality. Hempel regularly reported on Dillon's Dáil clashes with de Valera on the subject. Dillon's florid prose was countered by de Valera's flat Co. Limerick polemic. They were perfect foils for one another. Dillon did not have de Valera's political acumen but he was far from being the West British buffoon that his opponents made him out to be. His affectations and rolling anglicised accent concealed a keen geopolitical realism which identified fundamental British and Irish interests. He lacked the talent for getting on to the popular wavelength to make common cause with the plain people. He roasted Hempel at every opportunity. The Envoy retaliated by calling him a German hater, a Jew, and a bitter enemy of de Valera for good measure.

De Valera automatically extended a protective wing to the legation when it came under fire from Dillon. Hempel also took up the cudgels on his own behalf. On 29 January 1942 he lodged a formal complaint that the Speaker in the Dáil had not intervened to restrain Dillon when he made an intemperate attack on Germany, falsely based he claimed on the so-called confesssions of the IRA Chief of Staff, Stephen Hayes.

Ironically one of Dillon's interventions had the effect of taking the heat off Hempel. The Irish parliamentarian waxed indignant about an attack on the Irish ship, *Kerlogue*, in October 1943, and pressed hard for an enquiry. Hempel was gleefully able to report that the ammunition fragments found after the attack were British but he quietly added that the British had admitted their error and offered to pay compensation.

The British were unrepentant about the attack: whether by accident or design they had riddled with gunfire the *Kerlogue*'s tricolour. The ship had been off course and their *ex gratia* payments to the wounded men were made without prejudice. The British Admiralty probably regretted a couple of months later that the RAF had not finished off the job as they were at it. The *Kerlogue* rescued shipwrecked German sailors after a battle in the Bay of Biscay and sailed straight for Cork with them, ignoring British instructions and frustrating attempts to interrogate and imprison the German survivors, who were interned in the Curragh (see chapters 9 and 10). They attracted no attention as they shuffled through the gloomy camp into captivity.

The thousand-year Reich had shot its bolt; the main threat to Eire's neutrality now arose from American hot-headedness. The United States was the one now throwing its weight about.

Irish-American support for de Valera did not mute Roosevelt's antagonism to Irish neutrality. He was as vindictive as Churchill and grew more waspish from the time in April 1941 when he swept the delft and cutlery off his dinner table in a fury with Frank Aiken's nationalistic points of view! Aiken felt that the Americans despised Irish neutrality; they had given him the run-around. No love was lost between them; he thought the Germans were decent enough fellows by comparison and he found nothing to choose between Roosevelt and Churchill. They were birds of a feather as far as he was concerned.

The Americans reacted to this lack of Irish understanding by putting unconventional diplomatic pressures on de Valera well before they entered the war. On 17 July 1941 Hempel reported a visit to the Taoiseach by U.S. Colonel Donovan.[11] The following November, with an account of the American-Irish Defence Association and the activities of Senator Wheeler, he elaborated on the intervention of Donovan's propaganda staff in Irish affairs. He endeavoured to counter one aspect of the propaganda, highlighting the Nazi war against the Catholic Church, by issuing bulletins of his own.

He was not aware that what was at the back of Colonel Donovan's visit was an allegation made by MI5 that the Irish authorities had refused to co-operate or have any contact with them. Donovan first came in March 1941 but made no contact with Irish intelligence at that time to propose that an

American intelligence officer could be organised to act in a liaison capacity. The liaison officer would be apprised of certain information on condition that he did not pass such information *directly* to MI5. It took until 1942, during a visit by Colonel David Bruce, Chief of OSS Operations in Europe, to agree that there would be liaison with the OSS and Spike Marlin was selected for the job. Irish intelligence thereby found its way to Hubert Will, chief of the counter-espionage branch of the OSS in Europe, who was then able to reassure MI5's Cecil Liddell that the Irish had indeed taken all the necessary precautions to control German espionage in Eire.[12]

Marlin was inclined to be irreverent about David Gray's more extravagant claims concerning security breaches. A rift developed between them and Marlin was replaced by Edward Lawler in the pre-invasion days of 1944. Contact with Irish intelligence improved. This is no reflection on Marlin. Lawler got on well with a young intelligence lieutenant, Douglas Gageby.[13] Gageby's charm and sophistication was a factor in ironing out difficulties. He was married to Sean Lester's daughter and spoke fluent German. His Belfast background was untainted with conventional bigotries. Misunderstandings were resolved: 'frostiness' towards the British thawed, if it did not altogether melt. Goertz would have scoffed at the suggestion that 'frostiness' had ever existed. He was convinced Colonel Bryan was pro-British to the bone. Whatever about that, the G2 chief had no difficulty in working out liaison arrangements with the American Hubert Will.

There were other portents besides Colonel Donovan's visit that America would enter the war if a suitable pretext presented itself. On 9 August 1941 Hempel reported the arrival of a further 400 technicians and workers in Northern Ireland to build a base for 'Lease and Lend' (Hempel's phrase) operations. The previous month he reported Dillon's call for full help, short of sending troops, for the Allied cause because it was a fight for Christianity and Ireland should be on the side of the democracies. He also reported on 1 October 1941 that Irish Senator Frank MacDermot was campaigning in the USA, 'with a small group of Irish-American renegades', for Ireland's entry into the war on the Allied side. His inside information seemed to have been so good that he was able to relay de Valera's exact words to describe Gray: 'an impossible man'. Rather extravagantly, Hempel claimed that Gray, being a relative of Roosevelt's, had full power to acquire bases for US cruisers to counter German U-Boat and Luftwaffe attacks. Quoting Cordell Hull's expressed intention not to seek port facilities from Ireland for the present, the Envoy then thought that America had enough on her plate with the war in the Pacific; that the heated atmosphere was cooled after de Valera's friendly neutral speech in Cork on 15 December 1941, and that there would be no US attack on Ireland. Gray, he held, was a malevolent influence but he was unable to say whether the American representative was pressurising de Valera on his own initiative, or whether he was acting on Washington's instructions to test the Taoiseach. Sumner Welles would give no official guarantee that US troops would not be used against Ireland. His account on 16 December 1941 of sharp words used to de Valera by Gray and Maffey on a joint call a week previously confirmed Allied pressures for the use of the ports. Hempel held that de Valera's friendly neutral speech was made as a concession to these pressures.

Eight days earlier, on 8 December, one of the most melodramatic incidents of the Emergency had occurred. At 1.30 a.m. in the morning Walshe rang de Valera's house to say that Maffey was on his way to see the Taoiseach with a message from Churchill which he had been ordered to deliver immediately. De Valera was naturally alarmed at what the message might contain, since it was obviously too important to wait until morning. Maffey arrived within the hour. He handed de Valera the telegram from Churchill which read:

> Following from Mr Churchill to Mr de Valera. Personal. Private and Secret. Begins. Now is your chance. Now or never. 'A nation once again'. Am ready to meet you at any time. Ends.

This extraordinary communication seemed to be — and was understood by the Taoiseach to be — a coded offer of a united Ireland in return for the abandonment of neutrality. It was apparently one of a large number of euphoric telegrams which Churchill had fired off to all corners of the globe in the wake of America's entry to the war. (Pearl

Harbor had been attacked the day before.) De Valera's habit-
ual reserve stood him in good stead at that moment: neither
then nor later did he seriously entertain Churchill's offer. It
was an offer which de Valera had to refuse: the shadow of
John Redmond, the Irish Parliamentary Party leader, who
traded an unfulfilled promise of home rule for similar commitments in the First World War, inhibited the ready acceptance of such British suggestions by Irish politicians. In truth,
he had his mind made up on his preference for neutrality.

The Taoiseach was very much on the defensive on this
point from December 1941 onwards. Not alone were there
the constant pressures from the Allies and tirades, goads and
jibes from Dillon, but he was also getting trouble from his
own ministers. Hempel reported that dissenting voices were
becoming louder in the cabinet (he did not name them) when
de Valera was alleged to have rebuffed Allied suggestions that
he enter the war on their side in return for a united Ireland.

Nevertheless, maintaining a fine equipoise, de Valera, with
varying intensities, had seen to it that protests continued to
be made concerning the recurring German violations of neutrality. The Third Reich was again reminded that further
failure to accept responsibility for the bombings and to offer
speedy reparation aggravated the bad effects of such incidents
on the relations between the two countries. The Irish government once more stressed the necessity for giving the German
airmen the strictest instructions to avoid flying over Irish
territory and territorial waters. The tone of the protests
became increasingly sharp and there were no longer any
soothing accompanying remarks from Warnock or Walshe.
Hempel recommended that concessions be made to the Irish
representations: the bombs must be German, the Envoy
stated, and all the Irish government really wanted was a
friendly answer. But the Irish government wanted something
more than that. They wanted immunity from German attacks
and they wanted reparation. These instructions were a constant source of worry and provided inflammable material to
fuel the Allies' hostility to neutrality. The presence of the
legation was a constant source of friction with the British. It
infuriated the less suave Americans and eventually bothered
a couple of de Valera's own cabinet colleagues.

The Japanese presence, probably for reasons of distance from the Pacific war, did not arouse the same rancour. Beppu San, the Japanese representative, did not seem to present much of a threat. After Pearl Harbor even IRA sympathisers would have nothing to do with him. He was ostracised by the Irish social set and could not even get a golf partner for the duration. The full extent of the secret war against Japanese intelligence is still obscured but the Japanese consulate in Dublin was at most a minor cog in the network. The Allies had the ability to crack the secret codes of both Germany and Japan. Tapped and deciphered Japanese signals revealed their intentions before their attack on Pearl Harbor.[14] Japanese war plans were no secret to American intelligence.

With such unbelievable good luck that one is tempted to call it providential the British — with vital help from Polish cryptoanalysts — broke the German *Enigma* code. With all this intelligence at their disposal the blind spot at the Irish back door became increasingly frustrating for the Allies. They had the outward signs of the Reich's intentions for muddled unconventional operations in Ireland. Schutz had connections with RAINBOW (a crucial link in the double-cross system) in London. He could give valuable information about how RAINBOW's reports were going down in Hamburg. Schutz had been given the tasks of making daily weather reports and observing coastal movements by the Abwehr. But the Irish would not play ball and allow the British to question him directly.

The Allies also knew Goertz was in contact with Germany and that if there was one Goertz there could be two or more like him. As the war progressed, they were able to read many of the secret communications of the enemy. Goertz's uncertain methods of communications were too elementary to come into British intelligence's sophisticated scanning span: in this emotional uncertainty lay the dangers that they could avoid detection. The British might muddle through but the Americans were unhappy about situations which they could not 'tie up'.

One of the first things the Americans did on entry into the war was to land troops on Irish soil, in Northern Ireland. That foothold satisfied their needs. Roosevelt no longer doubted that what was at stake was the 'conquest of the entire world and the enslavement of all mankind'. Now that the United States was in the war the British were no longer much worried about American reaction to a possible seizure of the ports. Gray advised Roosevelt that a *fait accompli* offered the best prospect of success for an Allied seizure of the Irish bases. The Third Reich kept a wary, but increasingly impotent, watch as unconventional operations by both sides increased.

The landing of American troops in Northern Ireland caught Hempel, the reporter, unaware. He put the first reports of it down to journalistic sensationalism. He quickly grasped that the reality of the landing presented de Valera with an added complication. The Taoiseach had been restive from the spring of 1941 when the Americans started to work on bases in Derry and Belfast. He now stiffly stood on his constitutional rights to claim jurisdiction over the whole of Ireland. The Americans did not inform him that they were coming, he complained. They snapped back that if that was the way he felt about the six counties, he should have protested when the Third Reich bombed Belfast. The inexorable demands of war extinguished any sympathy for Irish neutrality even among Irish-Americans.

It was obvious to de Valera that American entry into the war had tipped the scales in favour of an Allied victory. He made his 'friendly neutral' speech which transmuted considerate neutrality for Britain into benevolent neutrality for the Allies. He explained that the statement he made at the time of the landings in the North should not be taken as a protest. That's all it was: a statement. He knew better than to insist on interning crash-landed US airmen. A form of words covering 'non-operational' flights provided the necessary semantic fiction. They were given red carpet treatment and their return to Northern Ireland facilitated in every face-saving way possible. It was different, but only in degree, with the British. Superficially they were the old enemy: in the public perception the United States was an old friend.

That did not stop the Americans from waging an unscrupulous campaign in the press against Irish neutrality and from using the Goertz affair for all it was worth as proof of an impending Third Reich invasion which if successful, would provide the key to defeating Britain. Roosevelt's reassurance to de Valera that he had not 'the slightest thought or intention' of invading Irish territory merely heightened fears especially when, with the British, the American President stymied every suggestion to supply additional arms to the Irish army. In a memorandum to Welles, Roosevelt indicated his low opinion of the military capability of the Irish Free State. Gray thought that a few well placed bombs on the Curragh and Dublin together with explanatory leaflets would neutralise opposition to his cherished *fait accompli* to seize the ports. He would, in the interval before a government was formed, instal a puppet general to take control; he contemplated that either Major-General M. J. Costello, a Fort Leavenworth graduate, or an American general would be in charge. There were good reasons for not considering Major-General Hugo MacNeill for this job although he too had received his military training in America. Fortunately for Eire, Gray was not aware of the full extent of these reasons.

Gray made the threat from the Third Reich seem remote by comparison: Allied troops were already poised on Irish soil and Gray had an insensitive amateur's appetite for action. Such action would automatically attract intervention by the opposing forces. So Irish neutrality, determined to take on all comers, had also to continue to take the Third Reich into account. As Frank Aiken put it, neutrality was not a condition of peace with both belligerents but rather a condition of limited warfare with both! It was a close run thing.

A single false move, if exposed, could have brought the walls tumbling down, as they would assuredly have done if Hempel's part in the Dieppe disaster had been known. In August 1942 he reported the Canadians were massed on the south coast of England for a probable invasion of France. The Third Reich's representative in neutral Ireland was also able to relay that retired seamen with a knowledge of the French coast were being called up in England. The Dieppe raid was carried out on the night of 19 August 1942. It was an operation criminally lax in security measures. Initially in April 1942 Montgomery was responsible for the army side of a plan to raid Dieppe using a Canadian Division for the purpose. On 4 July the troops were embarked and sealed in their ships but the weather turned out to be unsuitable and they were unsealed and disembarked. The 5,000 troops involved had all been fully briefed so it was obviously no longer possible to maintain secrecy. Montgomery reckoned that with security breached, the essential element of surprise for such a raid was lost and so the operation should have been cancelled. His advice was disregarded. The price was heavy in killed and prisoners. Canadian casualties of all categories aggregated 3,369: nearly 2,000 of the total casualties were prisoners of war. The Germans had been waiting for them: it is a fair assumption that Hempel's report was a factor in forming the German intelligence estimate of the situation. But hard evidence eluded Gray, and his arrogant methods did not help his case. In fact he had a strong case both about the transmitter and Hempel's role.

The sprawling nature of unconventional operations in neutral Eire, apart from the obviously clownish agents, defies precise description. German efforts in the field may occasionally have bordered on the farcical but Hempel was none the less able to garner the Dieppe piece of information from various sources, and German intelligence put it together with disastrous consequences for the Allies. Dieppe was more a large-scale critical reconaissance-in-force than a mere commando raid. It demonstrated that minor unconventional operations in remote areas had the capability to affect major conventional battles. It is also well to remember that corroborating information almost certainly flowed from mainland Britain, in spite of the plugging of holes by the double-cross system. The real trouble lay in the ill-conceived nature of the operation. There was no unity of command, no single task force commander. Apart from the security leaks, it was doomed operationally by the elimination of preliminary bombing and paratroops such as were in Montgomery's original plan. But Hempel's leak had been an important element in the Allied failure. That knowledge may have spurred him later on to try a repeat performance with a hotter tip about Arnhem exactly two years later in September 1944. For all the sound and fury about him, Goertz had never supplied information remotely comparable in quality to the diplomat's cloaked contribution.

That did not diminish the menace which the agent's presence had provoked. The British, actively engaged in infiltrating into Europe, were keenly aware, from their own Special Operations Executive, how much even one daring agent could accomplish behind their backs.

EIGHT

High Stakes

Goertz's links with the IRA constituted a grave danger to the security of the Irish state. Other entanglements of his were no less dangerous: his cloak-and-dagger contacts with General Hugo MacNeill were potentially among the most dangerous elements of the entire Emergency period. The magnitude of that danger has yet to be comprehensively evaluated; but for a mixture of chance and de Valera's skilful leadership, the policy of neutrality must have foundered on this point.

Gray claimed that the Americans could be cruel if their interests were affected and that Ireland could expect no sympathy if the British felt compelled to take the ports. America's entry into the war was only a matter of time and the U-Boats were proving to be a greater menace than had been anticipated. In the second half of 1941, up to one and a half million tons of shipping were lost due to German submarine action. In the second half of 1942 this had risen to around three and a half million tons. These losses occurred mainly in a gap in the mid-Atlantic which was accessible to U-Boat packs but out of range of Allied bombers. By 1943 Dönitz was mass-producing seventeen U-Boats per month. What Churchill termed the massacre of the U-Boats was yet to come. The stakes were high. Bases in France had increased the U-Boats' range. The possibility of havens in Eire increasing their capability further would have been intolerable to the Allies. The chance of such a possibility arising could have been construed from Major-General Hugo MacNeill's dealings with Goertz. The actual landing of German arms would certainly have triggered off Allied intervention.

Goertz, selected by Abwehr II, was perceptibly an authorised instrument of the German high command: that he was an imperfect Abwehr II instrument does not lessen the lethal implications of that authorisation. MacNeill was a senior serving Irish general: that implied that he too could speak with authority. Goertz was quixotic and impractical. MacNeill had a taste for flamboyant publicity and projected, together with his extrovert divisional chief of staff, the ex-Royal Flying Corps Colonel Tony Lawlor, a colourful, even swash-buckling, image that his more down-to-earth colleagues felt was more appropriate to showbusiness than to soldiering. During the period it was not unusual for generals to project colourfully: MacArthur, Rommel, Patton, and Montgomery are examples; the difference was that they had success in battle.

Politically MacNeill was a product of his generation and upbringing. His uncle was Eoin MacNeill, founder of the Gaelic League; Professor of Early Irish History at University College, Dublin; nominal head of the Irish Volunteers; former Minister for Education; and, fatally for his political career, Free State representative on the 1925 Boundary Commission. In de Valera's later opinion the Professor had been sadly miscast in his military role. His nephew Hugo, on the other hand, considered himself to be a dashing military man, bristling with martial creativity. He had been in the Fianna Éireann, the boy scout movement of the IRA. The jibe was that psychologically he never left it; when a general he was dubbed an overgrown Fianna boy.

During the economic war with Britain he caught Frank Aiken's ear with the proposition that it was possible with small mobile columns to worst the British militarily as well as economically! On his Command and Staff course in 1935 Dan Bryan wrote a thesis demolishing that contention. Conceptually, these two were on a collision course that climaxed during the Emergency when MacNeill tried to bypass and belittle Bryan in intelligence work. Colonel Bryan stressed, however, that while he distrusted MacNeill he never had any concrete evidence linking him to Goertz.

The natural aspiration of ending partition was now enshrined in the Irish constitution. Lip service was paid to that aspiration on each and every political occasion and whoever succeeded in accomplishing the misty mission would join the pantheon of nationalist folk heroes, and MacNeill was steeped in the green flag traditions of Irish history.

However, the hard fact was that the Irish army would have to be adequately armed and equipped if it were to be regarded as a credible deterrent by any would-be invader. This lack of arms and equipment was a constant worry to the general staff of which MacNeill was a member for a period.[1] It was difficult if not impossible in the circumstances to procure weapons. Britain was obstructive; the US was unco-operative. Previous arms purchasing missions to America by General Costello initially and later by Frank Aiken had failed. Frank Aiken's flights of fancy about an ammunition factory in Clare[2] notwithstanding, Ireland was too small and too poor to afford an arms industry of its own. Still the realisation that the Irish would resist with whatever weapons they had was a bottom line deterrent: there was a long tradition of taking the pikes down from the thatch. The government were continually compelled to seek ways and means of procuring arms: credible deterrence or meaningful resistance depended on their ability to do so.

Hempel's telegram of 10 November 1940 stated that, due to lack of heavy weapons and proper defences on the Irish side, occupation of the ports by the British would be relatively easy: holding them, he said, would be another matter and guerilla warfare could tie down strong British forces. On 6 December 1940 he reported that one of the highest ranking officers in the Irish army had, on his own initiative, made contact with Thomsen, the legation secretary, and apprised him of the Irish army's expectation of a British attack. Arising from their meetings Hempel reported three possible axes for this attack:

1. Occupation of Lough Swilly, which was by far the most important objective. The comment (it is not clear whether it is Hempel's or the army officer's) was that, as a glance at the map indicated, defence against such a land attack was pointless.
2. Occupation of Lough Swilly and a further assault by land on the airfields at Rhinanna and Foynes combined

with a seaborne landing at the mouth of the Shannon.
3. Cork, Wexford, Dublin and eventually Berehaven were also possible objectives.

The army officer further explained that in the event of a British attack the Irish cabinet would probably seek German assistance but first, it was necessary to find out the answers to certain questions as soon as possible. Hempel incorporated the questions in this report:

1. Was Germany prepared in principle to render assistance? To reply if answer affirmative.
2. Did Germany require Irish airfields? In that case the Irish army would hold them for as long as possible though heavy casualties would be unavoidable. Airfields at that point — apart from a few small fields in use by the Irish themselves — had been rendered unusable by sowing obstacles and spiking them with angled railway tracks, and those would have to be cleared if the airfields were required. However if Germany did not need the airfields, they would be only lightly defended. It was not possible to put them out of action for any length of time due to shortage of explosives: Rhinanna was eight times as big as Tempelhof; Fermoy was very poor, and Collinstown and Baldonnel could hardly be held against the British.
3. Could Germany, in the event of an Irish request for help following a British attack, parachute in anti-tank guns, which were in very short supply in the Irish army? Vickers heavy machine guns, anti-tank rifles and French Brandt Mortars — generally captured British weapons. This material should be prepared for dispatch, was the Army officer's advice, according to the German Minister.

In a second phase, weapon deliveries by sea was the requirement indicated by the army man who said that Irish ships were not available for this purpose. And in the third phase the officer envisaged active German support from a force of 100,000 to 150,000 men. Hempel remarked that these conversations took place in the presence of the leader of the disbanded Blueshirts, General O'Duffy,[3] who was a friend of the army officer. As he thought O'Duffy to be reckless and impractical, Hempel felt that he should not be made privy to any replies to the army officer's queries; that was also the wish of the 'high ranking officer', he said.

Hempel sent off that part of the telegram at 13.35 hours. Twenty minutes later, when he was writing the second part, his doubts about the business were apparently increasing. Direct contact with the legation in such an obvious manner, without the knowledge of the Irish government, could, the Envoy felt, bring about a difficult situation particularly when what he repeatedly referred to as the Irish propensity for indiscretion was taken into account. He recommended that, in future, contact should be effected only through Thomsen. In the meantime he would continue to try to influence de Valera as he had been doing, he added, distancing himself from Thomsen's contact with the army officer and indicating his own initiatives in sounding out the ground with Walshe and de Valera. Hempel's reckoning was that de Valera would treat any undertaking of this nature with caution and reticence and in a purely exploratory manner. The Envoy's concluding reference was to political rather than military aspects of the situation.

Hempel's own efforts at this time, coming up to Christmas 1940, were directed to augmenting the legation staff with an officer experienced in military reconaissance. The Irish army officer had himself expressed a wish for this, as it would make his liaison task easier and more meaningful. The determined efforts to do this had been adroitly rebuffed and circumvented by de Valera (see p. 132) The then Irish army chief of staff (General Dan McKenna) was at lunch at Hempel's on 17 December 1940 and was pressurised by the German Minister, with uncharacteristic aggressiveness, in connection with this bid to augment the legation staff. The Envoy's report on 26 January 1941, however, that a British pilot overflying Lough Swilly had been shot down by Irish anti-aircraft fire, indicated that the British too were still regarded as potential aggressors: in that event, German assistance would still be sought and welcomed. So the rebuff about augmenting the legation staff did not quench the question of rendering aid by supplying arms.

By February 1941 the plot involving the Irish army connection had thickened to the point of exasperating Hempel. The Envoy refers to 'L' – a single letter which he had arbitrarily chosen to designate Thomsen's army contact. He reported that 'L' now wanted to make contact with the IRA because they were in touch with the German high command and they could tell him about the German stance in the event of a British attack. 'L' was getting frustrated waiting for a reply from Thomsen. Hempel conceded 'L's military professionalism but found him to be 'typically Irish, and lacking in balance'. Again he counselled caution in dealing with him, even though Thomsen had a good impression of him. If 'L' invoked the IRA, the position of General O'Duffy, friendly with 'L' but not so friendly with the IRA, would further complicate an already dangerous situation. Indiscretion and the presence of British agents were always possibilities with the IRA, the report went on. Hempel now recommended, however, that 'L' should be given an answer.

In a continuation of that telegram from the German Minister, Goertz, referred to in the Envoy's telegrams as 'K',[4] enters the scene. In spite of optimism to the contrary in Irish government circles, Hempel felt that a British attack had still to be reckoned with. This obviously was 'L's interpretation too and the reason why, according to Hempel, the officer had made direct contact with Goertz in order to get in touch with the German high command. Hempel was uneasy and recommended that he should nominate an intermediary who would also be known to Goertz. The German Minister pointed out the risks he ran if he communicated with him: and he sought to separate the contact between the high command agent and 'L' while avoiding revealing the links between Thomsen and 'L'. If Goertz were not suitable, Hempel suggested that he himself communicate with him, through an intermediary. It might be better, the Minister Plenipotentiary remarked rather abruptly, if Goertz went home. Without de Valera's acquiescence the German Minister saw little prospect of any success: however, he was doubtful also of the Irish government's chances of success in seeking to buy weapons in the US. Hempel's eternal reservations again served to sidetrack firm conclusions: the fact remained that he reported that the Irish army still needed weapons to counter a possible British attack.

Open relations between the legation and the Irish army continued – on the surface at any rate – to be cordial and they may be taken as an index to official attitudes and diplomatic relations at this point. A company from the 31st Infantry Battalion with the No. 2 Army Band rendered military honours at the burial in Bantry of five German victims of an aircrash. Thomsen represented Hempel and gave the funeral oration in German. He laid a wreath in swastika shape on the grave. Many high ranking Irish army officers were present. As Thomsen was short of petrol, Hempel reported that the Irish chief of staff had put his own car and a high ranking officer at the legation secretary's disposal to make the journey from Dublin to Bantry. It may not be too cynical to observe that such solicitude was not so demonstrably evident five months after the Führer had committed the Wehrmacht to combat in Russia and the German threat of invasion had receded as a consequence. But at this earlier stage – February 1941 – there seemed to be nothing definite that should deter Hempel from allowing Thomsen to remain in clandestine contact with 'L' and the friendly Irish army, potential allies of the Germans in the event of a British attack on Ireland.

The German Minister, however, remained apprehensive. He reported that 'L' had hoped to obtain the top army job but the Irish government had selected a more solid personality who enjoyed their full trust. In this report 'L' is clearly identifiable as Major-General Hugo MacNeill, unlike a previous report which seemed to refer to Reserve Officer Colonel Nial MacNeill, a first cousin of Hugo's. Hempel mentioned again that 'L' was acting without the knowledge of the Irish government. 'L', he said, acknowledged the risks he was taking but maintained that he was acting in the best interests of his country. Hempel was not so sure that he was not just an anti-de Valera adventurer and the links with O'Duffy and the IRA, both of whom wanted a tougher stand against the British, continued to cause the Envoy disquiet. Though he thought it improbable that 'L' was working for England, still he felt it was worth mentioning such a fleeting disturbing thought. Irish impatience and inclination to indiscretion and exaggeration still continued to worry Hempel and he claimed that the British had very good contacts in the Irish army. He did not reckon that contact with 'L' gave the German side any guarantee of protection and he now had reservations about involving the legation in providing answers for his questions: it was dangerous, he repeated. The Minister recommended that they await the outcome of his own conversations with de Valera before proceeding further.

He recommended, after further agonising, that it would be better to leave the matter of sounding out to himself and in the same breath, almost as a sigh of relief, he reported (erroneously as it turned out) that Goertz had left Ireland.

It is difficult to reconcile the timings in the three parts of this telegram, No. 154 of 19 February 1941. The first part is timed 17.20 hours, while the second part is timed 11.25 hours. The third part, however, is timed for that evening 21.30 hours and by that time Hempel seemed to have become fully disenchanted with the whole idea of delivering weapons. He said that the pro-British element in the population was strong and he saw little prospect of keeping such a delivery of weapons secret. The Americans and British, the Minister continued, would exploit the situation as evidence of a German plot. Then using a different tone to the distrustful one he used when speaking of 'L', the Envoy said that he knew that the Irish army chief of staff (General McKenna) — whom he looked upon as a dependable national Irishman — took a similar viewpoint. He did not see any opportunity of further discussions with the Irish government wherein the hard facts of German capability to help would be concealed. It is intriguing to speculate how Hempel and General McKenna got around to the topic of supplying arms without either of them, as far as can be evidenced, breathing a word about General MacNeill's initiatives with Goertz.

However, Hempel undertook to explore the possibility of manipulating a conversation with de Valera to bring up yet again the subject of German aid, with the intention of establishing the contingency liaison required for the delivery of weapons. He linked this approach with the unofficial queries put forward by 'L' and recommended that further assurances be given of the German intent to respect Irish neutrality and Irish national aspirations after the war.

Acting on his own initiative, 'L' was probably relaying the tentative contingency plans of the Irish government to oppose the first violator of neutrality. But a tune played inexpertly at the wrong speed sounds distorted: this was probably the case in 'L's interpretations of the government's ultra-cautious contingency planning. It was a complex matter of extreme delicacy, certainly one for which either MacNeill's bravura or O'Duffy's bluster were appropriate qualities. They did not possess the necessary *savoir faire*. If the British had attacked — and de Valera, it seems, was never able to rule out that possibility — 'L's theatrical approaches to Hempel and Goertz would have provided a useful basis for liaison.

It also seems that 'L' had tentatively sought permission to proceed with his covert probing. There were no indications that anything so positive was forthcoming, but it seems that no one shouted 'stop' either. MacNeill was commander of the 2nd (Spearhead) Division deployed in the northern half of the state. Unlike his counterpart in the southern counties, Major-General Mickey-Joe Costello, 'L' did not stick to his military brief. Costello's intelligence officer, Commandant Florrie O'Donoghue, rounded up Goertz's collaborators of Kerry who were supposed to help the German agent to escape by sea. According to Costello they would have captured Goertz too except that he was under the protection of a uniformed member of the Garda Siochana. The garda in question was subsequently disciplined and sentenced to five years imprisonment. The story was that the detective in the matter was a spy planted by Stephen Hayes of the IRA. (The detective's brother-in-law had the unlikely name of Hess.) It was not so much apparently that Goertz was not arrested. He was deliberately allowed to escape through the backdoor of the house he was in. Whatever about the truth of the suggestions, it should be observed here that there were many unsung heroes in both the army and the gardai to whom the Irish state owed a great deal for preserving security in these years: men such as Captain Nick Leonard of the army and Sergeant (later Superintendent) Micky Gill of the gardai.

The Broy Harriers Special Branch had been infiltrated by

five or six IRA men. The gardai had already botched, some alleged deliberately, four attempts to capture Goertz. The cryptic GHQ comment was that they had made a balls of it. Crofton, the IRA spy who had infiltrated the Broy Harriers and who was in league with Goertz, was arrested on the spot.

Hempel, as far as his telegrams went, did not seem to have been fully *au fait* with all these machinations. He did not know the full extent of MacNeill's acquaintance with Goertz. But at a higher level, the Envoy scotched the notion that de Valera would personally liaise with Goertz. He realised that it was inconceivable that de Valera himself would be so involved. Stooping to that sort of hugger-mugger would be out of character for one so conscious of protocol.

In view of his sympathies with the Central European powers, however, it would not be inconceivable if such an adventuresome impulse were to come from Frank Aiken. He did, apparently, contact Goertz: though he was later said to have alleged that Goertz had broken into his house.[5]

Hempel went on to state that Goertz, and particularly the IRA, needed money badly. The Envoy suggested a U-Boat deliver £200 to an unnamed island off the west coast of Ireland. This was a daring suggestion for the German Minister to make and one which could indeed have compromised him. However, he warned against further developments of the contacts between 'L' and Goertz, which, he said, could jeopardise a new situation which had arisen since the Envoy's discussion with de Valera. After praising Goertz for his work with the IRA, Hempel then said that in his own opinion the man was too credulous and that the legation did not want to be mixed up at all in the mechanics of transmitting any money. He knew on good authority, he continued, that the IRA were riddled with government and British spies who knew about Goertz. The Envoy at this point indicated his own increasing concern for the Abwehr agent's safety. The fact, he said, that Stephen Hayes, who had been in contact with Goertz, had made a confession and was now under police protection, compounded the danger.[6] Hempel reported that Hayes had been working for the Irish government and that he had warned Petersen not to report the matter. The Abwehr acknowledged the Envoy's request about the handling of the money and sought other means of getting £500 to Goertz in Dublin. This memo identified the 'H' of Hempel's telegram as Stephen Hayes, who had replaced Russell as chief of staff of the IRA during the latter's trip to the US in 1940.

The Hempel telegram conveying the allegations of Hayes on the latter's involvement for provocation purposes with two cabinet ministers (Dr Jim Ryan and Tom Derrig) and an unidentified senator, goes on to be more explicit about Goertz, whom Hempel expected to be apprehended shortly. A copy of the Hayes confession, the German Minister said, had been found in a house which the police had raided. He further stated that he had it on good authority that the British secret service were also involved, so the legation had perforce to distance itself from Goertz: otherwise the British and Americans would be able to prove a link and would demand the expulsion of the legation. The case of Hayes, the Envoy concluded, emphasised the need for the greatest circumspection. The implication was that only he, the Minister Plenipotentiary, possessed it. It illustrated the risks that MacNeill ran, apparently obliviously. The German Minister had repeatedly outlined the pitfalls in becoming involved with the IRA. He reported that in early 1940 Hayes had informed Dr Jim Ryan, the Minister for Agriculture, that Russell was going to Germany.

Dr Ryan was greatly perturbed at the potential for damage to the Irish state that Russell would pose in Germany and said, according to Hempel, that if Russell returned to Ireland he would be subject only to nominal arrest: otherwise he would take steps to have Russell arrested on the high seas by the British and Americans. The Envoy repeated the false rumours of Russell's arrest, murder and burial at sea by the British secret service in Gibraltar and recounted Dr Ryan's concern at the problem of quelling Russell's activities without offending Irish-American susceptibilities, as their support was essential to sustain the policy of neutrality. Hempel thought that it would be a good propaganda move to confirm Hayes's story about Russell's murder and circulate it in the US – if this could be done without exposing the Irish government.

It was in Germany's interests, the Envoy maintained, that de Valera remained at the helm. Here we have a positive clue that the possibility of de Valera's removal could actually be considered. Hempel advised that intrigues against de Valera's government could only benefit the British and Americans. The German Minister's message was that the Irish government viewed Russell's links with Germany as an intrigue against themselves. They were not sure whether he was alive or dead. They were sure, however, about Goertz and Held because, as Hempel reported, Hayes had given Dr Ryan first-hand information on this and Hempel's report indicated that while the Irish government had Held arrested they allowed Goertz to go free in order, on the one hand, to discredit the IRA by associating their organisation with fifth column activities and, on the other hand, to keep Goertz under observation and thus keep tabs on IRA-German liaison activities. Another reason proferred by Hempel was that, if the situation arose, the Irish government would use Goertz as a liaison officer to effect a secret treaty with Germany in the event of an attack by Britain on Ireland. Held, the Envoy continued, had told the police of his talks with the Germans and of the plan of German assistance to the IRA for the Northern Ireland operations: on this point the report alleged that Dr Ryan had conveyed to Hayes that the Irish government would not get involved so long as the Irish state (i.e. the twenty-six counties) itself was not attacked; but that weapons destined for the IRA, badly needed by the Irish government, would be confiscated and further, that the business of Held and Goertz and the link with the IRA had made a bad impression.

This telegram went on to relate that Hayes's information of the $6,000 brought in for the IRA by an Irish woman living in Spain was taken as a sign by Dr Ryan that Germany was not taking the illegal organisation all that seriously.[7]

He repeated that when the Irish government foiled Goertz's attempt to escape by boat they took care to allow Goertz himself to remain at large: that tallies with General Costello's version. GHQ told it differently. The maintained that their instructions to arrest Goertz were unequivocal. But Costello was his own man and did things his own way. His forte was simple straightforward soldiering: he was not given to MacNeill's flights of fancy.

This report of the German Minister concludes with a reference to cabinet ministers, Dr Ryan and Derrig, taking Hayes into their confidence as to the contingent circumstances in which the Irish government was determined to offer 'real resistance'. (Hempel used the English words thus in his report.) In the circumstances of an imminent Allied attack on Ireland, the Envoy stated, Goertz would have his uses in reaching a secret understanding between Ireland and Germany. The tantalising question remains: was there any official knowledge of a role for General MacNeill in arriving at such an understanding? None at all, according to Colonel Dan Bryan, who said that MacNeill had absolutely no authority to act as he did. Bryan's view was that the whole affair was another manifestation of MacNeill's boy scout personality.

Hempel had been fast losing patience with both Goertz and MacNeill but especially with the mercurial Goertz. He referred again to contacts between Hayes, Ryan and Goertz and came out bluntly with the opinion that the activities of Goertz were undermining his own position, which he claimed was the more important of the two. To emphasise the dangers the Envoy drew attention to the fact that a brother-in-law of Hayes by name of de Lacy, who worked in the *Irish Times*, played a highly suspect part in the Goertz business.

The German Minister cautioned that any pre-arrangement involving Goertz could only be unofficial and would have to be conducted with circumspection because if it came to the ears of the British government it would furnish them with an instant pretext for the occupation of the ports. He had already warned that, as official German representative, he must keep Goertz at a distance to avoid giving the British an excuse to attain another of their objectives, the expulsion from Eire of the German legation.

From Hempel's telegrams it would seem that he used the letter 'L' to describe not one but two different persons with the same surname: Colonel Nial MacNeill in one instance and General Hugo MacNeill in the other. The Envoy was aware of Thomsen's liaison with an Irish army officer and he himself seems to have met other army officers including General Dan McKenna, the chief of staff, to whom, however, the German

Minister always referred in a respectful manner. Interest in the Irish army would have been normal practice for the German representative: his predecessors had established that practice. The advent of Goertz, however, introduced a new dimension to the legation's involvement in this area which could have seriously compromised both Hempel and the Irish army.

After his contacts with Iseult Stuart, Helena Molony, Jim O'Donovan, and subsequently with Miss Maisie O'Mahony (who acted as his chauffeuse/secretary), Goertz moved into a house in Dalkey which had been got for him by a Miss Maura O'Brien. She moved there from Strand Road in Sandymount where she had been living with Mrs Austin Stack. She was picked for this fronting job because she looked innocent. Goertz also stayed from time to time with the Farrell sisters in Dun Laoghaire: they idolised him. For a while, the house in Dalkey became his headquarters and it had a transmitter installed: Anthony Deery was the signalman. Many people, some allegedly TDs, met Goertz during this period, including one of whom Goertz said that he was 'very like a farmer'. His identity can only be a matter for speculation: Dr Ryan's name crops up. More knowledgeable sources inclined to the opinion that the visitor was the late Cristóir O'Byrne, Fianna Fáil TD for Wicklow.

General Hugo MacNeill visited the German agent on several occasions. Maura O'Brien remembered him well. From Hempel's telegrams the indications were that the momentum leading to this encounter came from MacNeill. But it seems Goertz had the Irish army in mind from the beginning of his mission and he had had an address ready appealing, over the heads of the government, directly to the Irish army to co-operate with a German landing when it came. Hayes, according to Hempel, had told the German agent that the Irish Defence Forces were to be strengthened through collaboration between the army and the IRA and had offered the German agent information about the Irish army. This address referred to, which in all probability increased the apprehension of the Irish government, was confiscated when the Special Branch raided Mrs Stack's home at 167 Strand Road. It is not known if the MacNeills were aware of the existence of the Goertz address document.[8]

Hempel remained agitated about Goertz. But the IRA plan, sponsored by Goertz, to march on the North appears to have worried more people than Hempel including some IRA members. MacNeill, on the other hand, seemed to have shown some sympathy towards this move, as did O'Duffy; and Thomsen, the contact man, evidently did not demur. Hempel's reservations about contacts with MacNeill were confined to what he reckoned to be a personality instability in the army man.

German foreign policy makers, judging by their actions, were convinced that as far as Ireland was concerned, sections of the army were at one with the IRA in favouring an aggressive anti-British policy. All that needed to be done, according to that Berlin train of thought, was to repair the relations between the illegal organisations and the supposedly sympathetic government leaders. Hempel reported that Goertz had contacts not alone with mavericks like the MacNeills but also with the head of the Irish army intelligence. When half the country seemed to be meeting Goertz it would not have been extraordinary to learn that the legitimate Irish army intelligence should have made it their business to find out what in fact was going on. But Hempel's report was misleading in one respect: the head of Irish intelligence at the time was not a major; he was Colonel Dan Bryan and he emphatically had not met Goertz at that stage.[9] However it might not be unreasonable to assume that surveillance over Goertz was exercised more or less continuously or that contact of some description would have been made with the circles in which the German agent seemed — up to now — to be able to move freely.[10]

Hempel's opinion was that Goertz was now becoming too hot to handle and the Envoy accurately predicted the agent's arrest. After that arrest the German Minister hastened to seek advice from Berlin as to how he should proceed to avoid having his association with Goertz compromise his position. It would have been particularly embarrassing for him if, in addition to his own contacts with Goertz, it came out that General MacNeill had also established links with both Goertz and the legation, with illicit gun-running operations in mind. It would have also been a major embarrassment for the Irish army.

When General McKenna had found his feet in 1940 as chief of staff of the Irish Defence Forces he quickly set about imposing his will. He was a down-to-earth Ulster man given to plain speaking. He demanded efficiency and he was ruthless in dealing with subordinates who failed to meet his standards. He curtly insisted that commanders get on with their jobs with the weapons they had, and not with the ones which they would like to have. Outdated artillery pieces consisting of French 75mm guns; 18-pounders of varying marks and 4.5 inch howitzers were grouped and whipped into regiments with capabilities ranging from single gun employment to putting down mini-barrages and concentrations. The British joke was to hand over to the Irish two obsolete 60-pounders which were incapable of integration into the miraculously efficient and mobile fire units which Dan McKenna's drive developed. It is not clear whether the British had the cheek to charge for these museum pieces.

The Irish army had few illusions apart from a tendency to inflate the tactical advantages of guerilla warfare. They realised that they could only wage war within their means. Their readiness to make the supreme sacrifice and to master minor tactical and small arms skills were their main assets. The homemade Molotov Cocktail was a substitute for an insufficiency of anti-tank guns: they had no tanks worth talking about; air power was nominal. So the rifle became king of the infantry. Rifle marksmanship became a religion and McKenna its high priest as he rode roughshod over resistance to his demands.

McKenna had his hands full in dealing with his two divisional commanders, Costello and MacNeill. He was comparatively circumspect in handling Costello on account of Costello's Fort Leavenworth reputation and dedication to soldiering. MacNeill, also a product of US military training,[11] was difficult to handle in a different way. McKenna was suspicious of his showmanship; he disliked anything that bordered on the bizarre or the flashy.

MacNeill's name kept turning up in matters extraneous to simple soldiering. In messages to Veesenmayer his name is mentioned as being sympathetic to notions relating to sabotage in the North of Ireland. Copies of the messages are

on record. There is, however, no corroboration of the allegations about MacNeill which appear in them. The furthest
confidential sources would be prepared to go was an indication that Joe Andrews knew what was going on in Thomsen-
MacNeill-Goertz circles. In the same context Andrews thought
it possible, through O'Duffy, to organise circles among
sympathetic Irish army officers who were dissatisfied with
Britain's continuing presence in Northern Ireland.

The reference to MacNeill, a senior serving Irish army
officer, intrigued Veesenmayer who knew a lot about MacNeill
but remained reluctant to develop any specific conspiratorial
links with him. He saw MacNeill in the context of his dream
of fomenting rebellion by letting the Irish do it themselves.
This vision was also in tune with the type of audience Goertz
imagined he was addressing when he prepared his manifesto
appealing directly to the Irish army to support a German landing. It was all geared to a *coup d'état*. The messages could be
interpreted as indicating that MacNeill might fit Veesenmayer's
bill. He seemed tailor-made and had the stature, the charisma
and the training for what the *coup d'état* specialist had in
mind.

More conservative views in Irish army intelligence circles,
as represented by the director, Colonel Dan Bryan, would
naturally be less adulatory of MacNeill. There was a nervous-
ness of the non-specialist general's tendency to interfere rashly
in intelligence matters which in command and control terms
were not his concern. The extra-curricular dabblings in intelligence affairs were a cause of disquiet to the cautious director.
Colonel Bryan frowned on amateurism in intelligence. His
bland, gentlemanly, roundabout way of getting to the point
concealed a steely professionalism which won the respect of
friend and foe alike.[12]

Regarding General MacNeill, as with everything else,
Veesenmayer believed what he wanted to believe. Veesenmayer
was a different proposition to the airy, temperamental Goertz.
He disconcerted loose talkers with his immediate propositions
for translating their talk into action. He was obsessed with
making 'big politics' out of Ireland. Typically, he drew encouragement for his speculations from Hempel's telegrams. Two
high officials of the Third Reich, Hempel and Veesenmayer,

drew radically different conclusions from the same material. Veesenmayer's myopic misreading of Hempel's reports were wilful and directed towards his own and Ribbentrop's nefarious ends. He never fully grasped the significance of de Valera's consideration for Britain; Hempel did.

Veesenmayer, to give him his due, supported Hempel's view that the Abwehr should have Foreign Ministry clearance before inserting agents in Ireland. But Veesenmayer's motives were different from the German Minister's, who was professionally and temperamentally averse to such adventures. Veesenmayer's objections were not made in principle (he had mooted the injection of 120 specialists to advise the IRA), but primarily on efficiency and unity of command grounds. But even here he revealed his political limitations.

It may not be entirely fair to blame either Veesenmayer for his failure to interpret de Valera correctly, or Hempel for his contribution to such a misinterpretation. Though Hempel may be faulted for presenting a less than penetrating analysis, the events he reported towards the end of 1942 spoke for themselves and had indicated, on the surface, a state of turbulence in the country, with the people in no mood to show much consideration for Britain. After the hanging of IRA man Thomas Williams in Belfast on 3 September 1942, Hempel reported unrest North and South of the border 'even in strongly pro-British Cork'. He noted the strong criticism of the Irish government's reticence in making any representations to the British in the affair. He further reported on the 24th of that month that the situation in Eire was delicate with the frustrations there aggravated by economic stagnation. Notwithstanding all this, Hempel gave as his opinion that de Valera was convinced that he was a man of destiny — the only one capable of shielding Eire's neutrality policy and of shepherding the country through the war. Hempel was inclined to agree with that assessment. Perhaps he did not sufficiently distance de Valera from the prevailing waves of anti-British sentiment when he was reporting what he found. The Third Reich's error was to confuse such anti-British sentiment with pro-German feeling. This confused thinking was a factor in tempting the Abwehr to persist in efforts to commit yet another agent. Veesenmayer, in his own handwriting, had intimated on 2 September 1942 that this was in order, but only if a full guarantee were given that Isebart (the agent in question) worked exclusively in Northern Ireland and that the Hamburg Abwehr branch reported regularly to the Foreign Ministry department of progress and results, as these were of importance to him with regard to his special assignment. But from the beginning of 1943 Veesenmayer had taken active steps to discourage the proposition to employ John Francis O'Reilly and a companion as agents (Mulally was mentioned initially as the companion; eventually John Kenny was sent). He complained bitterly to Canaris when his advice was not taken and the two ill-trained agents were landed by parachute in December 1943, equipped with transmitters for a spying mission. Veesenmayer and Hempel shared the same sense of outrage that such a thing could be done without consultation with the Foreign Ministry. Veesenmayer passed on Haller's unflattering memorandum on O'Reilly to the Foreign Ministry. Haller described O'Reilly as a pig-headed opportunist whose father was an RIC man.[13] O'Reilly's erstwhile companion, Mulally, was depicted as an irresponsible, albeit affable, chatterbox.

On 22 December 1943 Hempel reported the landing of the two Irishmen. Two transmitters had been brought in, the report went on, and one of the agents was alleged to have told of SS training before being sent to Ireland to carry out espionage against England. They got no chance to operate as they were picked up at once. A telegram of protest from Hempel on the matter on 7 January 1944 was instrumental in securing a rebuke from Ambassador Ritter, not for the Abwehr, but for the Security Service (*Sicherheitsdienst*). They were the ones, the ambassador's reproach ran, who contravened Veesenmayer's admonitions about clearance and co-ordination. Nor did the German Minister encourage Irish agents. His assessment of a retired British major, K. E. Fitzgerald Lombard, allegedly a homosexual, who offered his services to the legation, was harsh: 'a senile, garrulous, political snob', the Envoy called him; yet, typically, he did not fully eliminate him, and left the matter open by mentioning the retired officer's good connections.

In the case of the other would-be agent, Joe Andrews, the

German Minister had great reservations, which, however, were neither specific nor timely enough to deter Veesenmayer, who by 1943 was clutching at straws, from pursuing the connection. Andrews, it was true, did hold out very attractive bait: there were his alleged contacts with General O'Duffy and General MacNeill and O'Duffy's supposed rapport with the IRA in the North. There was the O'Duffy proposition of raising a Green Division to fight on the Russian front, which Veesenmayer saw to have no military merit but which he felt could be manipulated for propaganda purposes. The prospect of organising cells of Irish army officers who were sympathetic to Germany and antagonistic to Britain was irresistible bait for Veesenmayer.

Andrews sent another message (No. 14) stating that he had a contact with the supervisor in the Short and Harland aviation works in Belfast, a personal friend of O'Duffy's. He added enigmatically: 'Major-General MacNeill sympathetic'. There were extenuating circumstances for Veesenmayer's dalliance with Andrews. His remaining hope of fomenting rebellion in Ireland after the death of Sean Russell in August 1940 had been Frank Ryan. He did not like Ryan but Ryan was then all he had got for this purpose. But on 13 January 1943 he reported that Ryan had had a stroke, was hospitalised and would be out of action for months. To spurn Andrews would have seemed, in the circumstances, like looking a gift horse in the mouth. On 5 May 1943 he decided to persist with a progression of Operation 'Mainau', the codename of the mission originally given by Abwehr II to Goertz in the spring of 1940, which would involve Andrews. Hempel put that enterprise in perspective when he reported the arrest of Andrews on 6 December 1943: the Envoy wired that Andrews was totally unsuitable. But that was too late to deflect Veesenmayer and it must be remembered that it was Hempel's legation that had put Andrews in contact with Veesenmayer, albeit with reservations, in the first place.

Another factor possibly influencing Veesenmayer was Hempel's apparent softening towards the IRA in Northern Ireland. He was surprisingly venturesome in recommending the sending of three Northern Ireland IRA men, if necessary by U-Boat, to Germany for training. He also wanted to woo the Northern Ireland IRA away from Marxist influences. He seemed to be veering towards the mistake made by the Political Department in Berlin that subversion was acceptable, provided it was not directed specifically against Eire. That, as illustrated repeatedly, contravened a fundamental tenet of de Valera's neutrality policy: but Eire was in no way and in no circumstances to be used as a base for hostile actions against Britain.

Hempel's reports were factors which helped to heighten Veesenmayer's expectations of making 'big politics' out of Ireland in that manner. Hempel was probably unaware that these particular reports had this effect. Indeed, with regard to his reports, it eventually got to a stage where Ribbentrop had to have explanatory notes from his staff to elucidate Hempel's telegrams. It is interesting to note that by the end of 1942 Ribbentrop was trying to replace Thomsen who was said to be sick. Whether it was on account of the sickness or whether, dissatisfied with Hempel's reports, he wanted a first-hand pre-invasion account of the situation in Ireland from Thomsen, is not clear. The ill-planned insertion of O'Reilly and Kenny occurred a couple of weeks afterwards to the great embarrassment of Hempel. Gray saw to it that the government were embarrassed and Hempel abused.[14]

Veesenmayer had already accepted Hempel's assessment that he, as the official Envoy, was more important than the secret agent Goertz. The *coup d'état* specialist was also aware that Ribbentrop had his own reason for wanting to protect his German Minister in Dublin: although the Foreign Minister supported giving monetary aid to the IRA, he did not want Hempel to be involved in this matter. Then Veesenmayer was informed by Woermann that Clissmann, who was to be Veesenmayer's emissary to Leopold Kerney, the Irish Minister in Spain, had deduced from a Hempel telegram that 'L', in his opinion, was the Irish Minister for Agriculture, Ryan. That had the appearance of 'big politics' indeed. It is not clear how Clissmann arrived at this alleged conclusion, or what part repercussions of the Hayes confessions played in it. It does not, in any case, seem to be exactly what Hempel had said, unless Clissmann's guess that Jim Ryan was the real 'L' is correct. Hempel's arbitrary use of capitals could confuse and he had previously used 'L' to designate separately both the MacNeills.

Woermann thought that Hempel's telegrams had a bearing on the Spanish excursion planned by Veesenmayer so he sent him copies of them, having first shown them to Clissmann before the latter departed on his authorised mission to Kerney. In a memorandum to Woermann on 24 November 1941 Veesenmayer had indicated the conclusion he had drawn from Hempel's telegrams. As a result, he said, the communications which Clissmann had brought back from Spain arising out of his contacts with Kerney merited far reaching consideration. In other words Hempel's telegrams had thrown a new light on that development.

Veesenmayer opened his assessment by quoting from a Hempel telegram (No. 367, p.3) that the IRA had elite potential and were a rallying point for the spirit of Irish nationalism. This view, Veesenmayer said, coincided with Kerney's opinion, as allegedly expressed by Clissmann, and with the last radio message from Goertz: so he stressed that this message indicated that the IRA were an organisation of extraordinary importance. The pervading view was that the differences between IRA policy and government policy were more cosmetic and semantic than fundamental. Clissmann had alleged that Kerney minimised the Hayes affair by surmising that the latter might have had a role as a go-between for some of de Valera's colleagues. Veesenmayer's summary extolled the IRA's fighting record but he felt that now de Valera was more in tune with the changing times and since 1926 had scored many successes against Britain. The fact that the IRA men who captured and 'court-martialled' Hayes came from Northern Ireland where, Veesenmayer intimated, the British secret service had a wide influence, made them suspect: they were either paid agents, provocateurs or infiltrators, he said. However, he did not think that the time had yet come for a British attack, and if it did, contrary to Kerney's alleged opinion, he did not believe that the Irish army was capable of prolonged resistance. He saw the deterrent to Britain lying mainly in Irish-American reaction, as Roosevelt had also to take this factor into account. Veesenmayer had no difficulty in writing off Goertz. He had outlived his usefulness. In this matter Hempel could be satisfied that his damning reporting had the desired effect. Goertz was subsequently arrested: this confirmed Veesenmayer's judgment and Berlin branded the agent's aberrations as being due to a nervous breakdown, resulting from his long period of isolation in Ireland. The high command were convinced that Goertz was under close observation from both the Irish and British secret services: he had become a liability. Hempel had recommended the agent's repatriation but he did not say exactly how this was to be effected.

An important deduction which Veesenmayer managed to draw from Hempel's reports — over and above what the Envoy intended — was the implication that it was possible for de Valera to assign an undercover role to Dr Ryan to foster liaison with what Veesenmayer deemed to be a more tractable wing of the IRA, namely that led by Hayes. If that supposition were correct, Veesenmayer thought it merited special attention. The impression he had got from Clissmann's report of his meetings with Kerney was that in an emergency Kerney would be empowered to make representations for aid to Germany. Kerney, he said, was a careful and reserved Irish nationalist and a close friend of de Valera's: the implication therefore was that this was indeed a serious business, to be conducted at the highest level.

Veesenmayer had given priority to the healing of the rift between de Valera and the IRA and he had Frank Ryan in mind as the agent to effect this rapprochement.[15] He could see no good reason why de Valera and the IRA should be fighting each other when they could combine to everyone's advantage against the common enemy, Britain. It is doubtful if Hempel would be in accord with all Veesenmayer's attitudes. The German minister, who deduced his mission as being the preservation of Irish neutrality, could hardly have approved of Veesenmayer's resolve to strengthen the manipulation — no matter how prudently — of the *'Irland Faktor'* against the England 'bastion', as Veesenmayer described it. The *coup d'état* specialist intended to discuss further ways and means of fomenting the revolution with Frank Ryan as his chief instrument for that purpose. Part of Veesenmayer's problem in making a complete estimate of the situation on fomenting this rebellion stemmed from his difficulty in harmonising his interpretation of Hempel's telegrams with what he understood Clissmann said that Kerney said. Eventually Sonnleithner, according to a report from his special train in Westphalia, sent Veesenmayer himself to meet Kerney and informed the Führer of that position. The proposed adventure was thus mooted at the highest level on the German side.

Veesenmayer's eventual meeting with Kerney did little more than confirm accounts of previous meetings. According to Veesenmayer, Kerney said that Ireland's only hope of eventual reunification lay in a decisive German victory. The wife of the ambassador to the Vatican, Mrs Kiernan (ballad singer Delia Murphy), was alleged to have expressed similar sentiments. Allegations of pro-German utterances by the Irish Catholic clergy and other representatives abroad during the earlier part of the war were also recorded. The impression given in the telegrams was that Cardinal McRory was allegedly pro-Axis and anti-British. However, when the undertaking foundered in the end, Veesenmayer felt that he had been misinformed by Hempel and misled by Kerney. There was a point of view that Kerney's exchanges with Clissmann and Veesenmayer could be interpreted as constituting the gravest threat to neutrality of the entire war. When Professor T. D. Williams analysed Kerney's actions in this vein in *The Leader* (3 January 1953) and in the *Irish Press* (7-18 January 1953), he was sued by the ex-Minister. The matter was settled out of court. Coupled with MacNeill's activities, however, the dangers of the discussions to neutrality can hardly be over-emphasised. Kerney had been an old comrade of de Valera's but he was out of touch with the pressures bearing on the Taoiseach and de Valera's necessarily pragmatic responses to changing situations. It would have taken a British pre-emptive invasion to create the situation Veesenmayer had been hoping for, with the Germans, the IRA and de Valera being drawn into a common front against the British. Veesenmayer could never distinguish between de Valera's aims and methods and those of the IRA. He could not conceive of de Valera's consideration for Britain. He was not alone in this. Official Britain did not believe it either. Therein lay the greatest danger. Veesenmayer's potential to foment rebellion in

Ireland was far more explosive than that of Weisbach, who brought Casement to Ireland by submarine in 1916, or of Zerhausen, liaison officer to the Irish Brigade in the First World War. There was substance in Veesenmayer's angry dismissal of Hempel's dismissive comparison with 1916. In the final analysis he was stymied by de Valera who never neglected to keep Britain's welfare at heart. Veesenmayer regarded de Valera as the arch-priest of wiliness but fundamentally an insurrectionist. That was his error: he never appreciated that the insurrectionist had become a convinced constitutionalist. For Veesenmayer, it was an immutable fact that Britain was the mutual enemy of both Ireland and Germany. He never adequately evaluated the effect of the changing war situation on the Irish position or appreciated Irish determination to pursue their own brand of neutrality in what they reckoned to be the national self-interest.

If the British knew (and there was not much they did not know) they would have approved of the manner in which the German Minister dragged his feet in matters which would have promoted Veesenmayer's adventures with the IRA. It is a sombre question as to how the dutiful Envoy would have reacted had he been aware that his master Ribbentrop was the author and formulator of Veesenmayer's mission to foment rebellion in Ireland. Mere expediency had induced Ribbentrop to keep Hempel out of direct involvement with the IRA. Such direct involvement would have finished the German Minister with de Valera. If Hempel had encouraged the Irish adventure the resultant shattering of the policy of neutrality would have been inevitable and disastrous, though of course Veesenmayer and his blinkered confidants did not see it that way. Hempel was correct in his diagnosis that the majority of the Irish people had put their trust in de Valera to pursue a policy of neutrality and in his conclusion that de Valera was the man of destiny to see that policy through its difficult tortuous course. If Hempel had behaved as Veesenmayer apparently wished him to behave, de Valera would have had little option but to make more manifest his considerations for Britain and deal accordingly with the Third Reich representation.

Of course if Bewley had had his way, a rebellion such as

Veesenmayer wished to foment would first and foremost have ousted de Valera, whereas Veesenmayer's idea was to encompass and incorporate the Taoiseach, 'the last surviving commandant of 1916', in the unfinished struggle against the British.

As far as de Valera was concerned, Veesenmayer's hope was, from the outset, a vain one. But the ground was not unfavourable for sowing the seeds of insurrection. The Goertz-MacNeill liaison on the importation of arms to be used against the British was fraught with dangers.[16] Hempel's reports which seemed to implicate cabinet ministers with a wing of the IRA added a necessary political dimension which Kerney's alleged initial assertions to Clissmann were interpreted as confirming. Irish army intelligence was uneasy about Kerney and in hindsight felt that de Valera should have recalled him. They found it hard to know what Kerney was up to but they did know that 'other international agencies', presumably the British, had him under observation. Therein perhaps lay the greatest threat to neutrality: British intelligence, while technically accomplished, is not renowned for its finesse in interpreting Irish situations; a preconceived stereotyped approach and a congenital contempt seem to stunt their evaluation.

The landing of American troops in Northern Ireland brought home the realities and compulsions of war. Under the pressure of events, there was bound to be a less scrupulous observation of the details of neutrality. Furthermore, Gray was less than scrupulous or sensitive in his waspish blatherings about Irish breaches of neutrality endangering the Allied cause. Evidence of the exploits of MacNeill; or interpretations of the actions of Kerney; or, above all, word of the Veesenmayer connection would have given substance to the American Minister's accusations. An unstoppable momentum could have been generated: Churchill would have had the pretext he professed to desire to move against Eire.

NINE

End of Messages

Collecting information was one thing: transmitting it was another. Shortly after the war broke out the British became concerned that Germany was receiving news with remarkable rapidity. The UK authorities asked the Eire authorities to investigate and prevent the possibility of leakages, offering to train the personnel to do it. They noted that 'it may happen that the Eire authorities do not recognise as dangerous a telegram of harmless appearance.' They took steps to sew up the three cable services from Eire which did not pass through Britain.[1] They stressed that what they were seeking was not in conflict with neutrality: on the contrary, they felt virtuous at not insisting on setting up a censorship of all traffic — having concluded that to do so would probably invoke a violent response from the telegraphic service. Mr Connolly, the official in charge of censorship, felt that they were going too far in requesting a hand over of copies of all cables to Germany: Dulanty was instructed to return them to Dublin. The British read them anyway but still pressed for the possibility of Allied wireless stations being set up in Eire.

The Irish government agreed to the Cobh service being routed through London. With regard to the commercial cables a direct approach to the companies by them was deemed to be discourteous but Dulanty informed the British that his government would have no objection to a direct approach being made by the UK in an endeavour to agree with them that all cables should be routed through London. There would be no need then to ask for the formal approval of the Eire government of the step taken: only to inform them to make sure that they would raise no objection!

Dulanty also indicated that they would be glad to buy machines for intercepting wireless messages at a price of £500 each but he was shocked to find out that it would cost between £5,000 and £10,000 for the complete equipment. Maffey's naval attaché Greig reported that Colonel Liam Archer (then head of intelligence) assured him that they were doing their best to locate and confiscate the illegal IRA transmitter but that they were handicapped by having only Post Office detection instruments; more up to date equipment was on order; all known private transmitter sets had been confiscated.

Greig was conducted around seventy-nine coast-watching stations. He found them equipped with binoculars and a telescope but with no telephone link to the nearest police station. (He attributed this omission to the expense involved in laying telephone lines to remote areas). He recorded that throughout his conversations Colonel Archer was very friendly and appeared to be ready and willing to co-operate. It was later reported that Germans and German sympathisers were making great efforts to diversify and secure their telegraph and postal communications.

In June 1940 the British were worried that a crisis could prevent communication between the UK and their representative in Dublin. The threat of German invasion at the time induced a coincidence of concern and the Irish side bent over backwards to accommodate them. The British installed an extra transmitter in the house of the air attaché and considered plans to use communications from British ships in Dublin port. If Stormont proved to be difficult on the question of a direct line to Belfast they aimed to use a carrier pigeon service to the Air Ministry station at Aldergrove. The Dominions Office were looking for a direct line between the Air Ministry itself for Fighter Command and the appropriate Eire military authorities for the purpose of passing on operational air information, as well as a third direct line between Fighter Command and Irish army GHQ for the purpose of passing on air raid warning information. By the end of August the direct line between Maffey and Belfast was working but there were still some staffing difficulties.

The setting up of the pigeon service presented more problems. A suitable loft had to be acquired in or near Dublin to accommodate a regular supply of good birds from the West of England. Arrangements then had to be made to find a local trustworthy fancier.[2] They arranged for two birds to be taken over daily and released next day irrespective of whether a message was to be carried or not. No one in Eire got too excited about what the British were up to about communications. Eire was not neutral in this field. The British had three transmitters and receivers plus direct telephone lines to London and Belfast — and carrier pigeons. Their biggest problem was in persuading the Foreign Office to purchase a bicycle in order to maintain contact with the reserve set and the pigeons.

With the Germans it was different. The Third Reich's representative was continually harassed over the possession of his transmitter. His fond hope that the Irish would collaborate in the erection of a radio station had been quickly dissipated.[3] The Irish authorities closely monitored his set to the best of their technical abilities. The British deciphered the messages, which ranged from weather reports to random items originating from Goertz and Andrews. The uncovering of an assortment of agents equipped with transmitters sharpened the invigilation. Hempel realised the risks he ran and constantly preached the need for restraint and selectivity in transmission.

He regarded the sending of weather reports as an unnecessary risk. Canaris took the same point of view, and dissociated himself from them. He did not need them, he said. He had his own means of getting this information more accurately. He placed more reliance on bleeps from weather buoys[4] positioned in the Atlantic. Veesenmayer suspected his motives.

Preserving the set for Ribbentrop's purposes presented problems. The technical snags became such a nuisance that Hempel had to look for a special Signals Officer to service the troublesome set (he never got one). He was forever bombarding Berlin with maintenance and operational queries. The IRA likewise had technical problems but on 29 October 1939, after many frustrations, Jim O'Donovan restored communications with the Abwehr.

This restoration was a mixed blessing both for the Abwehr

and for Hempel. O'Donovan's first messages were calls for weapons and special items of equipment. Lahausen remonstrated that these requests gave no idea as to how a landing was to be effected. The lack of rapport between those two organisations affected co-operation. Liaison between them was bedevilled by more than technical faults. Hempel's grievance was that the IRA were misusing their set and jeopardising his position. They were capriciously conducting personal vendettas on the air and broadcasting crude propaganda. In his opinion it was only a matter of time before they were caught out. This would endanger the mission he had got from Ribbentrop to preserve his set for operational purposes.

Hempel's complaints were not confined to the IRA. He commented that their own propaganda techniques were at times flat-footed and he criticised the research and analysis that went into the broadcasts. He told Stuart to make a plea to the proper authorities in Berlin to show more sensitivity in their transmissions.

The laconic Stuart was not the most lucid of messengers. In Berlin he confirmed that abuse of transmission time had made it easy for the Irish authorities to locate and seize the IRA set: he reassured them that codes and ciphers had remained intact and mentioned that Jim O'Donovan was looking for a replacement.[5] Woermann was puzzled by Stuart: he found him reserved on Irish nationalist aspirations. He did not appreciate that Stuart was more interested in art than in politics.

Routing cables through London enabled the British to eavesdrop. Up until America's entry into the war the Envoy sent some messages nominally via Washington which were specifically designed to conceal the existence of his secret transmitter. Afterwards the British permitted the legation to transmit via Switzerland! They had a good read first and such messages only reached their destination after they had been well milked and had lost their news value. The British never informed the Irish authorities that they had cracked the German diplomatic code. The attractions of the secret set were obvious and Hempel did all in his power to keep it intact for the big day Ribbentrop dreamed about.

His transmission procedures were models of efficiency compared to IRA practices and he repeatedly relayed his restiveness that their amateurishness and recklessness must inevitably draw unfavourable attention to his own set which he was nursing as ordered until the time came to use it. He also protested at IRA tendencies to encroach and avail of his set.

From time to time they passed information to the legation for transmission. He was unhappy about the content and the style of the messages: he did not like their referring to the Irish government as 'the enemy'! Woermann, however, told Hempel not to worry, that it was unlikely that the Irish authorities would get a fix on a short wave transmitter: it was, he held, an extra-territorial matter and the internal business of the legation: if a disavowal of the transmitter had to be undertaken he would tell Hempel what to say.

That did not satisfy Hempel. He replied that if the government had British-supplied proof of the existence of the transmitter, then a denial by him would result in a loss of trust which he felt would be serious. He enquired as to the position in other countries, his diplomatic instinct leading him to seek refuge in a precedent.

Hempel's fears as usual were well grounded. The British located the IRA transmitter in Wicklow and he reported that they had informed the Irish government that a German code was being used. British suspicions had been aroused by an unexplained volume of radio traffic. At first it was thought that the untracked transmissions were coming from Drogheda. The transmitter in Held's house was not operating and transmitters in Rathmines, Sundrive Road Mills and Clanbrassil Street were only used intermittently. Hempel's own set was not pin-pointed at this stage: he was careful in regulating the volume of radio traffic.

His reaction to the news of the discovery of the IRA set was to lie low and suspend legation transmission until things cooled down. He got the impression from Walshe that the Irish government did not want to know about his transmitter. In the early part of 1940 the British were waging intensive psychological warfare against Eire and, possibly because of his realistic perception that an Envoy without links of his own government is useless, it took de Valera up until the spring of 1941 to grasp the nettle of doing something about the legation's transmitter. Even then the demand was only that radio traffic to Berlin be cut to a minimum. Hempel resolved, if he were pressed, to take the line that the cutting off of telegraphic facilities before the war had been insup-suportable; that several unsuccessful attempts had been made with the Irish side to establish communications with Berlin; and that anyway it was in Irish interests to have such a link. He continued to use the set selectively for confidential communications, including receipt of instructions relating to Goertz.

He reminded Berlin that he had warned Goertz about putting his trust in unreliable people. In the case of Held, he was able to say, 'I told you so'. But he could not get away from the fact that the Abwehr had contacted Goertz through *his* secret set: thus messages from Goertz had gone out from it in the official code for which he was responsible.

Curiously enough, the efforts of the Italian Axis partner in Dublin to make use of the transmitter had been roundly rebuffed by Hempel, with Berlin's backing, even though they had had to use the Rome channel via London before Italy's entry into the war. It was impossible to comply with the Italian request at a time when Hempel was constrained to keep the use of the set down to a minimum and he was angry at Ribbentrop for his rashness in letting the Italians know of its existence.

The British were even more secretive and circumspect. In their obsession to concel their trump card of being able, for most of the war, to read secret communications of the German armed forces, no price was too high to pay. They rarely revealed summaries of their intercepts of Hempel or the IRA to the Irish government except when they wanted to embarrass or compromise them. Hempel was sending telegrams on troop movements and troop locations, post problems, censorship, the searching of the diplomatic bag, telegraphic delays and — as an illustration of the extent of the scope of his coverage — he recounted that a camouflaged concrete ship was blocking Belfast harbour to deceive and lure either U-Boats or the Luftwaffe. One of his more specious messages pretended to draw attention to the artistic merit of photographs in the *Irish Independent* by a photographer

"Ph . . . ew". There was no photographer's name which could be associated with "Ph...ew", but there was a very good photograph of an RAF 'Fairey' battle bomber with good air photographs of Norwegian cities. This was at the time of the invasion of Norway in April 1940, which Hempel later put about was done to prevent a British attack and to aid Finland.

There was no regular complaint from the British to the Irish authorities. Hempel had got into hot water over passing on information leading to the sinking of the *Iroquois* but that complaint was seen to emanate from the US. Later the British chose not to complain about the damaging element of information concerning the Dieppe operation which Hempel managed to slip through. In no way were they going to draw attention to the possibility of the existence of ULTRA.

In some British circles there had been accusations that the Irish had been less than vigilant in their surveillance of German activities. As against that on 13 April 1940 the Dominion Office sent the following note to Maffey:

> Incidentally the Admiralty have told us that the Eire government have been fully alive to the connection between the German legation and the IRA and that they believe that certain members of the legation are almost too thoroughly watched already.

There was no clue there as to the extent of their own interception. The hint was that if Eire surveillance was a little less suffocating there could be more to intercept, more to keep tabs on. Hempel gave insights into the behaviour of the Irish government and the Dominion Office wanted to keep an eye on that.

As an instance of that, Hempel indicated that in the summer of 1941 the outbreak of the war with Russia brought a swell of Irish feeling in Germany's favour: by the end of that year he was reporting that that feeling had evaporated and that no one in Ireland had sympathy for either the Germans or the Japanese. As he saw it, the entry of America into the war had increased the danger for Ireland but whether the British or Americans were yet prepared for an Irish adventure he found it difficult to say. He concluded that the widespread expectation in the Irish army was that there would be either a British or American attack but that there were no significant military indications of this happening. On 14 December 1941 he confirmed de Valera's reiterated determination to defend Irish neutrality. The Taoiseach had used Ulster 'no surrender' phraseology when he asserted with all the vehemence at his command that 'not an inch' of Irish territory was for sale. The way Hempel interpreted this provided useful information for the British.

What really worried them were the 'Irish-style' channels that defied interception. Interception of traffic between Eire and the Third Reich gave clues and revealed inconsistencies which could be played on by the psychological warfare arm. One report disclosed a surprising channel of communication between Britain and the Chief of the Security Police in Berlin which gave its own interpretation of happenings in Ireland based principally on Church sources. This report indicated: that de Valera was pursuing nationalist anti-British policies, instancing the wrecking of British efforts to come to an understanding with the 'Free State' and the continuing ban on the import of British newspapers; that the propaganda of the BBC was decried as being ineffective, and the report compared it unfavourably with the more 'factual credible' German radio; that there was a considerable resurgence of the IRA and that closer co-operation between them and de Valera was expected; that British communist circles were trying (unsuccessfully) to exploit church-state relations in Germany to influence Irish public opinion; that an American attack on the 'Free State' was expected in early 1943; that the presence of American troops in Northern Ireland shocked the Irish public and indicated how impossible it was for the 'Free State' to pursue a policy of neutrality after this occupation. The conclusion from this report, however, was that the anti-British attitude in Ireland (which was aggravated by British economic pressures such as restricting the export of coal), did not automatically mean a positive attitude towards Germany. The Third Reich, the report said, had been rejected because of its attitudes to the Catholic Church. While it depicted the Irish as being undoubtedly anti-British, it nevertheless stated that they remained in sympathy with the US even though church circles in Britain felt that it was the American intention to make a strongpoint of the country, and that they would attempt initially to accomplish this by diplomatic approaches.

A report by Woermann on 23 December 1943 points to the existence of a different ecclesiastical link and to a Vatican connection through Bewley. Bewley, surfacing again, warned about de Valera's pro-British schemings, holding that there was no danger of an Allied attack. It was his contention that the Northern Ireland base sufficed for Allied needs. The report showed him to be making use of Vatican contacts to communicate with Ireland through a church-cloaked information gathering service. A Premonstrant monk named Noots visited convents in Europe, including a convent of nuns of a Belgian order in Kilnacrott near Ballyjamesduff, Co. Cavan.[6] Information, including some from Hungary, was then brought by a Swiss lady (a nun?) named Verviers or Ververs to Rome for dissemination to Scotaland and Ireland. Monsignor O'Flaherty, a Papal diplomat (though by no means of Nazi inclination; in fact Hempel reported him as being the reporter of German atrocities in Poland) also acted as a courier for Bewley. Hempel got a copy of one of Bewley's letters brought by him and querelously demanded to know whether Bewley had sent similar letters to anyone else.

Monsignor O'Flaherty was the famous 'Pimpernel' of the Vatican who succoured and saved Jews and Allied prisoners of war.[7] When accused of being pro-British he exploded that he remembered the Black and Tans! He later lent a hand to the Germans when the tables were turned. His relationship with Bewley sprung from their both having being expatriates and nationalists.[8] The fact that Bewley was a convert, and a Latin scholar, with fundamentalist beliefs and an emotional attachment to Church symbolism, helped the relationship and induced the priest to carry messages for the extremist ex-Minister. Mrs Sheehan, the Monsignor's sister, said that he only got home once during the war and that he looked worn and thin: they never realised the danger he was in or the risks he ran. But his bringing messages for Bewley did not please Hempel.

It is difficult to detect the nature of the messages the Monsignor brought for Bewley which annoyed the German Envoy so much. The Germans, especially Gestapo chief Colonel Kappler, regarded him as an arch spy. He was warned by the German Ambassador, Weizacker, that if he put a foot outside the Vatican he would be arrested. That was an additional reason for making him *persona non grata* with Hempel, a friend of Weizächer.

More than Hempel were puzzled and peeved by the crossing of wires. The Irish government asked MacWhite, the Irish Representative in Rome, to check Bewley's story that he was representing a Swedish press agency in Rome. He reported back that no such agency existed but that the Swedish ambassador told him that Bewley's paymaster had a club-foot. Irish intelligence could never make up their minds whether 'Clubfoot' was Goebbels or Veesenmayer. 'The Swedish ambassador was more likely referring to Goebbels. He did not refer to either Hempel or O'Flaherty. O'Flaherty apparently did not call on Hempel during his visit home.

Having got his grievance off his chest Hempel carried on reporting. He recorded Walshe's doubts about a British-American attack and the Irish official's hopes that America's entry into the war would not have changed German attitudes to Ireland: the reference was to the existing German consideration for Irish-American reactions. When Hempel sought elucidation of this observation Walshe promptly quenched the Envoy's patient query by again counter-attacking about Goertz's activities, which, the Secretary said, had greviously affronted Irish sovereignty. He was never going to be allowed to forget it. If the Allies had found the Goertz affair a convenient stick with which to beat the Irish government, they in turn made full use of it to belabour the German representative.

The best Woermann could do for Hempel was to supply him with the old lame excuse that Goertz was only operating against England: that no one was ever sent to operate against Ireland. That did not mollify the Irish government though there was an unexpected easing of pressure on the Envoy. Perhaps there was a renewal of apprehension as to what the Germans might get up to next.

As if operating in a different orbit, a Lieutenant-Colonel von Falkenstein of the army planning staff telephoned Eisenlohr in the Foreign Ministry to say that, following the

...g of American troops to Northern Ireland, the question ...f delivering weapons to the government of Eire was considered and that the execution of this concept was deemed by the special staff to be feasible. The army wanted to know whether there were any political snags!

Woermann had already dealt with Hempel's queries in this matter and had ruled out, for the time being, the further pressing of arms on de Valera. If Ireland were attacked, however, he foresaw that the Irish and the Germans would be drawn into a common front and he envisaged preparations being made for such a contingency. Kapitan z.S. Bürkner (*OKW Abteilung Ausland*) was informed of this position. The fact was that the Irish authorities, while remaining careful, had become less indulgent in entertaining German arms proposals.

The reality of the Goertz threat to neutrality had been exposed. Furthermore, America was not only in the war but her combat troops were on Irish soil. In addition Gray and Maffey had spread the rumour that a German invasion of Ireland had been planned for March 1942 and on 18 February 1942 Warnock presented another protest giving details of further German violations of Irish air space. All this meant a build-up of pressure on the German representative and in those circumstances the presence of Hempel's secret transmitter was becoming less and less tolerable to the Allies. The Irish government were constantly on the defensive for permitting its existence.

The changing attitudes towards tolerating the transmitter on the Irish side symbolised the changing fortunes of the war and the consequential changing relationships between Hempel and his Irish counterparts. It was a long drawn out story. In April 1941 Walshe intimated to Hempel in a 'careful, understanding, and friendly' fashion that they were aware of the existence of the transmitter. By August 1941 Hempel reported that since the end of June the British House of Commons and press were making a fuss about the danger of the legation's transmitter and that de Valera had requested him in friendly terms on 18 December 1941 to restrict its use to cases of the utmost urgency and importance. However, in the following February 1942, when there were accusations that weather information transmitted by the legation radio had helped the German battleships *Scharnhorst* and *Gneisenau* to break through the St George's Channel (Operation 'Cerberus') issues became more important and Hempel's description of Walshe's representations as friendly could not disguise the seriousness which de Valera attributed to the matter.

Walshe had confronted the German Minister with texts of recent transmissions which had been supplied by the British. When Hempel pleaded the Hague Convention to support his legal entitlement to use the transmitter de Valera's adamant instructions were that Ireland would not be used as a base to damage Britain. Hempel quoted from an *Irish Press* leading article to prove that the weather report could not have emanated from Ireland as the weather in question came from the north-west! That point of view seemed to have had more political motivation than meteorological substance.[9] Irish army intelligence also adopted this defensive line. Hempel's version was that the British were merely looking for Irish neutrality as a scapegoat to salve their loss of prestige in permitting the ships to escape. The set was not confiscated there and then but the Envoy was made fully aware that any further misuse would lead to its immediate confiscation. He advised Berlin to give up using the set for the time being. Remembering Ribbentrop's charge he repeated that it was extremely important to hold on to it at all costs. Lie low, he advised, until things blow over.

Other happenings in 1942 served to push the transmitter to the background. The story of Lieutenant Thornton of the Irish army air corps claimed attention for a while. Hempel said that he had been charged with the unlawful acquisition of a military aircraft. The background assumption, though Hempel made it clear that this did not come out in the court-martial, was that Thornton intended to fly Goertz to Brest in accordance with a plot hatched between Goertz and MacNeill. The court martial sentenced Thornton to one and a half years hard labour[10] but Hempel stressed that overtly this conviction was for conduct to the prejudice of good order and military discipline rather than to any contacts Thornton may have had with Goertz through MacNeill. That was an aspect he felt the Irish authorities would prefer to keep quiet about, knowing the propaganda mileage the Allies would get from it.

But enough came out of the investigation to convince the government that the time had come to put a stop to compliance. Back on 25 April 1940 they had expressed fulsome appreciation of a U-Boat's friendly handling of the ship *Irish Willow* off the the Donegal coast. Subsequently they looked for excuses for German transgressions. When a German aircraft attacked and sank the *City of Bremen* on 2 June 1942 about 130 miles south-west of Mizen Head, the time for bowing and scraping had passed. Although the crew were picked up and landed at a Spanish port the Irish government vigorously expressed their profound resentment. They strongly protested that the sinking showed a flagrant disregard for Irish neutrality and sovereign rights by wantonly depriving her of sorely needed tonnage and supplies.

A fortnight later, however, Warnock took the sting out of that protest by surmising that the pilot would never have attacked if he had known that the ship was Irish and Hempel passed on a rumour in the Irish army that it was a British pilot who did it. When it was conclusively proved that it was a German attack Boland quietly pointed out to Hempel that he hoped that it was an accident. The ship, which ironically had been thanked by the Reich in 1939 for rescuing a German crew, was sailing outside convoy and conspicuously and unmistakably identified as Irish. Thus confronted, Hempel's advice to Berlin was to handle the affair in the friendliest fashion possible and to pay compensation.

The soft soap approach of Warnock and Boland did not spare the Envoy from the suppressed Irish backlash. He told of a run-in he had with Walshe who rebuked him (in French) for failing to answer the telephone promptly when he summoned him. That must never happen again, the Irish official sternly admonished.

He inferred however that other pressures to account for Irish irascibility could be read from a flying visit which the American representative Bullit paid on de Valera. He was unable to explain fully the political significance of the visit which, he said, was totally unexpected and caused much concern. It was with obvious relief that he turned away from

from trying to unravel the imponderables attaching to policies and personalities and dealt instead with bread and butter issues such as the drastic fall in tillage in 1942 due to a shortage of fertiliser, and a return to cattle raising. This, he explained, had the effect of increasing unemployment and the unemployed were forced to go to England where they were welcomed: also, in his opinion, a reversion to cattle from tillage meant increased exports of cattle, bacon and butter which was to England's advantage. On Boland's representation, he recommended that the Germans contact the French government in order to facilitate the import to Ireland of phosphate as imports had fallen from approximately 96,000 tons in 1939 to almost 9,000 tons in 1941. In the first six months of 1942 only 598 tons of superphosphate and no rock phosphate was imported. He added that an attempt to develop phosphate production in Co. Clare had met with little success. On 9 April 1943 he observed that the economic situation was nevertheless not so bad as to give credence to the rumours that de Valera was showing signs of deviating from his neutrality policy; though he did remark that he had heard of a good new airfield being built at Cashel, Co. Tipperary; for whom he did not say.

At the same time he never took his eye fully off the political scene. He reported the results of the general election held on 27 July 1943 in which Fianna Fáil lost their absolute majority but still formed the government. The Cosgrave Fine Gael party, branded by Hempel as pro-Allied, lost thirteen seats. Hempel attributed the Fine Gael losses to that party's pro-British leanings, pointing out that the losses were incurred despite a clever, well-conducted 'National Government' campaign. He cited the *Manchester Guardian*, which was the only British paper to support his own view, that the results represented support for de Valera's policy of 'strict neutrality'. He advised the German radio and press to take the line that de Valera by his clear, energetic and successful policy had earned the trust of the people. Only for this, he felt, Fianna Fáil losses would have been much higher, especially if all the hardships that the people had to endure were taken into account. As a leader of a minority government de Valera was in a precarious position and more vulnerable than had pre-

viously been the case. He did not noticeably trim his political
sails but he did have to modify his attitude towards the Reich's
representative.

Prior to the Italian surrender in 1943, the Irish government
had, with German agreement, chartered an Italian ship — *C
Gerolimich* — from the Italian government. The Germans,
after the surrender, were in no hurry to release the ship as
had been arranged, and de Valera had perforce to go to
Hempel, to solicit his good offices in facilitating the release.
According to the German Minister de Valera explained that
the 1943 harvest had been bad and that if they did not get
this ship, he would be left with no option but to ration bread,
which would disadvantage him politically, having lost his
overall majority in the Dáil in recent elections. Hempel did
not let the opportunity pass and he let it be known that the
difficulties may well have been of the Irish government's own
making and may have been caused by a weakening in the
Irish resolution to maintain neutrality. He reported de Valera's
protestation of their intention to maintain neutrality to the
end of the war but alleged that de Valera again expressed his
doubts that small countries could remain neutral in a future
war. The Envoy had reported Allied pressure to change the Irish
neutrality posture to a stance of technical non-belligerency,
which would be designed, he said, to permit the Allies to use
the ports. He had also reported James Dillon citing Portugal
as an example for Ireland to follow as, in spite of being neutral, that country was able to assist in countering the U-Boat
campaign by leasing bases in the Azores.[11]

However, having made his point and got in a complaint to
de Valera about the inadequacies of telegraphic communications, Hempel indicated a willingness to help. To do otherwise, he said, would only serve to increase Irish dependence
on the Allies. He was instrumental in procuring the ship and
the Italian representative later contributed towards having
the charter renewed. Wheat was imported accordingly, and
thanks, in part anyway, to Hempel's intervention de Valera
did not have to ration bread and so run the risk of a defeat in
the Dáil and the possible loss of a subsequent general election.

Nevertheless, German-Irish relations remained uneasy. On
15 August 1943 Hempel telegraphed that he had good grounds

for an official protest at the manner in which the Irish government were releasing Allied pilots. This pragmatic connivance – not to be confused with collusion – on the part of the Irish government was covered up by making a ruling that only those who made forced landings during operational flights would be held. Hempel again found the distinction between operational and non-operational questionable and he cited numerous instances to illustrate the benevolent attitude shown by the Irish authorities to Allied landings, though he acknowledged that the geographical situation militated against according reciprocal treatment to the Germans.

A badly damaged 'Liberator' landed in Galway on 15 January 1943 with six high ranking officers, including four generals from North Africa (but not Eisenhower, as Hempel had originally speculated). It was transported, he reported, to Northern Ireland. Hempel was perplexed by Freddie Boland's quiver of excuses, especially the Assistant Secretary's assertion that this was normal passenger traffic; that they were only following the examples of the Swedes and the Swiss; and that, anyway, they would never allow the Foynes airlink to be used for military purposes. Previously Hempel had found Boland to be co-operative; now he found him unhelpful and evasive. British and American mechanics, he complained further, flew in civilian attire to get Allied aircraft back in the air. Although he acknowledged that he could not indicate how the Irish government could correspondingly compensate the Germans, on 27 July 1943 he still presented a formal note of protest. He had previously protested at British violations of airspace, including a protest to Walshe at the shooting down of Hauptmann Bernt and his crew by pursuing Spitfires. They made a forced landing in the Tramore area. But de Valera was increasingly less forbearing to the Germans. The legation quoted the Taoiseach's reaction to the torpedoing by the Germans of the *Irish Oak* on 19 May 1943. In a Dáil reply de Valera said it that it was a wanton and inexcusable act; there was no possibility of a mistake; the conditions of visibility were good and the neutral markings were clear. There was no warning given.

On the other hand the Irish approach to the problem of what attitude to adopt to Allied air crews, who were winning the war, was one of realism. De Valera demonstrated that he could bend a little under pressure and this lack of rigidity in the successive adaptations of policy was projected as being no more than common sense. In Hempel's eyes, however, it was evidence of yielding to Allied pressures for a milder application of the rules governing internment to their servicemen and, as such, was construed by him as a breach of neutrality.

De Valera rejected Hempel's protestations that the Irish government's conduct was scarcely neutral: he held that parity of treatment was not possible as returning Germans could bring back significant military information and, in that connection, he instanced German links with the IRA. He refused to accept that German pilots in this area could possibly be classified as non-operational though Hempel and some crews did try on the line that the pilots concerned were on training flights. He made it sound as if neutral Ireland was only in earnest about neutrality when it was directed against the Third Reich. Unlike the halcyon days early in the war when the Nazis bestrode Europe, the tide had turned and there was little the Envoy could do about it.

To emphasise Irish discrimination against them in breach of neutrality Thomsen charged that nine RAF internees had been allowed to escape from the Curragh. Hempel pursued that and referred for guidance a request from the German internee Oberleutnant Moldenhauer that representations be made to the Irish government to free a corresponding number of interned Germans. This tit-for-tat expectation of the German internees went on throughout this period until, after a transfer of RAF internees in November 1943, Hempel reported that only eleven British remained out of the original forty-five interned and that he was looking for an interview with de Valera to complain about this.[12] He had previously protested to Boland at the transfer of a batch of eleven RAF pilots to Gormanston, a base convenient to the border.

While nominally conditions regarding leave and parole were the same for all internees this move could be seen as positively favouring the British, poising them for escape. It made Hempel more determined than ever to oppose 'operational' and 'non-operational' interpretations which he continued to insist was a transparent device to bend neutrality in favour of the Allies.

He was surprised therefore to find that the Irish government had been actively negotiating with the British government to arrange the return of German internees. The British Foreign Office was prepared to negotiate accordingly as, in that case, the remainder of the British pilots would be released. Hempel's supposition was that the Swiss practice was based on releasing two Germans for every three British. He later reported that the British secret service scrubbed any such arrangement.

Discovering this benign Irish intervention did not assuage Hempel. He warned de Valera in no uncertain terms that the operational/non operational categorisation was clearly working in the Allies' favour and constituted a definite infringement of neutrality. De Valera was not easy to pin down and Hempel's difficulty in knowing what to make of him was apparent when he attempted to analyse a speech of 5 October 1943 in which the Taoiseach reasserted in tones reminiscent of 1940 that if they were attacked by one side they would seek aid from the other. This did not indicate any overt change in maintaining the policy of neutrality but all parties were by now keenly aware of Germany's reduced military capabilities. The Taoiseach was really setting his stance for the defensive posture he was to adopt when the situation came to a crisis arising from Gray's persistent pressures.

An air of defeatism can be noted in Hempel at this point, as he observed the incontrovertible weight of Allied power. He diagnosed de Valera's main concern as being for the fate of Ireland after the war should she become embroiled in the conflict against the Allies and should Germany not emerge a clear-cut victor. The unthinkable, a possible defeat for the Third Reich, could now be contemplated and expressed.

In Hempel's opinion de Valera's expectations of help from Germany had diminished if not vanished. De Valera never lost sight of his anti-partition policy and Germany's possible use towards achieving that aim had all but disappeared. A growing irritation with Germany on the part of the Irish government, in contrast with the forebearance shown when the Germans were winning, could be discerned in the telegram expressing their annoyance that Francis Stuart had used the German radio to interfere in Irish elections. They had no objections to Germans discussing Irish affairs but when the opposition party was attacked on German radio it could seem as if the government had sought German assistance against Fine Gael. Whatever use might once have been made of the German card to bring about reunification now obviously no longer obtained. There were no dividends any longer in adopting a conciliatory position.

The landing of two agents in Kilkee in December 1943 after all the talk about Goertz and the others was the last straw. It gave substance and impetus to Gray's exertions to have the diplomatic representatives of the Axis nations removed. Anything that gave the abrasive Gray grounds for accusations aggravated de Valera's embarrassment. It brought the transmitter issue to a head.

Walshe summoned Hempel. The Envoy refuted de Valera's interpretation and his stern demand that the legation transmitter be handed up at once as it *now* undoubtedly constituted a threat to neutrality. The situation had altered dramatically. It was hard for Hempel to believe from the tone of representations that he and Boland had once upon a time chatted affably about the prospect of a joint radio station. Those days were gone, as was the luxury that, according to Hempel, the Irish government had indulged in, of regarding the right to permit — or not to permit — the existence of the transmitter as being symbolically associated with their concept of sovereignty. The invasion of Europe was then in the desperate throes of preparation and Churchill was very anxious lest the Axis mission in Dublin could imperil that momentous undertaking. He was particularly worried that the 'German ambassador' there 'would send a wireless warning of zero though it was the last he was able to send'. Sophisticated interception would be of little avail if the critical operation had started to roll when the warning was flashed. Such was the understandable concern with security at the time that Churchill went to extraordinary lengths to suppress Sir Basil Liddell Hart on the grounds that one of his memoranda revealed the D-Day plans.[13] De Valera appreciated that he would have been prepared to suppress

Hempel too. Nothing was going to stop Churchill now setting Europe really ablaze and destroying Hitler.

Hempel bleated that the loss of the transmitter would ensure their total dependence on their enemies for communications. He had also threatened that they would consider reducing the status of the legation to that of a trade representative as the Irish had done with their office in Berlin, implying that he would be recalled. The concluding remark of the Minister's report on this stage of the transmitter saga related to Walshe's remarks about deciphering problems (presumably British) with messages from the Dublin legation and the Vatican. He did not refer further in his telegram to Monsignor O'Flaherty or to Father Thomas O'Shaughnessy who had been brought to the Irish Brigade headquarters by Jupp Hoven to act as their chaplain for six months from July 1941 (the British did not tell the Irish everything!). The message for Hempel was that the transmitter's days were numbered and his huffing and puffing about retaliation cut no ice with the Irish authorities.

On 25 January 1944 Hempel reported the mounting Allied disquiet over security in Eire. The British remained angry about the landing of the shipwrecked German sailors. They saw them as additional ears, mouthpieces, potential leaks. Anglo-Irish tensions increased and the Irish authorities reacted by kicking the German cat. Walshe was brusque and rude to Hempel, who continued to try to preserve his self-respect by putting this treatment down to Walshe's poor health.[14]

A complaint from Hempel underlined the Irish change of attitude and tone towards the Third Reich. The Envoy reported an attack by Irish soldiers on an internee, Hauptmann Müller. Irish military policemen manhandled Müller with less than kid gloves when he proved to be intractable on returning late to camp after a night's revelry. When the Germans were winning the war he might have got away with it. The senior internee, Hauptmann Mollenhauer, indignantly sent Müller's jacket to Curragh Camp headquarters for cleaning. It was returned uncleaned.

Hempel's greatest fears now were that Allied pressures would lead to breaking off diplomatic relations with Germany, destroy Irish neutrality and end his diplomatic immunity. In

that light he continued recording the cross-talk between Dillon
and de Valera in the Dáil. In language reminiscent of knock-
about comedians the two politicians made treasonable
charges against each other. Dillon accused de Valera of con-
doning the sending of secret radio messages from the German
legation in Northumberland Road. De Valera's retort suggested that Dillon was in the pockets of the Allies, but when
pressed further on the secret set he curtly replied that he had
given all the information on that subject that he proposed to
give.

Less publicly, however, the Taoiseach had already — according to Hempel's version — prevailed on the German Minister
to part with his cherished transmitter and to go through the
charade of depositing it in a Munster and Leinster Bank safe
on 21 December 1943. The set was jointly deposited by
Boland, for the Irish side, and Thomsen, for the German
side, in a box with a security lock for which, as Hempel
reported it, only the German held the key. That box was
then put in a jointly opened steel deed box which was placed
in joint custody in the bank safe. Only four bank directors
operating jointly could open the safe. Hempel, keeping himself covered to the last, sought provision for redress in the
event of the destruction of the transmitter! It was a ceremony that symbolised facets of the unreal facade involved
in the implementation of the policy of neutrality. De Valera
told Hempel that he was extremely sorry that this step was
necessary and Boland told Thomsen that the Irish government would return the set in the event of an emergency,
which Hempel interpreted to mean in the event of an Allied
attack on Ireland. The last paragraph of this report is laced
with realism: he advised against any attempt to try to replace
the set; such action, he said, would be highly dangerous in
the light of an impending Allied invasion of Europe. The
Envoy seemed to be under no illusions by 7 January 1944
as to which way the tide of the war was flowing.

The transmitter figured prominently in the notorious
'American Note' presented on 21 February 1944 by Gray to
the Taoiseach, who, fastened on interpreting as an ultimatum
the demand — 'as an absolute minimum' — of the American
Minister for the removal of Axis representatives in Ireland.

The note referred to the possession of a set by the German Minister and to the radio sets brought in two months previously by the two parachutists. In Joe Walshe's opinion the trouble was directly attributable to 'those damned parachutists'.[15]

Two senior officials in the Canadian Department of External Affairs in Ottawa, Norman Robertson and Hume Wrong, would have preferred an informal approach to exert pressure on Eire and felt that it might have been helpful, from the point of view of saving de Valera's face, if the Note could have included some evidence against the Axis legations. De Valera told the Canadian representative Kearney that Eire would fight invasion from any quarter and — even though the outcome was hopeless — would resist to the last man.

In a previous report on 4 March 1943 on Gray's tactlessness, Hempel had reported that the American Minister had sent a letter to the 'American Irish' Cardinal McRory criticising de Valera's politics, but that the Cardinal had rebuffed Gray and accused him of using British-American cant.

In the short term Gray lost the American Note encounter: in a general election called in May 1944 de Valera gained seventeen seats and an overall majority again for Fianna Fáil. That, and Hempel's reassurance to de Valera that the German authorities would do their best to save Rome, brought a respite for the badgered Envoy, though for the Third Reich the sands were running out. In the longer term, Gray's political purpose — to smear de Valera by portraying him as having 'frolicked' with the Axis representatives — had its effect. The very word 'frolicked' was used by Churchill in his post-war victory speech to describe de Valera's attitude to the Axis diplomatic representatives in Dublin. The controversy surrounding Churchill's outburst and de Valera's celebrated reply to it prompted Maffey to this revealing observation:

To us it is sad indeed that Dev's speech should have got the limelight. However we must be philosophical about it and, since steam has been blown off, perhaps there is something on the plus side of the account. I sympathise very deeply with the Dominion Office. This temperamental country needs quiet treatment and a patient consistent policy. But how are to you to control Ministerial incursions into the china shop? Phrases make history here. Other views are expressed but there are reservations about Churchill's phrase of 'coming to close quarters'.

Up to mid-1944 neither de Valera nor Hempel had any disposition to be frolicsome about inter-govermental matters. After that, there was little left for either of them to frolic about. The nearest thing to sportiveness in the relationship was de Valera's attempt at a thin watery jest about the capability of the German high command to do its own contingency planning for landing weapons, if required, when he was fobbing off the German Minister's offer of arms assistance. For the greater portion of the war Hempel was frequently on the defensive. The atmosphere in inter-governmental relations was strained more often than not. The Envoy was frequently explaining German gaffes, transgressions and violations of neutrality to an increasingly exasperated and harassed Irish government.

The sequestering of the legation's set did not plug all the possible leaks or solve all the inter-governmental problems. All operations, great and small, require the passage of messages up and down the line: the message generally finds a way. However, some circumstances surrounding the passing of messages in Emergency Ireland remained clouded, and once more it is around Goertz that a fog generates.

Enno Stephan's version, that Goertz found a bribable army sergeant named Power in Athlone to pass out messages, only reveals the extent to which Irish army intelligence had duped Goertz. Goertz's cell-mate van Loon remained angrily adamant that Goertz was not duped; that the messages one way or another did get out, and he instanced a secretly coded advertisement in the *Irish Times* to prove it. According to Bridie and Mary Farrell the letters smuggled out of Athlone were delivered in Dublin to a Miss Cantwell who saw to their onward delivery either to Northern Ireland or to the German legation where Goertz's coded messages were transmitted to Germany. Confidential sources closer to the action smile indulgently at this and hold that Goertz's messages never got beyond an army officer's flat in Leeson Street, Dublin, after the involvement with Sergeant Power was heavily acted out. Van Loon's opinion of this scenario is that it is 'balderdash'.

Much earlier Walshe had been highly indignant when Hempel had asked him to convey news of Goertz's promotion to the agent. Walshe took that request as adding insult to injury and the message was not passed on at that time. Later on however, whether because they relented or were bereft of other ideas, those playing games with Goertz incorporated the news of his promotion in a message which overwhelmed the emotional Abwehr agent.

Dr Richard Hayes, director of the National Library, a gifted cryptoanalyst co-opted to Irish intelligence for the duration, had (*pace* Mr van Loon) broken the Goertz code and intercepted the agent's outgoing messages. He never comprehensively broke Hempel's codes. But the British did, and they lost no opportunity in putting the information to work to make trouble for de Valera and to denigrate the effectiveness of his neutrality.

Hayes' work in cracking the Goertz code gave rise to a series of revealing incidents: the question arose as to who was duping whom. It was not until a year after the code was broken that Bryan, the Director of Intelligence, was acquainted of the fact! When he remonstrated with Hayes over this tardiness he was given to understand that Butler, his own second-in-command, had put a brake on transmitting this information to him, cautioning that Bryan would only run hot-foot to the British with it. They were two good loyal officers with rather different ways of looking at things.

Colonel Eamonn de Buitléar (Butler) was an ardent Irish speaker and he had gone to Berlin pre-war to perfect his German. In a business where MI5 and SOE loathed MI6; where the competing Abwehr agencies came to regard each other as the enemy; where the Office of Strategic Services (OSS), later to become the Central Intelligence Agency (CIA), was riddled with hatreds, it is not surprising to come across incompatibilities in the Irish intelligence services. Clashes arose from time to time as officers vied to excel each other in professionalism and patriotism. There was also an element of dog-eat-dog for promotion.

Colonel Bryan regarded dyed-in-the-wood Gaelic Leaguers like Butler as being anti-British to the point of irrationality. He had fought against the British in the War of Independence (1919-21) so there was no need for him to either prove or to parade his patriotism. He also clashed with Butler on methodology. He gave him confidential work to do and Butler's way of tackling tasks would not have been his way; he felt that his subordinate was unable to keep more than one ball in the air at a time.

Butler for his part regarded Bryan as being far too pro-British. Bryan labelled Butler as anti-British but was rightly convinced that this was not the same thing as being pro-German. He brushed aside initially the moot point that Butler might have exercised official surveillance, without his authority, over Goertz. He refused to consider that it would have been bad intelligence work not to have shadowed Goertz and known about his movements. His reticence reflected the government's sensitivities to the accusations and abuse they had endured from the Allies over Goertz and his associates.

It would never have occurred to Bryan that he would be classed as pro-British simply because it was his job to get on with his British counterpart: that was Government policy. Affectations of any kind were foreign to him. He realised how much the British and Irish people had in common, historically and materially. He had a massive contempt for intellectuals and what he called 'theorisers'. He had no patience with flights of fancy. He was devastating about the IRA plans which projected German troop concentrations in impossible places. 'They weren't even IRA plans', he snorted, referring to Plan 'Kathleen': 'they were got up by an ex-teacher or an ex-Customs and Excise man. They planned to bring German warships where you couldn't bring a row-boat!'

There was, however, one element of danger in Bryan's no-nonsense approach, crucial as that approach was to steadying government thinking at the time and stopping panic measures. It arose from his previous successes. His intelligence work had aborted the army mutiny in 1924; he had been instrumental in defusing an incipient army revolt when Fianna Fáil came to power in 1931. These events conditioned him to believe that such activities were only all talk! While he acknowledged that 98 per cent of the Irish people were opposed initially to the 1916 Rebellion he would not entertain the idea that the Northern Ireland controlled IRA of the day and their German agents had the capacity to gather massive public support in the way of Sinn Féin after 1916. He regarded the Northern Ireland crowd as a bad bunch unworthy to identify with the freedom fighters of the old IRA. He admitted that an ever present danger lay in what the British would make of IRA activities and how they would react to them in times of tension and national danger. He had good reason, from his experience of the war against the Black-and-Tans, to know that the British could be tough and terrible. He kept them quiet by promptly passing on information to them as he had been half-detailed to do. As Butler predicted he instantly passed on the breaking of the Goertz code: he did not get much in return. Butler had another grievance, that Hayes got the credit for cracking the Goertz code which should, in his opinion, have gone to him. He could not blame Bryan for that.

There is no such thing as one hundred per cent security. The Allies had their own ways and means of finding out what they wanted to know. Bryan subsequently made no bones as to where his sympathies lay as between Allies and the Nazis. Notwithstanding this liaison, which had the sly concurrence of Irish officialdom, Nigel West wrote, 'The one European capital to remain completely closed to all British intelligence services throughout the war was Dublin.'[16]

For sound security reasons the British did not reciprocate the co-operation they received from the Irish. With ULTRA they decoded most German messages: only Czech codes and higgledy-piggledy Russian codes defied them. Hayes helped them break a troublesome German code during the Ardennes Offensive in 1944 and they were grateful but that's as far as it went.[17] When codes in canisters jettisoned from a German submarine were washed up on the Cork coast in 1944 they were decoded by Hayes, translated by Gageby and picked up post-haste by Ed Lalor of the OSS who flew in specially from France to collect them for American intelligence. Such consideration obviously could not be extended to the Germans. Was it neutral behaviour?

An awareness of prevailing attitudes was one of the reasons Hempel panicked so much when he heard that Goertz was planning to escape from Athlone. He knew that if the legation were caught putting a foot wrong in 1944 they would be instantly expelled and possibly interned. Goertz claimed to have a transmitter ('Ulrike') in the North of Ireland and Hempel realised that if the agent got his hands on that it would make nonsense of the sequestration of the legation set. Knowing the dangers such actions could still have for Irish neutrality he did his best to dissuade Goertz from his folly.

He had taken great pains (unsuccessfully) to avoid publicity about the Goertz affair, from the time of the agent's association with Held to his capture. He had repeatedly warned of the danger of the man falling into British hands. He had voiced his suspicions of the involvement of the British secret service especially in the matters linking Goertz with the Hayes confession. Now, even in internment, the troublesome agent contrived to keep the Envoy on tenterhooks.

Goertz no longer received the special treatment he got when he was interned initially in Arbour Hill, where it was alleged he occasionally got strawberries and cream from General MacNeill's wife, who lived next door in army married quarters. He was transferred to Athlone: he had become a nuisance to all but the most incurable nationalist romantics. The matrons of the movement still loved him. Hempel regarded him as a menace and dissociated himself from him where possible. He solicited von Grote in Berlin to persuade headquarters to direct that the legation should not become involved.

They had other things to do. The Allies were about to achieve decisive success in Normandy with the American break-out and the slaughter of Germans in the Falaise Gap. Hempel pressed the point and von Grote put in a word with Hitler. He got a very dusty answer: Hempel was the man on the spot; only he could properly evaluate the situation. That reply did not suit Hempel: he was happier being told what to do.

Through intermediaries, Goertz kept pressing him for £400 to assist his escape, and he could not make up his mind as to how he should respond. Once more he referred the matter to headquarters. He sent another telegram on the dangerous political complications and consequences of dragging the legation into the affair. Goertz, he said, was labouring under a misconception and the prospects of effecting a successful escape were practically nil. On 11 September 1944 von Grote again lent the Envoy his support. This time, on 18 September the *Reichsführer Reichsicherheitshauptant, Militärisches Amt* rebuffed him squarely. Hempel would have to make up his own mind; they were not going to take his decisions for him. With the war going so disastrously it is amazing that they found time to reply at all to what seemed to them to be Hempel's dithering.

In fairness to the Envoy, they did not take into account the difficulties he had to contend with. If Goertz had got access to a secret transmitter in Northern Ireland the fat would have been in the fire as far as he was concerned. Any suspicion of Hempel's involvement would have incurred de Valera's wrath and brought a final irresistible demand for his expulsion from the Allies. Conscious of this climate, the German Minister refused to entertain a plea from Weber-Drohl for release on medical grounds: he would not even recommend a visit from Drohl's son in London. He was painfully aware of the dangers the agents had posed and was content to see them all interned out of harm's way while the war ground on to its now predictable close.

The last German fling to try to reach Antwerp from the snow-filled Ardennes through the Meuse river in Belgium foundered in December 1944 in what became known as the Battle of the Bulge. It was more obvious than ever to the German Minister that there was nothing that inept agents could do outside except cause troubles and compromise him. Passing vital information on his own terms was a different matter.

The plan for the Battle of the Bulge was said to have originated with Hitler. The set-back now sent him scurrying back to Berlin in mid-January 1945 and almost immediately he opted for the troglodyte existence in the Bunker until the time came for him to carry out, for the record, his rehearsed suicide.

Hempel's reluctance to respond to the request to aid Goertz stemmed in part also from the increasing irrationality and arbitrariness with which the affairs of the Nazi state were now run. He was mortified to still receive communications under the heading '*Unternehmen Mainau*'. This was the Abwehr operation which linked the legation with Goertz and by extension to Veesenmayer, Andrews and MacNeill. The Allies would have had no patience now with this sort of indiscretion.

They had had to learn the hard way that the war was losable, especially in the Atlantic. The Geman U-Boat campaign failed by only a very narrow margin. If Hitler had not been so slow to accept the need for a large U-Boat building programme; if the British convoy and anti-submarine tactics had failed; or if the Americans had failed to reach their ship-building targets, the Allies could have lost the war. That stark fact put an edge on political debate about the rights and wrongs of neutrality. The Allies had to give top priority to anti-submarine warfare. If they had not got a Derry base, they would have had to get one. The prime need was to halt the loss to tonnage on the Atlantic approaches. Otherwise no offensive anywhere could succeed. More than half a million tons of Allied shipping was sunk in the first twenty days of March 1943. If remedial action was not successful defeat then had stared them in the face.

Technological advances and ULTRA code-breaking successes signalled the turn of the tide. Still, despite British possession of ULTRA, the Germans were able to pull off a *coup* like the 'Battle of the Bulge'. The Allies had all the elements of information pointing to the imminence of the attack. They failed to add it up properly. The German soldier proved again what a tough well-trained professional he was: the German general staff demonstrated once more their moral cowardice and strategic myopia. Patton reckoned that the further the Germans advanced, the more of them they could kill. He was right; but the Allies remained shocked by the turn of events. Any antics from Goertz in distant Athlone would have got short shrift and would have had reverberations for Hempel.

For him the cognotional scenario of the war was depressing and there was no one, either at home or abroad to whom he could turn for comfort. It was in such adversity that Hempel showed his best side and his behaviour merited de

Valera's favourable consideration. German addiction to day-to-day bureaucracy proved to be an antidote to disaster.

No matter how badly the war was going for Germany Hempel saw to it that Bruckmans, the member of his staff who looked after accounts, kept the books right: every penny was accounted for. But meticulous book-keeping did not prevent money from becoming very tight at the legation and Hempel and his staff found themselves in increasingly straitened circumstances. The Irish government helped out with an odd advance. Maffey reported that the German legation was hard up for funds. On 4 February 1944, the *Daily Sketch* reported that 'fat glib Eduard Hempel was flat broke!' and that he crawled to the Italian Minister for a loan and was refused: that Thomsen's wild parties would have to come to an end and that Petersen had married an Irish girl. Of Hempel's efforts to collect debts Maffey commented that any payment of this kind would 'infallibly' bring the name of the firm in question on a blacklist. The *Daily Express* on 10 March 1944 related with relish that Hempel had failed to get the cash when he sued in the Dublin District Court for money alleged to be owing by Irish firms to German firms. He also failed to shelve financial responsibility for the 162 sailors rescued from the Bay of Biscay battle early in the war and interned at the Curragh.[18] No one wanted these unfortunate sailors and the unkind thought was expressed that the master of the *Kerlogue* should have minded his own business and let them drown.

The financial situation got more and more dire for Hempel, as if he did not have enough problems. Counsel representing the Irish firms pleaded that the legation could not act as a debt collecting agency for its nationals and that it had no legal powers to sue them in the courts because, he contended, that would be a negation of diplomatic usage; that the legation was a building and a building could not sue; that the power of attorney only gave the right to demand payment of debts. On 1 February 1944, the *Daily Telegraph* had reported that the legation was sending back to Germany for amendment of the power-of-attorney by which debts contracted by Eire firms to German companies before the war might be collected in order to provide payment for German agents in Eire! In the end there was only one place they could turn to for money. The Taoiseach arranged for the Irish government to give them a loan. The normally frugal de Valera was moved to sympathy by their plight. That did not mean that his chariness about their capability to make mischief, even at the eleventh hour, had been dissolved.

Events proved how right he was to remain wary. They confirmed as well that British apprehensions about the legation as a channel for sending secret messages prejudicial to their security were not unfounded. Hempel knew that the Third Reich had lost its gambles but fierce battles were still raging and more were still to be fought: the war was not over yet for Germany. Some Germans, even after the reverses in Normandy, still nourished notions of salvation from a *deus ex machina* intervention. They were closer to it than they realised with their progress towards atomic weapons and in particular in their possession of nerve gas. They did not use nerve gas to repel the Normandy invasion in the mistaken belief that the Allies had a corresponding nerve-gas capability.[19] Similarly, German development of rocket bombs was not to be lightly dismissed. Churchill was undeniably right in asserting that it was in shipping and in the power to transport across the Atlantic Ocean in particular, that the crunch of the whole war was to be found. Yet the German capacity to produce a secret weapon to turn the tables remained a serious threat. A week after D-Day, V-1 guided missiles started to fall on England. Paris was liberated on 25 August but on the 8 September the Germans retaliated with a V-2 rocket attack on Britain.

The V-2s were more unpredictable and nerve-wracking than the V-1s. It is doubtful if the target acquisition data which Hempel had been instrumental in collecting and supplying would have been a decisive factor in the launching of these buzz-bombs and rockets. They were inherently inaccurate and erratic; fall of shot was haphazard and the zone of dispersion random. They had a devastating effect on civilian morale. The climate in Britain was right for finding a scapegoat and a finger could always be pointed at Hempel to make a whipping boy of de Valera.

If the following sensational claim is correct they had enough material to do so. Hempel usually behaved correctly but 'when the chips were down' de Valera, diplomatic discretion, and neutrality considerations alike were all set aside by him.

During the summer of 1944 a cousin of Hempel's friend Dr Gogan came home on holidays from England where he had been working in the aircraft factory. His name was Russell: he had been a Royal Flying Corps pilot in the First World War and later officer commanding of the Irish Army Air Corps. He told Gogan of preparations in England for an airborne landing in Holland. Gogan immediately rushed Russell out to Hempel's house, where, he said, the Envoy interviewed the cross-channel worker at great length and reported accordingly. By what means Hempel reported, Gogan did not say. The absence of the transmitter, it seems, did not prevent the messages getting out. Gogan was convinced that the information supplied was responsible for the repulse by the Germans on 17 September 1944 of the Allied attempt at an airborne landing at Arnhem: Operation 'Market Garden'. The 2nd SS Panzar Corps were in fact in position in the Arnhem area, not limping and badly mauled as Montgomery had anticipated, but poised in a high state of combat readiness. They did not just happen to be there for refitting.

There are loose ends left in trying to assert authoritively that Hempel's information was an essential element in the German success at Arnhem. Frau Hempel seemed to be pleased to imagine that such could have been the case and that her husband could have been an instrumental warrior in bringing about such an historical Allied reverse. She remembered the visit well, recalling that Russell had only one eye.

The incident proved that if the stakes were high enough Hempel could be daring enough. If 'Sealion' and *'Grün'* had materialised he might not have disappointed Veesenmayer after all. It gave some substance to Gray's arraignments and to Churchill's fears that the security of the Normandy landings could have been imperilled by a last minute leak from Dublin. Messages *could* get through. Dieppe in 1942 and Arnhem in 1944 are sombre indicators of the possibilities.

If Gray had come to know of these messages there would have been no holding him. Although Gray's intelligence gathering was faulty, merely keeping an ear to the ground would not have detected such leaks. The requirement was for underground information. Irish intelligence never knew about them, not to mind Gray, who continued to remain out of touch with simple everyday affairs and moved principally in *haut bourgeois* circles.

As the war drew to a close, Ribbentrop was out to save his own skin. He was aware that the Vatican was apprehensive about the political consequences of the Soviet armies irresistibly advancing towards the Elbe. He tried to capitalise on this by priming the German ambassador to the Vatican, Ernst von Weizächer, in February 1945 to probe for a separate peace with the Western Powers with the inducement of leaving Germany free to fight the Bolsheviks. It was Ribbentrop's last forlorn bid to pull the chestnuts out of the fire. His themes were: that National Socialism was the only real capitalist antidote to Communism, a line which could have struck a sympathetic chord in certain anti-British circles in Ireland; that the Jewish problem was soluble and was anyway an internal German matter; that the Nazis need not necessarily be in control in post-war Germany; that this was the only way to avoid World War III. Fritz Hesses was given the mission of making soundings in Stockholm. Friedrich Möllhausen was despatched to Madrid. There were secret encounters with Roosevelt's emissary, Robert Murphy. Hempel was alerted in Dublin. On 24 March 1945 the *Daily Telegraph* reported that de Valera had relayed peace feelers on the above lines to the American Minister. Gray hotly repudiated this. In any event the Casablanca and Yalta conferences had made abundantly clear that the only response now acceptable to the Allies from the Third Reich was unconditional surrender. Neutrals such as Turkey were reassessing their positions accordingly.

De Valera, for Eire's part, was determined not to be seen to jump on the bandwagon. But that did not mean that he was going to disoblige the Allies to prove the simon purity of his theoretical neutrality. As the following story illustrates, he knew when to adapt.

A large quantity of meat for the Allies Expeditionary Force France came from the Roscrea Meat Factory. This factory had been set up by Sean Lemass and a Herr Fäsenfeld. An Allied intelligence officer somehow or other found out that it was a German in Ireland who was supplying meat to the Allied forces. A pinch of noxious powder in each tin, some superior officer divined, could cause havoc during a campaign. Representations were made to de Valera: the German would have to go.[20] Lemass explained to Fäsenfeld that there would have to be at least a paper hand over! There was no hold up. The German went: the Allies got their meat.

In the RAF use of the Donegal corridor was a more serious affair. Here a breach in the letter of neutrality had to be condoned but not until after RAF planes had been fired on. German planes on the other hand were fired on as they presented themselves. Even Lewis guns on ack-ack mountings in outposts had a go. De Valera had to consider the courses of action open to him when the Allies were not disposed to take 'No' for an answer over the Donegal corridor. Possession of the air space was nine points of the law. Eire had no means of interception and forcing down. The Allies were winning. He took the only practical course open to him and acceded to Allied requests to use the corridor.

When German defeat became a certainty, Don Quixote-like, Gray rode out again. Without any ado he peremptorily demanded physical possession of the archives in the German legation. Maffey, the British representative, did not think that was such a good idea as he felt that Hempel would have taken the necessary action to nullify any steps of this kind, and that the Eire government could hardly be expected to be genuinely helpful in this regard. De Valera would not hear of such a proposal. Anthony Eden, while he too wanted to seize the archives, did not think much of Gray's demand either, as he shared Maffey's opinion that the Eire government would almost certainly warn the legation of what was in the wind and that they would no doubt inform Berlin who would issue a warning. Eden's inclination was to take the matter up with Washington to work out a joint plan. But in an 'Action this Day' memo Churchill snapped his entire disagreement with Maffey. He said that he was very glad that the US should send such an instruction to which they should conform. De Valera was to be left in no doubt as to how little support he could get from the US while he persisted in keeping the Axis representatives.

The sequestration of German archives generally spread to have international ramifications but Gray's pursuit of the Dublin ones did not abate. Walshe had informed him that the Eire government might at any moment instruct its representative Cremins to cross over into Switzerland. The American Minister suggested that the taking of such a step would provide a convenient opportunity to move against the German archives in Dublin.

In spite of Churchill's rocket Maffey still did not feel that this step would yield much though he fully endorsed emphasising objections to the presence in Dublin of the Axis missions. He was concerned that the US State Department was acting unilaterally in the matter and that it was in American interests that the US and the UK did not appear to be at loggerheads on an Irish question.

When Cremins did quit Berlin, Gray was authorised to proceed as he decided, involving the Canadians in his *demarche*. The Canadian representative, however, was instructed not to associate himself with any action which might follow from the US approach. General Eisenhower contributed to defusing the issue by disclaiming any responsibility for archives.

The arena was left to de Valera and Gray, with Maffey in reluctant support of the latter. The British representative minuted one interview in this connection: 'De Valera grew very red and looked very sour. This is a matter for my legal advisers, he said, it is not a matter I can discuss with you now.' Walshe pointed out the difficulty of handing over before a final declaration of the end of the war.

The VE Day announcement solved the predicament and made it possible for the keys of the legation to be handed over to the Allies. Nothing of importance was disclosed from the search of the archives. The Foreign Office concentrated on unearthing political rather than military information. The US disclosure revealed apparently only one or two papers of minor importance in relation to local personalities. Hempel had effectively carried out his shredding and incinerating instructions.

From the end of 1944 there seems to be no record on

Hempel's side of the *denouement* of diplomatic relations between Eire and the Reich although Frau Hempel said that he
carried on as usual and continued to send messages right up
to the end. The fact that the Envoy was an indefatigable
document burner does not explain the absence of the type of
telegraphic records which are otherwise available up to that
time. There is a phantom element here somewhere. Hempel
remained addicted to protocol for its own sake and meticulously adhered to complying with the external requirements
of his office.

In this rigid adherence to the protocol of externals the
German Minister Plenipotentiary and Envoy Extraordinary
was well matched — it not outmatched — by the Taoiseach
and Minister for External Affairs. De Valera's literal interpretation of protocol requirements is illustrated by his controversial call on Hempel to express sympathy on the death
of Hitler. This was to be the final act in the neutrality drama.
Consideration for Britain did not come into it. The play was
the thing. De Valera mentioned that he did it out of consideration for Hempel and because it was the right thing to do.

Hitler died on 30 April 1945 and, after his death was
announced, de Valera accompanied by Joseph P Walshe, the
Secretary to the Department of External Affairs, paid a
formal call of condolence on the German Minister on 3 May
1945. This action brought a cry of outrage from the
Allied press. A letter to *The Times* called de Valera the
'Casiabianca of the Protocol' and 'a totalitarian termite'. It
annoyed Frank McDermot so much that he was still referring
to it over twenty-five years later in a letter to his daughter
Patricia:

De Valera's call on the German ambassador was in accordance with strict protocol and did not shock majority opinion
in Ireland, which had been trained by the fantastically
strict Irish censorship to grant no moral superiority to the
anti-Hitler cause. The German envoy was, besides, a great
favourite of Dev's because he had fought against any
German infringement of Irish neutrality.

The envoy in question was named Hempel and he was
mildly pro-Nazi. His wife was extravagantly so. I met them

only once, dining with a leading Dublin surgeon called Meade. Chatting after the ladies had retired upstairs, he remarked that the Irish decision (taken a day or two before) to pay a salary to the leader of the Opposition was very illogical. I said 'Yes, I was the only Senator to oppose it in debate, but all the same I would rather give him a salary than send him to a concentration camp'. A deathly silence ensued.

On 30 April he returned to the theme, obviously in response to a query:

No, the German envoy made no excuse and shut up instantly. I don't think de Valera had charm but he was that rarity in politics — a man of principle. He also had what it takes to be a leader despite his great defects as an orator. All in all I thought more highly of him than of Cosgrave or Costello. Fundamentally he bores me and I never go to see him.

De Valera remained unrepentant. At the time he justified his actions: his point of view was that so long as Eire retained diplomatic relations with Germany to have failed to call upon the German representative would have been an act of unpardonable discourtesy to the German nation and to the Envoy himself. He did not intend to add to the German Minister's 'humiliation in his hour of defeat': ironically that seemed to have been just what he did do.

He held that during the whole of the war Hempel's conduct was 'irreproachable and that he was always friendly and invariably correct — in marked contrast with Gray'. He felt that it was important that it should never be inferred that these formal acts imply the passing of any judgments, good or bad, on the Third Reich. He was quite sure that he had acted correctly and wisely. One contrary opinion was that for political purposes he was acting out his own idiosyncracies, his obsession with weaving complex geometrical political patterns and bending protocol to fit them. The more cynical muttered that the protocol was a pay-off for Hempel's accommodations which managed to put a face on his unprincipled pragmatic neutrality policy of a certain consideration for Britain. Others felt that it was his way of getting even with Gray, particularly in view of the recent tussle over the legation archives.

In any case the grand gesture fell flat. The condolers found Hempel in a distressed and inconsolable state. He kept wringing his hands and crying repetitively, 'It's all so humiliating; it's all so humiliating.' It is not clear whether he was referring to Germany having lost the war or to the implications of the visit. The visitors were disappointed in him. They had perhaps expected a more stoic, heroic composure: but his repeated use of the word 'humiliating' upset them. They tried to excuse the unhappy choice of word by allowing for the fact that Hempel was a foreigner, but had to remind themselves that the Envoy's English was very good. The dramatisation of the visit seemed to have been lost initially on the German Minister. The deputation came away, if not deflated, a little disappointed in Hempel.

It took Frau Hempel to put the record straight as to the location of the visit. The Taoiseach had visited Hempel's home rather than the legation: some subsequently saw a typical deviousness in his choice of venue, as if it made it less official. She vehemently refuted that version of the visit, saying that as she was present all the time so she ought to know. She denied that there was any wringing of hands on the part of the Envoy. She explained that he had a slight eczema between his fingers: a scratching of that might have accounted for the fidgetiness. The only humiliation they felt, was that Hitler did not die fighting in the streets instead of sordidly committing suicide. (Ribbentrop was holed up in his mistress's apartment in Hamburg.) She repeated that the visit never took on the tone referred to. She never saw her husband wringing his hands and in the course of the visit the conversation soon turned to matters other than the death of Hitler: de Valera solicitously enquired after the safety and well being of the members of their family still in Germany. They had expected that Mr de Valera would visit them and were also aware that he would be letting himself in for trouble by doing so. Her husband, she said, had seen defeat coming for a long time: it came as no surprise to him.

A week later Hempel visited de Valera to hand over his

legation: the war was over. The Third Reich was in ruins; there were no more messages to send and no one to send them to. According to one source, some members of the German colony (not the Hempels) relieved the legation of portable items like typewriters and duplicators before the close down. Frau Hempel discounted this and questioned the credibility of the source: what actually happened, she said, was that some Germans had left items there for safe-keeping and simply collected their own belongings. The contents of the legation later realised £1,760 at a sale in Belfast. A copy of *Mein Kampf* fetched a guinea while a copy of Goering's *Knights of the Air* went for ten shillings. On 10 May 1945 the key of the legation was handed over to Gray as the representative of the American Occupation Force in Germany — plenipotentiary of the new authority.

De Valera's attitude to the displaced German diplomat continued to be charitable and understanding. He granted asylum to him and his family. Frau Hempel rose magnificantly to the occasion and became the breadwinner. That is another story; a nice one. The Hempels were grateful for de Valera's consideration and helping hand. He was indeed a friend in need. Hempel's personal efforts to set up in business, according to Frau Hempel, were frustrated by British influences. Later, however, it was Maffey's intervention which smoothed the path for the ex-Envoy's eventual return to Germany for rehabilitation.

TEN

Epilogue

By August 1945 practically all the German belligerent interness, including the 164 sailors landed from the *Kerlogue* and airmen who had been shot down by pursuing Spitfires or had crash-landed, were returned to Germany. The agents/spies were not repatriated at this point, though the Allies were anxious to get their hands on them for interrogation.

In day-to-day dealings, resentment at Churchill's victory speech lingered on. Sections of Irish officialdom were in no hurry to facilitate the Allies. Suddenly and contrarily the Department of Justice, off its own anti-British bat, and without consulting the Department of External Affairs, announced on 10 September 1946, that they were granting the spies asylum. Gaertner, van Loon, Preetz, Simon, Weber-Drohl, Held and Goertz were released. They went their various ways. Schutz and van Loon married Irish girls and eventually became domiciled successful businessmen. Goertz got a small job as secretary of the 'Save the German Children Fund'. He made a mission of it.

This nose-thumbing gesture by the Department of Justice embarrassed External Affairs and annoyed the Allies. In April 1947, when the trials of war criminals began, demands for the extradition of the agents became more insistent. By that time de Valera had become more openly accommodating. He reversed the Department of Justice decision to grant asylum.

In this connection Goertz enters once more and, like the ghost of Banquo, continued to impinge on de Valera and to haunt Hempel. Goertz turned out to be a kind of Nemesis who, from the moment of his arrival in May 1940, had cast a shadow over the Third Reich's official representative. The events immediately leading up to the dramatic death of the Abwehr agent have been construed (misconstrued, contended Frau Hempel) to diminish the ex-Minister. That is not to say that he behaved less than correctly. Nor is it to imply pejoratively that he had been no more than 'the fixed person for a fixed job'; one of the technicians of diplomacy. The former diplomat did the best he could and retained some sympathy for Goertz in his conflict of loyalties.

Goertz had remained obsessively apprehensive at the thought of falling into either British or Russian hands. One was as bad as the other as far as he was concerned. It was a great relief to him when Gerald Boland, the Justice Minister, the man with a good record in the War of Independence, cocked a snook at the British, to the dismay of the Irish diplomats, and offered the spies asylum. He seized the opportunity to throw himself heart and soul into his crusade of saving German children. And now de Valera, it seemed, was going to renege on Boland's magnanimous gesture and yield to Allied pressures. They were to be rounded up and reinterned prior to deportation to undergo interrogation. No one could convince Goertz that the interrogation in question — helping the Allies with their enquiries — was not a euphemism for more dramatic treatment. He had had experience of British jails when he was imprisoned before the war for spying in Britain. As a German he was well aware that there were ways of making one talk.

From Mountjoy Jail he wrote direct to de Valera begging for asylum. He recalled the assurances that he had been given by the Department of Justice officials. They had told him that they knew what would be in store for him if he fell into Allied hands and that they regarded it as a matter of humanity and honour to grant him asylum. All Goertz now got from de Valera's officials by way of a reply was double-talk. A member of the External Affairs staff told him that his request to the Taoiseach was under consideration and that they would communicate with him on the matter in due course. Off the record, reassurance was whispered. He was told not to worry; unofficially, saying nothing, mind you, the official could tell him that he would not be deported. Goertz panicked at what he sensed.

He turned to Hempel for assistance in his predicament. De Valera's *volte face* had bemused him. The ex-Envoy dutifully intervened with his old friend Freddie Boland and with de Valera himself. Assurances were forthcoming that Goertz had nothing in the world to fear in returning to Germany into the arms of the friendly understanding Allies. Hempel and Boland visited him in Mountjoy. Their assurances only served to drive Goertz wild. He would not be pacified with any blandishments. He scented treachery.

Later he was released on parole. The first thing he did was to ring up ex-internee, Luftwaffe man, George Fleischmann who, with a little help from his friends, Dan Breen included, had managed to stay on in Ireland, when other internees were being shipped out. Goertz asked the ex-pilot what he could make of the situation. What did he think was going on, as he, a prisoner on parole, had been invited to dinner with the Hempels in Dun Laoghaire; Boland was also to be a guest. Fleischmann told him that, whatever it was, it could not be bad; that the best thing to do was to accept Hempel's invitation to dinner, see how things turned out and afterwards they would meet in the Royal Marine Hotel to discuss the position.

It was four o'clock in the morning when a very agitated Goertz met up again with the waiting Fleischmann who could not calm him. It seemed that the proposition put to him by Boland, with Hempel's backing, was to consider an offer from the Americans to work for them. It could not be termed an offer, Frau Hempel corrected. It had, in her opinion, at that stage only the status of a hypothesis; it was more a case of a possibility than a firm offer. Such fine distinctions were beyond the comprehension of an addled Goertz.

He had not taken the changed alignments in the Cold War situation into account and the prospect of working for his former enemies appalled him. He said that he would never change sides. Fleischmann advised him pragmatically: the Americans would look after his wife and son in Hamburg; he should play along for a while and then, if he found it too distasteful, he could take evasive action. Goertz was not convinced but agreed to think it over. They walked through the night tossing and turning the problem posed at Hempel's table.

Boland, according to what Fleischmann said that Goertz had related to him, had given the agent, in Hempel's hearing, until the following Saturday to make up his mind whether to accept the American offer or not and allegedly told him not to bother about his parole which was due to expire that same Saturday. Boland was alleged to have said that all that would be taken care of. According to Frau Hempel, Goertz then went off to the West of Ireland for the rest of the week to calm his nerves a bit. He had been invited again to lunch at Hempel's on the day that he was due to report to the Aliens Office. They waited and waited in vain: their unhappy guest was never to turn up. He had swallowed the contents of his phial of potassium cyanide under the noses of accompanying detectives in the Aliens Registration Office in Dublin Castle.

When he had duly gone along to the Aliens Office for an extension of his parole, a Special Branch man had met him and told him that a Dakota plane was waiting to fly him back to Germany. Another version is that he was told that he was being taken back to Mountjoy Prison. In Fleischmann's opinion, the hyper-sensitive Goertz felt that he had been betrayed, tricked, trapped and badly let down by de Valera, Hempel, and Boland. The latter pair in particular failed to get through and persuade him to consider throwing in his lot with the Americans.

Fleischmann had gone a good part of the way to repair these deficiencies and to reassure him. The trouble in the end was that there seemed to have been a slip up between the Department of External Affairs and the Department of Justice, which stopped putting into effect the undertaking given by Boland and Hempel. Incidentally, there was a feeling on the part of army intelligence that they would have handled the business better if they had been involved. For some reason, and they knew more about Goertz than anyone else, they were kept out of it. They would have asked him if there was anything else against him apart from his pre-war imprisonment in England. If the answer was in the negative they would have appealed to his sense of duty and patriotism — that the mission would not so much be working for the Americans as serving his country against the Russians in the only way possible in the circumstances.

Boland, the man who had done so much for Irish-German relations, was very upset at Goertz's suicide, though he could not be held responsible. Nor can Hempel be blamed: the fates had taken a hand in the game. A military funeral was sought. But the nearest Goertz got to having one was being buried in Fleischmann's old Luftwaffe greatcoat. Unaware of bureaucratic bungling, the Misses Farrell in Dun Laoghaire, with whom 'the Doctor' used to stay, bitterly blamed Hempel and de Valera for his death.

Following protocol to the last, the ex-Envoy sounded out the Irish government to see if approval would be forthcoming for his attendance at Goertz's funeral. The response was negative. Judge Wyse Power phoned informally to tip off the ex-Envoy not to go. He had intended going and was all dressed up to go. The judge did not reveal for whom he was speaking but he impressed on Hempel that it would be less than politic for him to attend. De Valera's hand was seen in the matter: he had a long memory and he still had his considerations for Britain to think about. So the ex-Minister duly stayed away. His non-attendance at the funeral did not enhance his reputation in Ireland, a country where funerals are special, and a feeling persisted in Goertz circles that he had been less than magnanimous or helpful (some went so far as to imply that he had been deceitful) in his treatment of the Third Reich's popular agent.

Goertz's coffin was draped in a swastika (should have been the black, white and red flag, complained Frau Hempel). The Farrell sisters wore Goertz's decorations and remained hostile towards Hempel. This was less than fair to the ex-diplomat: he was a far more humane man than they gave him credit for. It was impossible to counsel Goertz when the full realisation dawned on him that, unbelievably, de Valera had actually decided to hand him over to the Allies.

His subsequent re-interment from Dean's Grange to the German war graves cemetery in Glencree was carried out melodramatically under cover of darkness by Herr Achilles and some companions. The war still went on in the minds of some partisans — Irish as well as German.

It is easy to blame Hempel for being receptive to de Valera's relayed wishes about the funeral. But the ex-Minister was in a vulnerable position and de Valera never went out of his way to help those who had crossed him in any way. Very little official Irish help was forthcoming to Francis Stuart, for example, when he was receiving rough treatment from the French: his passport was not renewed. On the other hand, Thomsen, Hempel's second-in-command, was allowed to stay on in Ireland after 1945 in spite of his Nazi taint.

Thomsen never lived down the name he had got of having been the chief Nazi. His post-war railing against the defeated Nazis infuriated those who insisted that he had been the biggest Nazi of the lot. He would refute this. He pointed out that it was only after being cleared by a special Bundestag Committee that he was recalled for service by the Foreign Office.

Not alone was he recalled but he was promoted to ambassador rank and later served in Iceland and Africa. Either the denazification process washed whiter than white or else somebody was still looking after their own. The extent to which the denazification process might have diminished in the Cold War climate to a mere formality has yet to be fully analysed.

Hempel eventually went back to his prewar job — looking after Foreign Office furniture and accommodation. Warnock echoed a negative assessment of that post when he termed it 'some sort of Board of Works job'. Frau Hempel explained that no one who had held her husband's rank 'under Hitler' had been reappointed as an ambassador. Hempel's accreditation was made by Hitler. Protestation of lack of sympathy for Nazi aims and aspirations do not nullify that.

He was denazified in Slade near Hamburg, and classified as No. 5 category. That classification should not have debarred him from senior office. His age probably told against him: he was 63 years old; Thomsen was 46.

He served out his last two years in Bonn before he retired with his loving wife to his farm in Freiburg. It was an idyllic retirement. He died at the ripe old age of 85 on 12 November 1972. He and his wife had been completely happy. Their union had been a real love story from the time of the chance meeting at a ball between the staid settled bachelor and the handsome high-spirited young girl. Hempel's private papers were never found after his death, despite Frau Hempel's best endeavours to unearth them.

His second-in-command in Dublin, Thomsen, in spite of the Nazi smear, served on and progressed in the diplomatic service. Colonel Bryan ruminated reflectively and enigmatically that they had perhaps been too hard on him. He accorded no such indulgence to MacNeill's involvement with Goertz and bitingly dissociated himself from that whole business.

Dr Gogan insisted (and he knew the Hempels well) that Thomsen was the Nazi overseer and that he worked hand-in-glove with the influential Fianna Fáil TD, Dan Breen, the renowned hero of the War of Independence and old comrade of de Valera. A word from Dan Breen to de Valera about undue influence from ex-British and ex-Free State army officers in the Local Defence and Security Forces was enough, according to Gogan, to have the Taoiseach instantly react and put them under army control. Breen offered to harbour Fleischmann in a hideout farm in Kilkenny to dodge repatriation. As it turned out Fleischmann did not have to resort to that covert. According to him, an official blind eye helped him to dodge the column.

There was no sign of Dan Breen ever having been reprimanded by de Valera for giving aid and comfort to agents and internees of the Third Reich: Breen was a law unto himself. His intervention did not represent expressed policy or de Valera's thinking but he did reflect an attitude of a fringe of the Fianna Fáil party. Ambivalence was the name of the game: Thomsen, although officially given asylum, was unofficially given the cold shoulder. The Nazi slur stuck to him in the British-oriented Department of External Affairs.

On one post-war occasion, during Warnock's ambassadorship in Bonn, he was omitted from an invitation list to a function at the embassy there. Nevertheless he insisted on turning up, loudly demanding an explanation as to why he had not been invited. It is unlikely that Warnock acted either whimsically or arbitrarily. The omission mirrored the mood of the day about Thomsen and the fallen Third Reich. Hempel, on the other hand, remained in good odour and de Valera had no problems about soliciting Maffey's intervention to facilitate his return to West Germany in 1949.

De Valera also canvassed Maffey to intervene to save Bewley, even though he regarded him as an unaccountable pest. Bewley had been captured by the Americans in their advance up through Italy and was later interned by the British at Terni. He was liable to be shot; his fellow prisoner John Amery was hanged. De Valera may not have wanted to make a martyr out of Bewley: he may have acted out of deference to his people. Anyway Maffey vouched that Bewley came from a good loyalist family, that he was well connected with a brother in the British Treasury and that his execution would cause political embarrassment. It was more than a little ironical that his reprieve was due to the benign influence of his hated British establishment connections.

There was evidence enough against Bewley to have him executed. His peace-feeling mission to Stockholm in 1940 had espionage undertones. William Joyce (Lord Haw-Haw) was convicted although he was an Irish-American, because he obtained a British passport for the purpose of leaving England in the days before the war; that seems to have been precisely what Bewley also did. Anyone who travelled on a British passport, it could be argued, owed allegiance to the king. In any case, it could also be argued, Ireland was *more or less* a dominion until 1949. Bewley could have been brought to London to' stand trial for treason. Maffey's intervention avoided that.

In his autobiography (the unpublished *Memoirs of a Wild Goose*) Bewley does not give the impression of having been seriously interested politically in what happened in Germany and he doesn't report what actually did happen with either accuracy or depth. His impressions of the Nazi leaders he knew are superficial and he deals trivially with main incidents such as the Night of the Long Knives, or, years later, the July Plot. If Bewley, interned at Terni, heard something interesting about the use of the Mafia by Allied intelligence, this story would be worth telling, but he gives no details. His judgment on Sicily showed no appreciation of the fearsome difficulties in the planning and execution of the invasion.[1]

Bewley's denigration of the Sicily campaign is cited as an example of his pathological inability to give the Allies credit for anything. He gloated that Churchill's Mafia friends

had let him down. He did not understand the feat of arms
in achieving almost total surprise. Similarly his account of his
association with John Amery at Terni, intriguing as it is, com-
pares unfavourably with Rebecca West's first-class reportage.
What is intriguing is why Bewley was imprisoned along with
Amery. This does suggest that a serious charge against him
was under consideration at the time. Gibbon, master of the
art of handling complex material, warned historians 'never to
pursue the curious', but Bewley compels curiosity.

His memoirs are riddled with an embittered loathing of
England, and a passionate distrust of de Valera, combined
with a conviction that neutral Eire's considerations would
have been better channelled in favour of the Third Reich.
He was an unlikely custodian of the pure republican flame,
but this was notoriously an area in which attitudes and
inclinations were almost impossible to predict. Hempel
thought Sean MacEntee was pro-British. (He would not
repeat that to the fiery Belfast republican's face.) Frank
Aiken had the name of being pro-German! It was hard for
Hempel to distinguish between all the shades of green.
Bewley, with true-blue credentials, masquerading as an
incorruptible sea-green republican, merely added to the
confusion.

In spite of Bewley's mischief Hempel generally maintained
good relationships with de Valera. He kept the IRA at arm's
length and this was a great help in keeping up appearances.
Woermann said that Hempel was no great intriguer but neither
was he a tyro in the diplomatic art of simulation. Woermann's
reference was made in the context of internal Nazi politics.

The British did not disapprove of Hempel: they recorded
their esteem for his professional demeanour. Cranborne believed that on the whole he had behaved well. Perhaps this
implied satisfaction at the manner in which he appeared to
rise to their provocation. Their approval or disapproval is
not on record as a factor influencing his recall to service.

He may not have been so mildly treated by either de
Valera or the British had they known the full extent to which
he was prepared to allow his legation to be used to send subversive messages. This posed a constant threat to the maintenance of neutrality and encouraged Veesenmayer to see a

role for him. In the final analysis, however, the *coup d'état* specialist found the Minister Plenipotentiary inadequate for his purposes. Hempel refused to be used by him.

With a more creative and adventuresome Envoy than Hempel it would have been difficult for the Irish government to maintain its neutral position. If the German representative had been, on the one hand, a Minister with the predilections of a Bewley, or, on the other, a diplomat with the initiatives (no matter how tentative) of a Kerney, it could well have been a different story. In the event, neither Hempel nor Kerney measured up to Veesenmayer's expectations of them.

All this does less than justice to Hempel's character and even to his daring. One can sympathise with Frau Hempel's annoyance at her husband being so negatively projected as 'a stuffed shirt' and a 'softy', as she quaintly put it. One small example at the beginning of the Emergency is perhaps indicative of the Envoy being ready to stand up for himself when he judged it proper to do so: he was prepared to use more than diplomatic weapons to defend himself. He had reported that his staff and himself were armed with revolvers; one attendant with a loaded revolver slept in the legation; windows on the first floor were specially secured; there was continuous protection from the Irish police, but he also kept a vicious guard dog that bit! The German representative had no intention of turning the other cheek if it came to protecting his legation.[2] There was also another side to Hempel to the supine role in which Veesenmayer cast him: he invariably showed restraint and perception. The following story of Frau Hempel's illustrates his diplomatic tact.

She recalled him getting information from a reliable source of a German pilot, shot down over England, being apprehended by an excited overwrought mob and cast alive into a blazing furnace. He refrained from passing on this information as he felt that it could only stir up tit-for-tat revenge action in Germany resulting in some shot-down RAF pilot being similarly incinerated.

Veesenmayer was a complete contrast. It was easy to see how he had got a name for being a *coup d'état* specialist. Ribbentrop had chosen an able ruthless man to foment the Irish rebellion. He earned the epithet 'emissary of evil' for his record with the Hungarian Jews. But Nazi evil was not always patently obvious. Even concentration camp officials went home to their lunch, played with their children, kept house, were dutiful parents and said their prayers. Germans have little resistance to bureaucratic compulsions. A job was a job and orders were orders. *Befehl ist Befehl.*

Veesenmayer, the lower middle-class painter's son, was a typical product of Nazi meritocracy. He had a brilliant academic record and the new system provided him with an opportunity to break out of his environment and move up the social scale. He was quickly engulfed in a fanatical ideology that swept through an entire people and distorted their judgments. He lived into his seventy-fifth year, and died in January 1978.

Although his enemies will never be persuaded that he did not write with a crooked quill and speak with a forked tongue, de Valera's papers should provide definitive revelations when they are made available to scholars.[3] The former President, Taoiseach and founder of the Fianna Fáil Party died at Linden Convalescent House in Blackrock, Co. Dublin aged 92 on 29 August 1975. Full of years and honours he was accorded a state funeral. His body lay in state for two days before the funeral. His stature as a world statesman was widely acknowledged. He was a great charismatic figure who played an immensely significant role in the history of Ireland in this century. His greatest achievement was keeping Ireland out of the Second World War.

It was clear to him that for a small nation neutrality was almost certain to represent the purely national interest; a neutrality, he indicated, to be guaranteed by all sides if possible. This was the course pursued by all the small democratic countries outside the Commonwealth until attacked. He intimated that had the Second World War come about from a joint decision of the League of Nations his attitude might have been modified. As a matter of principle, his underlying motto was that if we wanted justice for ourselves we ought to stand for justice for others. In the League of Nations in 1935 he told the Assembly that if, on any pretext whatever, we were to permit the weakest state amongst us to be unjustly taken away, the whole foundation of the League would crumble to dust. The League did crumble but that was not de Valera's fault; he was prepared to adopt military sanctions against Mussolini when the Italian dictator invaded Abyssinia. He felt that Ireland should play its part, and the fact that the British happened to be on the same side did not deter him. He was not blindly anti-British. He was indicating that Ireland would be willing to take part in an internationally constituted force to uphold international law: he firmly believed in the concept of the League of Nations. He felt that it was not acceptable for disputes between nations to be settled by war. When the League, through lack of 'teeth' and British and French will, failed to function he pointed out that neutrality was the only alternative left for small nations. When sanctions against Italy collapsed he sensed and pronounced on the powerlessness of small states. All they could do was to determine not to become the tool of any great power or to be forced into a war against their will. The powerful states with the capability to do so failed to defend Abyssinia against Italy and they later sacrificed Czechoslovakia to the Third Reich. This failure of the necessary backing for the concept of collective security reinforced his arguments in favour of a policy of neutrality. But, inevitably, other considerations arose. The policy could not, on account of historical, agricultural and economic circumstances, lend itself to simplistic formulae. Rigid rules were obligatory in some areas; flexibility was essential in handling other day-to-day dealings. De Valera's consideration for the British during the Second World War can only be understood if the identity of the two countries' interests is recognised. 'A certain consideration for Britain' was nothing more or less than a definite consideration for Eire.

The British side had searched for formulae to preserve the Commonwealth principle, especially from 1929 onwards. They genuinely had searched for the words to create a formula which would enable Ireland to remain within the Commonwealth. 'His Majesty's Government in the Irish Free State' had been concerned for the 'diplomatic unity of the Empire'. In an earlier effort to accommodate the Irish, the Foreign Office remarked: 'the arrangement proposed would not denote any departure from the principle of diplomatic unity of the British Commonwealth of Nations, that is to say prior consultative co-operation amongst all His Majesty's representatives in matters of common concern.' By the time de Valera's neutrality policy was advanced in conception, Eire had become an external member of the Commonwealth. De Valera insisted still that Eire, like Britain, was a mother county and was proud of her Commonwealth achievements. He was before his time: he was the father of the present Commonwealth concept.

Those sentiments, however, were by no means received with universal acclamation at the time from either the Irish or the British sides. Words were the crucial commodity: verbalisation was nearly all. Words were always important to de Valera: a prepositional change enabled the appointment of Sir John Maffey to be made; a dictionary definition stilled for him misgivings about the republican status of the state. His sentiments for the Commonwealth struck a responsive chord in old Commonwealth members and they in turn acted as a brake on Churchill in some of his more headstrong moves on Ireland.

The two main differences nowadays for Ireland in attempting to follow a similar policy of neutrality in wartime are membership of the European Economic Community and the threat of nuclear war. Must Ireland now have 'a certain consideration for Europe' and, if so, what forms would it take? Would the implementation of such a policy follow the old 'ad hoc' trail?

Times have changed. Scientific fact is now stranger than science fiction. Galactic nuclear artillery exchanges, with laser weapons mounted on space satellites in support, now figure in the scenarios of command and staff school war games. The current 'yellow peril' is 'yellow rain': chemical warfare is part of conventional warfare vocabulary. How would Ireland stand in a European Defence Community set-up to counter what Henry Kissinger used to phrase as the uneasy 'adversarial partnership' between the United States and Russia?

De Valera's 'certain consideration for Britain', complex in its day, seems by comparison to have provided a simple solution. The application of sanctions by the EEC against the

Argentine gives some measure of the complexity and delicacy of today's problem of 'certain considerations'. Any 'certain consideration' for Europe would have to take in *en route* the abiding 'certain consideration for Britain'. Can that policy ever be implemented again so dextrously and with such finesse and adroitness as de Valera managed to do it? His considerations gave the trappings and trimmings of protocol to the doomed Third Reich while managing to give the substance of real assistance to a surly but victorious Britain.

Fundamentally neutrality is an attitude of impartiality which excludes such assistance and succour to one of the belligerents as is detrimental to the other and such injuries to one as benefits the other. It requires *active measures* from neutral states to implement, because neutrals must *prevent* belligerents from making use of their neutral territories, and of their resources, for military and naval purposes during the war. This applies not only to actual fighting on neutral territories (a possibility neutralists tend to ignore) but to the transport, provisioning, trade interference and so on. Joe Walshe had a point when he persistently held that the less put on paper at the time about Irish neutrality the better. Moreover, to be serious about neutrality, it is essential to be prepared to defend it. That was de Valera's trump card and both the British and the Germans knew he meant it. As he put it, 'if we had to die for it, then we had to die for it.'

National self-interest was de Valera's guiding motivation. While he was prepared to prevent belligerents making use of his territory, he also had the sense to judge limits and the sense to realise that in war the need to survive is the final arbiter of actions. What would have happened if he had taken steps to prevent the Allies using the Donegal corridor? Doctrinaire righteousness was not the key to the best national self-interest in that context. As de Valera himself with justification put it: none of the great powers went crusading until they were forced to. The United States did not come into the war until she was attacked in Pearl Harbor by the Japanese in December 1941. The war against the Third Reich had been in progress since 1939. Nazism is now acknowledged to have been a great evil. Eire has nothing to be ashamed of in its crusading record to combat it. Thousands of Irishmen died at the tip of the spear — that's where they generally were — on the battlefields. Eire got eight Victoria Crosses to prove it. Thousands more worked in Britain's munition factories, farms and hospitals. It was an extraordinary unsung contribution.

Neutrality is not absolute. De Valera had no equivocation about his principle of consideration for Britain though he did have to tell white lies about the extent of that consideration. Ireland learned a lot from its neutrality in the war against the Third Reich. It survived. Having successfully pursued national self-interest during the Second World War neutral Ireland came through practically unscathed from the ravages of that terrible time. The Third Reich is dead and gone beyond recall of the wildest revanchist! Neutral Ireland is alive. It now wants to avoid the nuclear winter, but there will be no hiding place, for small or large nations, in the face of a thermonuclear war. There would be no way of controlling the weather. There would be no way of holding down the world's sea levels, bottling up the volcanoes, coralling the ice caps, or checking the paths of asteroids travelling in outer space in the havoc wrought by an environmental holocaust. The lessons of 'traditional neutrality' as practised between neutral Ireland and the Third Reich would be irrelevant.

Appendixes

Appendix 1

SAMPLE LISTS OF PRE-WAR
GERMAN COLONY IN IRELAND

The following names and addresses were supplied as suitable agents to the Head Office of the Overseas German Maritime Union in 1927:

Dr Pilger, Hume Hosptial, Hume Street, Dublin
Professor Dr Sanger, Blackrock College, Blackrock, Co. Dublin
Franz Born, 135 Tullow Street, Carlow
Hugo Schmal, Church Street, Longford
Commandant Friedrich Saurzweig, Beggar's Bush Barracks, Dublin
Maximilian Scherer, Leinster Square, Rathmines, Dublin
Colonel Fritz Brase, Beggar's Bush Barracks, Dublin
Herman Rombach, 21 Adelaide Street, Cork
Hermann Binninger, 34 Nelson Street, Tralee, Co. Kerry
Joseph Koss, Patrick Street, Kilkenny
Friedrich Gleitsmann, Kilbregan Hill, Bandon, Co. Cork
Dr Robert Stumpf, 30 Fitzwilliam Place, Dublin
Otto Witting, 137 Leinster Road, Rathmines, Dublin
Alois Fleischmann, 6 Wellesley Terrace, Wellington Road, Cork
H. Ritter, 54 Morehampton Road, Dublin
Dr Kurt Tashauer, 17 Eustace Street, Dublin
Fr J. H. Koenig, Oatlands, Castleknock, Co. Dublin.

Appendix 2

The *Irish Times* of 21 January 1937 reported von Kuhlmann's memorial service conducted at St Bartholomew's Church, Clyde Road, Ballsbridge. In a simple service, Rev. W. Tanne, Malahide, said Herr von Kuhlmann had been 'like a father' to members of the German colony in Dublin. Present were the German chargé d'affaires [*sic*] Herr E. Schroetter, with Herr Muller and Herr Wenzel; Herr Muller-Dubrow, President of the German Society in Dublin; Dr Adolf Mahr; Dr R. Stumpf; Mr and Mrs Flactet; Herr S. Strecker; Herr Ernst Krause (Manorhamilton); Commandant and Mrs Sauerzweig (Army School of Music); Fraulein Babelle Retz; Frau Mahr; Frau Muller-Dubrow; Herr W. Olhausen; Herr O. P. Traenker; Frau K. Muller; Captain Halse-Busch; Herr T. Schroeder; Dr Valerie Stumpf; Herr Clissmann.

Also present were Mr W. Warnock, Department of External Affairs and Mr R. C. Ferguson, Assistant Secretary, Department of Industry and Commerce.

The Director of the Army School of Music, Colonel Fritz Brase, is not listed amongst those present.

Notes

Chapter 1
BACKGROUNDS
(pp. 11—34)

1. He presented his letter of credence to President Paul von Hindenburg (1847-1934). At the last moment there had been a symtomatic hitch in the ceremony; he arrived for the audience without the king's letter and had to dash frantically back to his hotel to retrieve it.
2. *Studies*, March 1933.
3. Aged 32 when he resigned: the youngest *'ancien ministre'* ever, he quipped.
4. *Studies*, June 1937.
5. Bewley was not appointed as successor to Binchy until 1933.
6. The *Auslandsorganisation* was founded in 1931 and after 1933 acted as if it were a foreign office on its own. In addition to fostering trade it exercised surveillance over German nationals abroad to ensure that they remained loyal to the Nazi party. It sent agents abroad to propagate Nazi doctrines and to extend party discipline. It also maintained contact with subversive organisations. From 1937 on, no Third Reich diplomat or consul could be appointed unless his National Socialist credentials were cleared by the *Auslandsorganisation*.
7. De Valera had his doubts about Casement's common sense, but in this case he adopted one of his ideas.
8. See *Irish Times*, 23/8/84, p. 9.
9. 'Neither revolutionary violence and the sacrilege of masses blinded by false prophets nor the sophisms of those who are trying to de-christianise public life have been able to conquer the resistance or check the words of censure of this intrepid patriarch.'
10 The *Irish Times* editor, Robert Smylie, never tired of recalling his POW escapades in Germany: his readers did.
11. Later repealed by referendum in 1972 (4th and 5th amendments).
12. Affectionately known in his family circle as 'Tody' (not 'Toady': that would be inapplicable to this able astringent minister). He even signed personal letters 'Tody'. It was a nickname given to him by a nursemaid, for nursemaid's reasons, in his Derry childhood.
13. A perjorative label for Irish who affected British manners.
14. Alfie Byrne, lord mayor of Dublin.

15. Catholic Young Men's Society, some of whose members had previously been responsible for attacks on left-wing premises.
16. See Appendix 2.
17. See chapter 3.
18. 'Re-education' is Thomsen's own euphemistic word though colloquially the expression did not gain currency until the denazifaction days under the Allies.
19. A coin then in limited circulation in the UK and Eire.
20. The pupil outstripped the master. Walshe had learned his French in Holland and could never master the French R just as conversely Sean MacBride was unable to shed his Rs.
21. Later Irish representative at the UN and Chancellor of Trinity College, Dublin (1964-82).
22. Bewley, a Quaker, had been converted to Catholicism in Oxford by the idiosyncratic Jesuit, Father Martindale.
23. Childers' yacht, *The Asgard*, had been used for the landing of arms at Howth in 1914. Before he died he shook hands with the Free State army firing squad. He was an Englishman, an ex-British army officer, and the author of *Riddle of the Sands*.
24. When John A. Costello became Taoiseach of the first coalition government in 1948, Bewley hinted that he was available, for no salary, for diplomatic service. That aspiration came to nothing: McGilligan was in the coalition cabinet.
25. Bewley had been educated at Winchester before going to Oxford.

Chapter 2
KEEPING THE REICH INFORMED
(pp.35—51)
1. 'Hardly true' remarked Frau Hempel: Thomsen was young and brash and ambitious and Hempel was careful with him; but that he was actually a Gestapo agent, she did not believe.
2. Hempel had previously attributed de Valera's appointment to this post as having been due to British support.
3. This ambidextrous style of reporting was the despair of officials in Berlin who were trying to draw firm conclusions from Hempel's reports. No sooner had he fleshed out a proposition with one hand than he conjured it away with the other. Frau Hempel's sour comment was that it was only officials of the Veesenmayer ilk who professed to be so baffled.
4. After the war Hempel explained that 'doctrinaire' was in no way meant to be pejorative but intended to convey that de Valera approached problems in a theoretical way.
5. He reported de Valera as saying '*dass die Aufrechterhaltung irischer Neutralität im Kriegsfall kaum möglich sei*' but added his own '*von Vornherein zu sagen Neutralität unmöglich sei*' (F & CO. 037360-5 17/2/39).

Chapter 3
OFF THE RECORD
(pp. 52–66)
1. See chapters 6 and 8.
2. Major-General H. MacNeill, Assistant Chief of Staff; Colonel M. J. Costello; Captain P. Berry; Lieutenant Charlie Trodden; Lieutenant Sean Collins-Powell (a nephew of Michael Collins).
3. R. L. Brandy also chose to involve himself with Frank Aiken in Turf Development.
4. *Hauptverband Deutsch Seevereine im Ausland.*
5. See Appendix 2.
6. There were four main divisions in the Abwehr: Administrative; Espionage (I); Sabotage (II); Counter-Espionage (III). See also chapter 7.
7. Captain Walsh has left some papers in the National Library (6539).
8. Director of Irish Army Intelligence.
9. Author of *Spies in Ireland.*
10. Colonel Dan Bryan asked the present author to enquire of Veesenmayer why Mill Arden's name was on Goertz's list of possible helpers.
11. Dr Thierfelder, Prof. Sieverts, Dr Steuber, Professor Riddell and Herr Bene.

Chapter 4
THE PHONEY WAR – IRISH STYLE
(pp. 67–90)
1. Hitler's Directive: 'Case White' (3 April 1939). Hempel had a good idea of the date.
2. His successors Lemass and Lynch interpreted it also in a broad federal sense. Purists in the Fianna Fáil party contended that the word 'federal' was misused if it were applied in that context to the party's proposal for a united Ireland as a unitary state with a devolved government in Belfast.
3. Deak and Jessup, *Neutrality Laws and Regulations* (New York 1940).
4. Mistaken for a cruiser and sunk by a German submarine in September 1939. Survivors landed in Galway.
5. Hitler's five points were: German retention of Bohemia, Moravia and Poland (the retention of Austria was regarded as 'going without saying'); renunciation by Britain of her demands to intrigue or exercise her influence in Scandinavia; disappearance of Britain's bases at Malta, Gibraltar and Singapore; a 'Monroe Doctrine' for Germany in Central Europe; return of Germany's former colonies.
6. B. Martin, *Friedensinitiaven und Machtpolitik in zweiten Weltkrieg 1939-42* (Düsseldorf 1974), pp. 64, 262, 315.
7. Forty-five pages of relating cabinet papers covering the period 4/5 October 1939 will be not released until the year 2015.
8. Enno Stephan told me that Petersen had died in tragic circumstances around the beginning of the 1970s in Bonn where he had been living with his niece. He had returned to journalism after the war.

Chapter 5
THE FOGS OF WAR
(pp. 91—113)
1. Longford and O'Neill, *Eamon de Valera*, p. 350. John Bowman, *De Valera and the Ulster Question 1917-1973*, conveys an opposite impression of de Valera's reaction to Hempel's conduct at this time (p. 213, n. 46).
2. The Danes had not opposed in arms the German invasion of their country. The Germans then called Denmark the whipped cream front. A secret army, primed by the Secret Operations Executive in London, sprung up which was three times the size of the token army that surrendered in 1940 and amply redeemed Danish honour by their heroic resistance. A black mark remained against the Danish police for their vicious collaboration with the Nazis.
3. Sir John Anderson, the Home Secretary, had been Under-Secretary in Dublin Castle in 1920 and '21. Hempel's informant obviously made no distinction between this bureaucratic role and that of the notorious British army unit deployed during the Irish War of Independence, so called because of the differing colours of the tunics from the trousers.

Chapter 6
A RETHINK FOR THE REICH
(pp. 114—143)
1. *'Militärgeographische Angaben über Irland'*.
2. Montgomery had a hard job dissuading Whitehall advocates of a retreat based on a defeatist 'scorched earth' policy as the Germans advanced inland towards London.
3. The British Foreign Office commented on de Valera's 'frozen mentality' and 'the fact that the Irish people are terrified'.
4. *Operation 'Grün' (Landung Irland)*.
5. *'Und wenn wir fur diese sterben müssen, so werden wir für sie sterben.'*
6. General Hugo MacNeill or his cousin Colonel Nial MacNeill. 'L' at other times was variously said to be Dr Jim Ryan, the Minister for Agriculture, or Dr P. J. Little, Minister for Posts and Telegraphs. See chapter 8.
7. War Cabinet's secret memo, 8 October 1940.
8. De Valera was not apprised of this theory. The allegation that Churchill refused to bend the beam to save Coventry from the November 1940 bombing in the interests of protecting the code breaking 'Enigma' operation has been contested but not fully refuted. (*Most Secret War* by R. V. Jones, Hamish Hamilton 1978, p. 147).

Chapter 7
UNCONVENTIONAL OPERATIONS
(pp. 144—179)
1. The following codewords give clues as to the span of the spy net-

work: 'mackarel' for Ireland; 'bulldog' for England; 'bullfrog' for Portugal. A new contact address had been found by the IRA for their couriers and agents in England but an attempt to establish a courier route through Portugal fell through and it took months to establish a secret link via Spain.

2. Jim O'Donovan is supposed to have got a large amount of dollars from him. He denied this to me when I interviewed him.

3. He cohabited with a soldier's daughter. The affair came to light when the Department of Defence happened to notice that the soldier's wife was claiming children's allowance for her daughter's child, fathered by Weber-Drohl.

4. His nephew, Mr Brian Lenihan TD, told me that his uncle was a 'loner'. He lived very much on his own and had a job in Manchester where he died a few years ago. The family brought him back to Esker, Lucan for burial. It may be significant that he was able to make his home in England.

5. *Spies in Ireland* (London 1963).

6. *The Shamrock and the Swastika* (Palo Alto 1977).

7. Previously MI5 were angry at being denied access to reports on the German agents. Under Bryan, an arrangement for filtering information without technically breaching neutrality was worked out.

8. But it could have been right, Frau Hempel insisted, proving the point. She was unaware that the story could have stemmed from the system by which German agents captured in Britain collaborated with MI5 to send back false information to Germany. This was known as the double-cross system.

9. He memoed to the Secretary of State: 'One cause of much misunderstanding and many tragedies in Irish history has been that the people have not been kept in touch with. What could Queen Victoria not have done? Disraeli never came here; Gladstone for two days. Dublin Castle was more of a screen than a mirror. If there had been a British representative here at the time of the 1938 discussions the ports would never have been handed back. There was no great feeling about them here. Indeed there was much doubt and hesitation. De Valera was not in a strong position. He had to end the economic war at all costs. He bluffed our negotiators and his success has been a tragedy for better relations.'

10. Greig had been sent to spot sheltering U-Boats off the west coast. The operation was code-named 'potatoes'. Irish intelligence cooperated in his coastwatching exercises. He cloaked his counterespionage activity.

11. Later head of OSS.

12. See letter from E. R. 'Spike' Marlin in the *Irish Times*, 25 June 1985.

13. Later editor of the *Evening Press* and the *Irish Times*.

14. Suggestions that Roosevelt for political and military reasons suppressed that knowledge are disdainfully dismissed by some historians and avidly espoused by others.

Chapter 8
HIGH STAKES
(pp. 180—205)

1. He was transferred to GHQ from the Military College where, before the 1940 expansion of the army and with the suspension of normal command and staff courses, it was felt that he did not have enough to do to keep him occupied.

2. Tipperary, according to Colonel Bryan; Hempel reported Clare.

3. O'Duffy, a sacked Commissioner of the Garda Siochana, had a reputation for vanity, publicity seeking and parading his piety. He was instrumental in sending an ill-equipped, ill-trained brigade to fight for Franco in the Spanish Civil War. He was an admirer of Mussolini and emulated the Italian fascist leader's bullfrog *braggadocio* style.

4. Derived obviously from Goertz's other pseudonym 'Lt Heinrich Kruse': that was the name found on the military paybook he was carrying when captured. His slip-up was to sign it 'Hermann' Kruse.

5. A friend of Aiken's alleged that he brought Goertz *as far as* the house. The break-in story was not given much credence in intelligence circles.

6. Hayes had been court-martialled by the IRA on charges of treachery and collaboration with the 'Free State government'. According to Hayes, his 'confession' was extracted from him by torture; according to the IRA, it was given voluntarily after he had been found guilty. One way or the other, Hayes later escaped from IRA custody and made his way to a nearby garda station. The gardai then raided the house where he had been held and recovered the 'confession', among other things.

7. Colonel Bryan insisted that while Hempel's information about the woman spy, cleared by Kerney to travel from Spain, was correct, his information about Dr Ryan seemed to be based on the distorted stories Hayes confessed to the IRA.

8. Irish army intelligence never were apprised. This omission may be attributable to initial inter-service rivalries, though the story goes that with the passage of time the police intelligence came to appreciate more and more their military counterparts and to seek their assistance: but they apparently kept the Goertz document to themselves.

9. Colonel Bryan was outraged that in a footnote the German edition of the *Documents on German Foreign Policy* (E1.27.12.41) falsely identifies the major who met Goertz as himself: he intended to have the error corrected.

10. Colonel Bryan vehemently refuted any suggestion that official Irish intelligence had any contact with Goertz while he was on the run. He asserted righteously, if somewhat illogically from an intelligence point of view, that Goertz was a non-person to them at that time. Perhaps he protested too much: for an intelligence officer, sources must be protected always and at all costs. See chapter 9.

11. The US assessment of him was alleged to have recommended his employment as Operations Officer: the implication being that, while able, he needed someone to sit on him occasionally.

12. He was poorly rewarded by the Irish establishment for his outstanding success as Director of Intelligence, though the Americans and especially the British were keenly appreciative of his professionalism.

13. O'Reilly's father was known as 'Casement' O'Reilly: he was a member of the party of RIC men which arrested Roger Casement when he put ashore in Kerry from a German submarine in 1916. O'Reilly caused a panic when he escaped through an unsecured window from Mountjoy prison at the time of the 'second front' in the summer of 1944. His father handed him up, collected the reward for doing so, and dutifully invested the money for John Francis!

14. While Irish army intelligence was getting on well with the OSS, relations with Gray remained bad. It was not until late 1944 that the first so-called exchange conference with him was held.

15. The friendship between de Valera from Bruree and Ryan from Emly (two neighbouring Co. Limerick villages) had odd origins. Ryan's uncle had bad arthritis: an alleviating 'cure' was available in Bruree. King Edward VII had a similar rheumatic complaint and, believe it or not, there was correspondence between Buckingham Palace and Emly concerning the 'cure'! De Valera and Ryan came into contact initially arranging the transactions for its procurement for the king.

16. Colonel Bryan would simplistically construe the German arms offer as being nothing more than a well-meaning gesture to strengthen Irish neutrality, a policy which happened to suit them at different phases of the war. He steadfastly declined to give the MacNeill/Goertz liaison the status of having been a menace. He remained encrusted in the party line on neutrality: everything was under control. The Irish were well able to defend neutrality.

Chapter 9
END OF MESSAGES
(pp. 206–244)

1. Western Union cables to America; commercial cables to America, Newfoundland and Azores; commercial cables to Le Havre.

2. Reputable fanciers were hard to come by. There was, they memoed, only one representative of the National Pigeon service in the whole of Eire who owned a loft and he was Mr R. Shaw of 29 Marlborough Avenue, North Strand. Mr Samuel Wells of Woodlawn, Malahide was also noted as dealing in pigeon fancying.

3. The mooted station was to be located in the West of Ireland. It would be nice, the line ran, to be able to keep in touch with the Vatican! It could also send weather reports! That sounded innocuous enough at the time and it provided a topic of conversation for Hempel and Boland on their tramps across the Dublin mountains.

The British Secret Service got word of the proposition and put a swift end to it.

4. Two of these were recovered by the Irish army and dismantled in Islandbridge by Commandant 'Webley' Doyle.
5. The 'Dr Sehmelzer' promised by Weber-Drohl to rig up a replacement set eventually turned out to be Goertz.
6. For 'church circles' reference, see PAAA 280072-79 (19/8/42). The particular denomination is not given, but is presumably Roman Catholic. For Kilnacrott convent reference, see F & CO, 91/101080 (2/12/42).
7. After the war he was honoured by the US, Britain, France, Canada, Australia, New Zealand and Italy. He received the American Medal of Freedom and he was made a Commander of the British Empire. His work for the Germans when their hour of adversity came has not yet been formally recognised.
8. Mr Hugh O'Flaherty, S.C., a nephew of the Monsignor, recalled that after the war, when he visited his uncle in Rome, they spent a most cordial evening calling on Bewley.
9. Ireland was an important base for relevant weather reports. A report from Blacksod Bay in County Mayo was a factor in the meteorological advice given to Eisenhower by Dr J. M. Stagg influencing the go-ahead for the Normandy landings on 6 June 1944.
10. He subsequently joined the RAF but later deserted. He was a wild young man at the time. He was an unlikely conspirator but his folly in allegedly allowing himself to get mixed up with Goertz could have had disastrous consequences. Luckily, the gossip did not get to Gray's ears.
11. Dillon did not say that Portugal was still sending wolfram to make German guns, shells and submarines.
12. Army records list forty-seven but two died in hospital before they reached camp.
13. Information received in an informal letter from Adrian Liddell Hart, son of the famous military historian.
14. Walshe had become more difficult to get on with. One of his staff, Mr McCarthy, only communicated with him by letter. He never got around to marrying Miss Sheila Murphy, which his friends held would have been the making of him. On the other hand, Dr Michael Rynne paid tribute to his stature and to his contribution to the formulation and implementation of the policy of neutrality.
15. There was a theory that the British had chosen not to inform the Americans about the fate of Hempel's transmitter and so let the Americans make fools of themselves protesting about it. British cabinet papers, which were released in 1972, disprove this. They show a previous exchange of ideas between Gray and Maffey as to the text of the Note and on how to proceed in the matter of forestalling the opportunity for de Valera to spread on record the sequestering of the set.
16. *MI5* (London 1981), p. 309.

17. Constantine Fitzgibbon, who was then an intelligence officer in the Allied HQ staff, was dismissive of this and of its source, Douglas Gageby. But after the war MI5 told Hayes to have a week on the town in London at their expense. He had the time of his life. They did not give him that for nothing. Fitzgibbon was not privy to all.
18. Hempel said 162: the correct figure was 164.
19. Post-war stories of anthrax experiments in the Scottish Isles (one still uninhabitable as a result) reveal that the British had something just as terrible and that Churchill was barely restrained from pushing further for its use. He did not view the anthrax experiment, by all accounts, as a deterrent but as a weapon to exterminate Nazis.
20. Fäsenfeld then turned his hand to the manufacture of pharmaceutical products and characteristically made a success of it. He used to ply the German internees from time to time with sides of beef and cases of whiskey for their periodical junkets.

Chapter 10
EPILOGUE
(pp. 245–259)

1. 'It was undoubtedly a smart deal on the part of the Americans and possibly saved the lives of some American soldiers. It would probably be considered puritanical to suggest that the handing over of seven millions of people to a gang of assassins and white slave and drug traffickers was an act which could not be justified even by the exigencies of war. In fact since 'liberation' the rule of the Mafia in Sicily has been a tyranny enforced by numberless murders and the absolute negation of the individual liberty for which the Allies had pledged their honour.' From *Memoirs of a Wild Goose*, by Charles Bewley, Part II, Chapter VI (unpublished).
2. Frau Hempel stressed the distinction as between their home and the legation.
3. John Bowman's *De Valera and the Ulster Question* gives a taste of things to come.

Bibliography

1. ARCHIVES

Note: items selected by the F & CO are included to indicate a difference in the scale of documentation available in the F & CO as against what is available in PAAA Bonn. For instance, in Serial No. 3730M (1[a] [3]) twenty-four items were selected at the F & CO and fifty-one items were unfilmed. Their comment on this was that the most important documents had already been filmed: that the reports from the German legation in Dublin which had not been selected filled in details concerning the Irish policy as communicated to Berlin, but that these with the exception of Item 20 (1[a] [3] [XX]) called for no particular comment. Many, but not all, of these unfilmed documents are in Bonn where relevant documentation is copious.

But even in Bonn there are limitations to the amount of documentation available. A note in the Kent Catalogue (Findbach: Vol. III) makes a general reference (not specifically to Ireland) that the great amount of material available made it necessary to condense certain listings, and that in the case of the *Neue Reichskanzlei*, the extensive and varied titles of files not filmed have been consolidated and thus indicate only in a general way the contents of these files. Such original files as have been preserved are accessible in the Bundesarchiv, Koblenz. A brief visit to Koblenz however, did not indicate the availability of any further substantial documentation.

Foreign and Commonwealth Office, London
(1) Serial 1612N 386396–386508.
Political relations between Britain and Ireland.
Vol. 1 (May 1936–April 1938).
Selected items:
(i) (24 November 1936). Eireann Minister in Berlin asks that in publications the name 'Irish Free State' should not appear under the general heading of 'England' but should be given separate space as in the case of other British Dominions.
(ii) (12 December 1936). Report on law abolishing post of Governor General in Dublin.
(iii) (19 November 1937). Secretary of State for External Affairs discusses with German Minister favourable political position of Germany caused by Italy joining the Comintern Pact.

(iv) (20 December 1937). Lengthy report on significance of new Irish Constitution and position of Eire within the British Commonwealth.
(v) (18 January 1938). Report on British-Irish Conference in London.

(2) Serial 1618 387528-387624.
Selected Items:
(i) (17 May 1938). Report from German legation in Dublin on Anglo-Irish relations as a result of Agreement of 25 April 1938.
(ii) (17 October 1938). Report on Ireland during and after Sudeten crisis.
(iii) German legation reports on Irish armament questions.

(3) Serial No. 3730 M
Supplementary to Serials 1612M, 1618H and 3158H (German Foreign Ministry: Pol 11 Po 3: England-Ireland). Twenty-four items selected; fifty-one items unfilmed.
Selected Items:
(i) (30 July 1936). E 037217. Ber. A42. Koester Dublin to AA. Statements by Irish politicians indicating that Ireland would be neutral in the event of a European conflict.
(ii) (1 August 1936). E 037300-303. Ber. A43. Koester Dublin to AA. Irish refusal to participate in the Coronation celebrations.
(iii) (25 February 1937). Schroetter Dublin to AA. Ireland and the Oath of Allegiance.
(iv) (18 May 1937). Schroetter Dublin to AA. Radio speech by de Valera on Anglo-Irish Relations.
(v) (21 May 1937). Schroetter Dublin to AA. De Valera's declarations re Ireland's non-participation in the Imperial Conference.
(vi) (17 July 1937). E 037315-17. Ber. A98g. Schroetter to AA. Political feeling in Northern Ireland.
(vii) (30 December 1937). E 037318-23. Hempel Dublin to AA. Proclamation of new Eire constitution.
(viii) (15 January 1938). E 037324-5. Ber. A192g. Woermann (London) to AA. Reaction in Northern Ireland to Eire constitution.
(ix) (18 January 1938). E 037326. Telegram 19 Woermann to AA. Progress of the Anglo-Irish talks; Northern Ireland and Irish unity.
(x) (19 January 1938). E 037327. Tel 21 Woermann to AA. The Anglo-Irish talks.
(xi) (26 January 1938). E 037328-9. Ber. A455. Woermann to AA. Northern Ireland and the Anglo-Irish talks.
(xii) (23 February 1938). E 037330-2. Ber. A871J. Woermann to AA. Northern Ireland elections.
(xiii) (18 March 1938). E 037333-336. Ber. A104. Hempel Dublin to AA. The situation reached in the Anglo-Irish conversations.
(xiv) (5 May 1938). E 037338-341. Ber. B1365G. Beilfeld (London) to AA. Northern Irish opinion and the Anglo-Irish Agreement.
(xv) (13 May 1938). E 037342-345. Ber. A152 Hempel to AA. Defence questions discussed in Irish Senate.

(xvi) (18 October 1938). E 037346-351. Ber. A417 to AA. De Valera on Northern Ireland.

(xvii) (20 November 1938). E 037352-354. Ser. A484. Hempel to AA. De Valera on Anglo-Irish relations.

(xviii) (16 February 1939). E 037355-9. Ber. A120G. Hempel AA. The suppositions on which Irish defence expenditure for 1939 would rest.

(xix) (17 February 1939). E 037360-5. Ber. A127g. Hempel to AA. De Valera's speech on Ireland's attitude in the event of war.

(xx) (15 February 1939). E 037366-9. Ber. A103g. Hempel to AA. Conversation with de Valera on the subject of the IRA and outrages in Northern Ireland.

(xxi) (23 February 1939). E 037370-5. Ber. A143g. Thomsen Dublin to AA. De Valera on Irish neutrality.

(xxii) (28 January 1939). E 037376-80. Hempel to AA. Renewed IRA activities.

(xxiii) (1 July 1939). E 037381-7. Ber. 1308. Hempel to AA. Dáil debate on neutrality.

(xxiv) (29 July 1939). E 037388-91. Ber. 1530. Hempel to AA. British measures against IRA.

(4) Collection entitled Eire Vol. I. Serial 91/I:100051-100510
(there are gaps in this sequence: some, but not all, of these missing telegrams are available in PAAA, Bonn).
Numerous telegrams between the German legation in Dublin and the German Foreign Office from *August 1939 to December 1940*, mainly regarding the neutrality of Eire.

(5) Collection entitled Eire Vol. II. Serial No. 91/II:100511-100945: 1 January 1941 – 31 March 1942.
Selected Items:
Telegrams between the German legation in Dublin and the German Foreign Office dealing with:
(i) Dropping of bombs on Dublin and other towns in Eire.
(ii) Question of resistance if neutrality violated.
(iii) Influence of Irish in USA.
(iv) Fear of invasion of Ports in Eire by Great Britain.
(v) Wendell Wilkie's visit to Dublin and report of speech by him in the National Press Club. Telegram from German Ambassador, Washington, No. 450 of 18 February 1941.
(vi) Offer of German assistance to Eire in case of attack by Britain – Ribbentrop to German Ambassador Dublin, No. 97 dated 24 February 1941 and reply to letter in Telegram No. 218 dated 11 March 1941.
(vii) A secret wireless station used by German legation, Dublin.
(viii) Activities of German agents in Eire.
(ix) Appeal of pro-German section of town of Derry in Ulster that that town should not be bombed.
(x) Appeal by Archbishop of Armagh that the town should not be bombed.

(6) Collection entitled Eire Vol. III: Serial No. 91/III: 100946-101324: 1 April 1942 – 31 December 1943.
Selected Items:
(i) German legation's connection with spies in Ireland.
(ii) Protests of Irish government against attacks on Irish ships.
(iii) Reports on military movements and numbers of troops in Ulster and England.
(iv) Former Irish Minister in Berlin, Bewley, discussing the future of Eire in case of a German victory.
(v) Reporting particulars of British preparations for invasion of the continent.

(7) Collection entitled Ireland (Veesenmayer) Serial No. 91/IV:101325-101470: May 1941 – 5 May 1943.
Selected Items:
(i) Plan *Mainau* of Mr Andrews for action with Germany in connection with Irish fascist organisation 'Blue Shirts'.
(ii) Reports of *SS Oberführer* Veesenmayer regarding activities of his group of 120 men in the matter of Ireland.
(iii) Report of dropping *Hauptmann* Dr Herman Görtz by parachute over Ireland on 5/6 May 1940 to carry out action with the IRA to assist German War Plans.
(Reference to '*Von Herr Clissmann der Abwehrabteilung II übergebene Telegramme* (Dublin): No. 289 (22/9/41); 342 (20/10/41); 367 (29/10/41); 371 (2/11/41); 387 (6/11/41); 443 (3/12/41); 442 (5/12/41); 443 (8/12/41).

(8) Collection entitled: Ireland Serial No. 1423: 362675-362691. August 1942 – October 1944.
Selected Items:
(i) (9 August 1943): telegram from German Minister at Dublin surveying series of alleged breaches of neutrality by the Irish Government. Hempel refers to the release of air crews, the granting of aircraft repair facilities, and reports on his various *demarches*.
(ii) (5 October 1943): telegram from German Minister at Dublin reporting on discussion with de Valera, during which he presumed that if Eire were the victim of aggression from one side, she would receive all possible assistance from the other.
(iii) (25 January 1944): telegram from German Minister at Dublin reporting ever increasing Allied pressure on Eireann government for severance of diplomatic relations with Germany. Hempel states that he is observing political trends very minutely in order to prevent any breach of relations.

(9) Collection entitled: Intelligence (Abwehr): Ireland. Serial No. 961: 301977-302176.
These documents are concerned with the activity of German secret agents in Ireland and with the help rendered by the German legation in

Dublin. Several names and addresses are contained in the correspondence. Agent reports that General O'Duffy prepared to send a 'Green Division' to Russia.

(10) Serial No. 957: 301141-301404.
Certain documents concerning the activities of German agents in Eire and help extended to those agents by German legation in Dublin. Several names are given ('including names of Eireann sympathisers').

(11) Collection entitled: Ireland (Ambassador Ritter Bundle 4): Serial No. 1005: 307436-307570.
Selected Items:
(i) (14 November 1940). General Warlimont informs Ambassador Ritter that in event of British attack on Eire the only assistance Germany could offer would be (1) Concentration of U-Boats around ports occupied by British, (2) Extension of air-raids to ports occupied by British. The use of airborne troops is ruled out owing to supply line difficulties.
(ii) (18 December 1940). German desire to send two military officers to be attached to German legation in Dublin as civilians.
(iii) (6 December 1940). High-ranking officer in Eireann army asks what help Germany could give in event of British attack; asks for deliveries of British weapons captured by Germans.
(iv) (21 December 1940). Eireann authorities request Germans not to strengthen staff of legation at Dublin.
(v) (25 December 1940). Ribbentrop instructs German Minister in Dublin to inform Eireann authorities that Germany will decide the strength of legation staff.
(vi) (29 December 1940). Ribbentrop instructs German Minister in Dublin not to press further in the matter of increasing staff of legation.
(vii) (18 August 1941). De Valera requests German Minister in friendly terms to restrict use of wireless transmitter in legation to cases of utmost urgency and importance.
(viii) (22 February 1941). Short report of conversation between Wendell Wilkie and de Valera on Eire's neutrality.
(ix) (24 February 1941). Ribbentrop instructs German Minister in Dublin to assure de Valera of Germany's readiness to aid Eire in event of British attack.

(12) Miscellaneous: Loesch collection: Serial 825: GB59: 6329: 3015: 3096: 3199.

Public Record Office, London
War Cabinet, Foreign Office and Dominions Office papers.

Imperial War Museum, London

CO. Ref. No.	Title	Date
AL 1933	Canaris/Lahausen fragments	(5/3/37)

CO. Ref. No.	Title	Date
MI 14/68	Deception measures	(7/8/41–28/10/41)
MI 14/81	Deception measures	(7/8/41–28/10/41)
MI 14/86	Deception measures	(7/8/41–28/10/41)
MI 14/87	Deception measures	(7/8/41–28/10/41)
1678 (2)	Lahausen's Diary	(12/5/37–12/4/41)
		(14/4/41–3/8/43)

The War Journal of Fritz Halder
AI 1770 Hitler's ideas of a British (19/3/43) Legion against Bolshevism;
John Amery.
MI 14/402 *Fall 'Grün'* (12/8/40-20/9/40).
Betr. Ausbildung der Pioniere
    Ausbildung der Artillerie
Organisatorische u. technische Vorbereitungen
Art der Durchführung
Anordrungen für die Verwendung der Artillerie
Aufgaben und Verwendung der Pioniere
Anordnung für die Geheimhattung
Erganzungen zur Bezugverfügung
See-Transportsmeldung
Vorlaüfige Stärkemeldung
(These are listed to indicate detail of planning deception measures.)
AI 1491. Letter of Hempel, German Ambassador (17/12/40) to Ireland
offering arms and German help against England.
AL 1048/2. Plans for invasion of British Isles. (The Führer's thoughts as
relayed by his Adjutant [AI 2828] and General Jodl's summary of the
situation with reference to the Invasion of the UK (MI 14/14/112) do
not refer to Ireland.)

Politisches Archiv des Auswärtigen Amtes, Bonn
Many of the items unfilmed in F & CO files are available in Bonn;
generally as per reference in the Kent *'Findbuch'*.

(1) General
PAAA, England Nr. 80 (Irland), Bd 11-16.
*PAAA, Politische Beziehungen zwischen Irland und Deutschland, Bd 1
    und 2*
PAAA Abt 111 Pol 1-13 (Irland) (1/9/21 – 3/4/36)
*PAAA Büro St. S., Deutsch-Englische Beziehungen (19/6/40 –
    31/12/40)*
PAAA Ha-Pol Clodius (Irland), Bd 2 und 3
PAAA Büro Akten St. S., Irland, BI 1-3
PAAA Akten Botschafter Ritter (1940-1944)
PAAA U. St. S., Irland (Veesenmayer)
PAAA Abt III Handelsbeziehungen Irlands zu Deutschland (Bdl; Bd IV)
*PAAA Pol Abt II Politische Beziehungen zwischen England und Irland.
    Bd I, II*

PAAA Bürostatsekretar Irland, BI 1, 2, 3, i.e.,
   1 (8.39-12.40) 91/100052-510
   2 (1.41-3.42) 91/100512-945
   3 (4.42-12.43) 91/100947-1324).
PAAA Rundfunkpolitische Abteilung 1939-45 Bd 7; 8; 27-42
PAAA Ha-Pol 1936 off I, IIa, IIb; III; P/ket 12
Fach 183-186 Paket 9-15

(2) Kent Catalogue Vol. II
Ireland file references: p. 10; 11; 28; 29; 163-168; 266; 879.

(3) Kent Catalogue Vol. III
Lists all important files of period 1936-45 except those of Missions and Consulates (Vol. IV). Ireland file references: p. 5; 20; 32; 41; 44; 53; 62; 171; 198; 208; 329; 336; 346; 382; 427; 471.

(4) Kent Catalogue Vol. IV
Lists the files of the major European missions and consulates and some non-European. A note indicates that deficiencies, especially of records in the non-European area, is due to the loss and destruction of entire sets of files during and after WWII. From the Hempel point of view this collection is disappointing and a further reminder of his compulsive burning of files. It brings to mind that Hempel actually wrote to the German Foreign Ministry, even though he was then out of office, seeking to suppress Stephan's book *Spies in Ireland*. Hempel feared that it would damage German-Irish relations. The AA in turn got down the line to Stephan's employers to seek to muzzle him. Stephan stood firm on his rights and refused to be muzzled. Aid came to him from an unexpected quarter: the *Bundesnachrichtendienst* (Intelligence) opposed Hempel and said that, on the contrary, publication of such a work could only improve relations by shedding historical light. Jupp Hoven (see Chapter 3) was another to indicate virulent dissent at the publication and indicated to Stephan, as an example to be followed apparently, that Goertz took the honourable way out rather than betray his comrades by revelation (conversation with Enno Stephan, July 1977). Hempel's actions indicated a suspicion that there was something to hide. Ireland file references: p. 41 (Bern); 315, 328 (Madrid); 386 (Oslo); 392, 434 (Paris); 563/4 (Rome); 713 (Vatican); 720 (Sofia); 760 (Warsaw); 678 and 558: political relations between Ireland and Italy 1938-39.

Bundesarchiv Koblenz
Sammlung Brammer (101-12); *Sammlung Traub* (110/11) *Sammlung Oberheitmann: Korrespondenz H. Clissmann's, Deutsche Akademie,* R57, DAM 932; R2 9914 (folio 1-98); R2/10013 fol 1; R2 10218 fol 1; R2/24603 (*Internationale Vertrage*); R. 4311/1445e *Irland; Akten der Reichskanzlei sowie des Finanz-und Wirtschaftressorts; Aktenbände aus*

der Adjutantur des Führers. SS Akten (Irland); Auslandsnachrichten dienst (Irland) Resort Schellenberg (Irland); Slg Schlumack, 291-296a NS15/15-26. NS22/485.

Militärarchiv Freiburg

Operation 'Herbstreise' (incorporating Operation 'Grün') Operations 'Seelöwe'; 'Haifisch' and 'Harpune'. Various political, economic and naval files referring to Ireland (e.g. RW5/v: RWG/V and Wi/1).

State Paper Office, Dublin

Files S9439 and S9884 not yet transferred to this office (4/2/77). Government and cabinet papers as available.

Public Record Office, Four Courts, Dublin

Frank McDermot's letters on Hempel: 999/84/5; 99/84/6
(20/4/71) (30/4/72)

Public Record Office, Kew

FO memos on Bewley covering protocol problems concerning Bewley's recall from Holy See; diplomatic difficulties of bestowing a Papal decoration and later his undiplomatic behaviour in Berlin.

FO 627 13 (1929) 'His Majesty's Government in the Irish Free State'; concern about the diplomatic unity of the Empire; the Commonwealth principle.

FO 371 16714 (1933): Air defence in Germany.

FO 371 17741 (1934): Pen picture of Bewley (benign enough at this stage) on his Berlin appointment (C251/131/10).

FO 371 8855 (1935): Foreign office criticism of excessive timidity of Papal Nuncio in Berlin (Mgf. Orsenigi): 'he looks around fearfully when he expresses himself. When he protested to the German government about the arrest of the Austrian press attaché in 1935 he did so so cautiously that nobody but himself seems to have heard it.'

FO 371 23042 Annual Report on Heads of Foreign Missions in Berlin (including Bewley). C/170/170/18 (1939).

CIII 40/170/18 Termination of Bewley's appointment.

C 5172/6/18 (1940) Conditions in Germany: reference to Bewley's visit to Stockholm.

FO 372 2970 (1933) et seq. Letter from Pius X to King George V re Bewley. King found it 'all very complicated'.

FO 372 2903 (1933) 'Bestowal of a papal decoration upon Mr Charles Bewley lately IFS Minister to the Holy See'.

FO 372/3097 (1935) Bewley's failure to attend King's Jubilee celebration at H. M. Embassy Berlin.

FO 372/3161 (1936) Withholding of information from IFS.

(Significantly, perhaps, FO 392/2978, which presumably refers to Bewley's covert operations, is not yet released.)

DO 130 (10/10/39) Peace-feelers.

DO 130 (18/10/39) Letter from John Hamilton Cannon to Special Branch Scotland Yard complaining about German Minister in Dublin.

DO 130 (23.11.39) Eire and the march on the North. Letter from A. Handly, Arklow Pottery.

DO 130/8

14.2.40 How Brendan Behan got into England without a travel permit.

6.7.40. IRA activities.

DO 35 German bad debts in Dublin; de Valera's condolences on death of Hitler.

WX 130/3/40 (1945) The Archives of the German legation.

The following refer mainly to Maffey:

DO 130/4 (1939) Correspondence re Lieutenant Michael Mason, British spy.

DO 130/5 (1939) Unity of Ireland: partition.

18.12.39 Frank McDermot to Maffey from 14 Burlington Road.

DO 130/6 (1939) Censorship of communications between UK and Eire; illicit wireless station; leakages; remedy.

DO 130/9 (1939/40) IRA death sentences; Bishop of Kilmore's letter to Dean of St Patrick's maintaining that 70,000 Irishmen were fighting for British army.

DO 130/13 IRA suspects: appeals against expulsion order.

DO 130/14 Additional communications between Maffey and UK (including carrier pigeon arrangements).

DO 130/17 (1941) Maffey on de Valera's 'frozen mentality'; Irish army establishments; nearing 'a parting of the ways'.

DO 130/23 Case of Stephen Hayes. References to: Roger McHugh, Assistant Professor of English, arrested for pro-Nazi views; to Dr Ryan; T. Derrig; Chris Byrne; and Laurence de Lacy.

WX 126/1 13.8.40 Liquidation and share out of German assets.

DO 35/1522 12.10.40 de Valera's approach on the subject of Nuremburg sentences.

DO 130/127 Maffey on de Valera: 'we are dealing with a mind that is not malleable'. Defence of Ireland.

DO 130/40 War Criminals Asylum.

2. MANUSCRIPTS

Bewley Memoirs. Dr Bewley.

Goertz letters etc. Enno Stephan.

J. O'Donovan (including letters from Goertz and Weber-Drohl).

Miss Maura O'Brien; Enno Stephan; Professor Williams.

National Library Ms 21155 Acc 3199

Liam Walsh's (incl. Eoin O'Duffy) National Library P6539

(Miss O'Brien kindly accepted my suggestion that the Goertz letters and other papers be given to the National Library and Mr O'Looney arranged for their collection.)

3. PERSONAL INTERVIEWS

Prof. D. A. Binchy; Dr Geoffrey Bewley; F. H. Boland; Col Dan Bryan; Miss Mona Brase; Joseph T. Carroll; Helmut and Mrs Clissmann; Horst Dickel; Misses Farrell; George Fleischmann; Douglas Gageby; Dr L. S. Gogan; Frau Eva Hempel; Mrs Caitriona Hertz; Jan van Loon; Seamus Mallin; Miss Sheila Murphy; Sean MacBride; Miss Maura O'Brien; Patrick O'Connell Buckley; James L. O'Donovan; Dr Harry and Mrs O'Flanagan; Anthony Powell; P. P. O'Reilly; Michael Scott; Enno Stephan; Francis Stuart; Arthur Voigt; Dr W. Warnock; R. R. A. Wheatley; Prof. Desmond Williams; Dr Edmund Veesenmayer.

4. LETTERS/CONVERSATIONS

Dr H. Becker; Lt Col D. Beglin; Dr David Bewley; R. D. and Thea Boyd; Mrs Carolle Carter; Fr S. J. Clyne (for Archbishop O Fiaich); Tim Pat Coogan; Con Cremin; Mrs Maire Cruise O'Brien; Col E. de Buitleir; James Dillon; Dr Reinhard R. Davies; Ruth Dudley Edwards; Bartholomew Egan OFM; Dr R. Fechter; Robert Fisk; Colonel James Fitzgerald Lombard; Dr Giessler; Mrs Hayes; Prof. Dr Klaus Hildebrand; Ken Hiscock; Harold Hoven; Dr Maria Keipert; Anthony Lampkin; Hilary F. Lawton SJ; Col F. E. Lee; Brian Lenihan TD; Adrian Liddell Hart; Herr Loos; Dr Bernd Martin; Ron Mellor; Lothar A. Merta; Anthony Marreco; Capt. Jack Millar; Mrs Caitriona Miles (for Professor Delargy); Sean MacEntee; Mrs Jacqueline McGilligan; Peadar O'Donnell; Mrs Kay Petersen; Dr Pretsch; Dr Felician Prill; Philip Reed; Dr Michael Rynne; Oberst i.g. Sauvant; Frank Selinger; W. K. Smurthwaite; Dr Franz von Sonnleithner; Kurt Ticher; M. Toomey; Rudolf Veesenmayer; Dr Ernst Woermann.

5. NEWSPAPERS, PERIODICALS, ARTICLES, PUBLISHED DOCU-MENTS, MICROFILM, MAPS

Newspapers

Irish Independent; Irish Press; Irish Times; The Worker; The Irish Worker's Voice; Daily Express; Daily Mail; Daily Telegraph; Sunday Chronicle; Manchester Guardian; The Times; New York Journal; New York Times; Allgemeine Zeitung; Völkischer Beobachter; Sunday Independent.

Periodicals

Archivalische Zeitschrift (1968); *Der Archiver* (1972) (n.b. *Zur Lage des Archivwesens in der Republik Irland* by P. Kahlenberg, pp. 175-182); *An Cosantoir; The Bell; Journal of Commonwealth Political Studies; Historische Zeitschrift; Journal of Modern History; Nation und Staat; The Leader; Der Spiegel; Statesman and Nation; Studies.*

Articles

Anon., 'MacNeill', *The Leader*, 28 March 1953.

Anon., 'Ireland in the Vortex', *The Round Table*, No. 121, December 1940.

Binchy, D. A., 'Adolf Hitler', *Studies*, March 1933.

Binchy, D. A., 'Paul von Hindenburg', *Studies*, June 1937.

Brennan, Robert, 'Wartime Mission in Washington', *Irish Press*, June-July 1958.

Brodrick, Charles, '*Gruen*: German Military Plans and Ireland, 1940', *An Cosantoir*, March 1974.

Cox, Colm, 'Wir fahren gegen Irland', *An Cosantoir*, May 1974, March 1975.

Dickel, H., *Irland als Faktor der deutsehen Aussenpolitik von 1933-1945: Eine propadeutische Skizze – Hitler, Deutschland und die Mächte Bonner Schriften zur Politik und Zeitgeschichte*.

Dwyer, T. Ryle, 'Wild Bill's Spooks in the Free State', *Sunday Independent*, 17 June 1984.

Dwyer, T. Ryle, 'The Irish diplomats used as U.S. spies', *Sunday Independent*, 24 June 1984.

Harkness, David, 'Mr de Valera's Dominion: Irish Relations with Britain and the Commonwealth, 1932-39', *Journal of Commonwealth Political Studies*, vol. VIII, 1970.

Goertz, Hermann, 'Mission to Ireland', *Irish Times*, 25 August – 10 September 1947.

Murdoch, J., 'Interviews with Dr Hempel', *Sunday Press*, November – December 1963. (These articles contained many inaccuracies and caused much distress: they were refuted.)

O'Reilly, John, 'I was a spy in Ireland', *Sunday Dispatch*, July/August 1952.

Rugby, Lord (Sir John Maffey), 'Lord Rugby remembers', *Irish Times*, 3 June 1962.

Stuart, Francis, 'Frank Ryan in Germany', *The Bell*, November 1950.

Van Hoek, Kees, 'Secret Agents in Ireland', *Sunday Chronicle*, June 1954.

Williams, T. Desmond, 'Study in Neutrality', *The Leader*, January – April 1953.

Williams, T. Desmond, 'Neutrality', *Irish Press*, June – July 1953.

Published Documents

Akten zur deutschen auswärtigen Politik
(ADAP) Serie E Band 1 Gottingen (1969).

Documents of German Foreign Policy DI-XIII
(DCFP) HMSO (1949-64)

International Military Tribunal Nuremberg (1949). Vols. 1-42 Nuremberg.
Dáil Debates 1939-45 Dublin.
Seanad Debates 1939-45 Dublin.

Microfilm

P. 4670
P. 4672   in National Library of Ireland and generally correspond
P. 4671   to 91 serial: see 1(4): 1(5): 1(6) above
P. 4672

Maps

Militärgeographisch Angaben über Irland Süd und Ostküste (von Mizen Head bis Malin Head); *Text-und Bildheft mit Kartenanlagen; Abgeschlossen am 31 Mai 1941; Generalstab des Heeres; Abteilung für Kriegskarten und Vermessungswesen* (IV Mil. Geo Berlin 1941 15 October 1941). (Military College Library.)

6. BOOKS AND UNPUBLISHED THESES

(All books are published in London unless otherwise indicated)

Anderson, M. S., *The Ascendancy of Europe 1815-1914* (1972)

Bell, J. Bowyer, *The Secret Army* (1970)

Blaxland, G., *Destination Dunkirk* (1973)

Block, Jonathan and Patrick Fitzgerald, *British Intelligence and Covert Action* (1983)

Bowman, John, *De Valera and the Ulster Question*, Oxford (1983)

Brassey, *Brassey's Naval Annual* (1948)

Brissard, A., *The Biography of Admiral Canaris* (1973)

Brissard, A., *The Nazi Secret Service* (1974)

Bullock, A., *Hitler: a Study in Tyranny* (1968)

Butcher, H., *Three Years with Eisenhower: Personal Diary 1942-45* (1950)

Carroll, Joseph T., *Ireland in the War Years 1939-45*, Newton Abbot (1975)

Carter, C., *The Shamrock and the Swastika*, Palo Alto (1977).

Chamberlain, N., *The Struggle for Peace* (1939)

Chatfield, A. E. M., *The Navy and Defence: the autobiography of Admiral of the Fleet Lord Chatfield*, vol. 2, 'It Might Happen Again' (1942, 1947).

Churchill, W. S., *The Second World War*, vols 1-6 (1960)

Cienciella, A. M., *Poland and the Western Powers, 1938-39* (1968)

Clarke, D., *Seven Assignments* (1948)

Colvin, I., *Canaris, Chief of Intelligence* (1973)

Coogan, T. P., *The IRA* (1970)

Cooper, Matthew, *The German Army 1933-1945* (1978)

Craig Gordon, A., *The Diplomats 1919-39* Princeton (1953).

Demeter, Karl, *The German Officer Corps in Society and State, 1850-1945* (1962).

de Valera, E., *Peace and War: Speeches on International Affairs*, Dublin (1944)

de Valera, E., *Ireland's stand: a selection of the speeches of E. de Valera during the War 1939-45*, Dublin (1946)

Donitz, K. *Deutsche Strategie zur See im Zweiten Weltkreig*, Frankfurt a.m. (1972)
Duff Cooper, *'Operation Heartbreak'* (1950)
Dulles, A., *Germany's Underground*, New York (1947)
Dulles, A., *The Craft of Intelligence* (1964)
Dulles, A., *The Secret Surrender* (1967)
Dulles, A., *Great True Spy Stories* (1969)
Dwyer, T. Ryle, *Irish Neutrality and the USA, 1939-47*, Dublin (1977)
Edwards, Ruth Dudley, *An Atlas of Irish History* (1973)
Eisenhower, D., *Crusade in Europe* (1948)
Farago, L., *German Psychological Warfare*, New York (1942)
Farago, L., *War of Wits: the anatomy of espionage and intelligence* (1956)
Farago, L., *The Game of the Foxes* (1971)
Fisk, Robert, *In Time of War* (1983)
Fleming, P., *Invasion 1940* (1959)
Fonvielle Alquier, F., *The French and the Phoney War, 1939-40* (1973)
Gallagher, Joseph Peter, *The Scarlet Pimpernel of the Vatican* (1967)
Garlinski, J., *Intercept: secrets of the Enigma War* (1979)
von Gersdorff, U., *Geschichte und Militärgeschichte*, Frankfurt a.m. (1974)
Halder, F., *Kriegstagebuch Bd III*, Stuttgart (1964)
Harkness, D. W., *The Restless Dominion* (1969)
Hildebrand, K., *The Foreign Policy of the Third Reich* (1973)
Hillgruber, A., *Kontinuität und Discontinuität in der Deutschen Aussenpolitik von Bismarc bis Hitler*, Düsseldorf (1971)
Hillgruber, A., *Hitler's Strategie, Politik und Kreigsführung 1940-41*, Frankfurt a.m. (1945)
Hillgruber, A., *Deutschland's Rolle in der Vorgeschichte der beiden Weltkriege*, Göttingen (1967)
Hitler, A., *Mein Kampf* (1939)
Hogan, V. P., *The Neutrality of Ireland in World War II* (unpublished doctoral thesis for University of Notre Dame, 1948)
Hull, Cordell, *The Memoirs of Cordell Hull*, 2 vols (1948)
Huntington, Samuel P., *The Soldier and the State*, Cambridge, Mass. (1972)
Ironside, W. E., *The Ironside Diaries* (1962)
Kahn, O., *Hitler's Spies: German Military Intelligence in World War II* (1978)
Kavanagh, Comdt. P. D., *Irish Defence Forces Handbook*, Dublin (1974)
Keatinge, P., *The Formulation of Irish Foreign Policy*, Dublin (1974)
Keatinge, P., *A Place among the Nations*, Dublin (1978)
Kehal, K., *Kreisen Manager im Dritten Reich*, Düsseldorf (1973)
Klee, K., *Das Unternehmen 'Seelöwe'*, Göttingen (1958)
Klee, K., *Dokumente zum Unternehmen 'Seelöwe'*, Göttingen (1959)
Kordt, K., *Nicht aus den Akten*, Stuttgart (1950)
von Lahausen, E., *Secret Service War Diary of General von Lahausen* (1958)

Langer, W. L. and S. E. Gleeson, *The Challenge of Isolation, 1937-40*, New York (1952)
Leverkuehn, P., *Der Geheime Nachrichtendienst der deutschen Wermecht in Kriege*, Frankfurt a.m. (1957)
Liddell Hart, B. H., *History of the Second World War* (1970)
Longford, Earl of, and T. P. O'Neill, *Eamon de Valera*, Dublin (1970)
Lukacs, J., *The Last European War* (1971)
Macksey, K., *Kesserling: the Making of the Luftwaffe* (1978)
Mansergh, P. N. S., *The Commonwealth Experience* (1969)
Mansergh, P. N. S., *Survey of British Commonwealth Affairs*, vol. 2
Mansergh, P. N. S., *Problems of Wartime Co-operation and Post-War Change, 1939-52* (1958)
Martin, B., *Friedensinitiativen und Machtpolitik in zweiten Weltkreig 1939-42*, Düsseldorf (1974)
McCracken, J. L., *Representative Government in Ireland* (1958)
McMahon, D., *Malcolm McDonald* (MA thesis, University College, Dublin, 1975; since published)
Montgomery, B. L., *Memoirs* (1958)
Namier, Sir L., *Diplomatic Prelude 1936-1940* (1948)
Neave, A., *Nuremberg* (1978)
Nowlan, K. and T. D. Williams, eds, *Ireland in the War Years and After*, Dublin (1969)
O'Donnell, J. P., *The Berlin Bunker* (1979)
Petersen, G. W., *The Limits of Hitler's Power*, Chicago (1968)
Von Ribbentrop, J., *Memoirs* (1954)
Seabury, P., *Wilhelmstrasse*, Berkeley (1954)
Schellenberg, W., *The Schellenberg Memoirs* (1956)
Schramm, P. E., *Kriegstagebuch des OKW (Wehrmachtführungstab)*, Frankfurt a.m. (1961)
Von Schweppenburg, G., *Errinerungen eines Militärattaches*, Stuttgart (1949)
Shebab, H. M., *Irish Defence Policy 1922-50*. M. Litt. thesis for UCD (1975)
Shirer, W. L., *The Rise and Fall of the Third Reich* (1960)
Smith, R. H., *OSS: The Secret History of America's First Central Intelligence Agency*, Berkeley, Calif (1972).
Stagg, J. N., *Forecast for Overlord: June 6 1944* (1971)
Stephan, Enno, *Spies in Ireland* (1963)
Stephan, Werner, *Joseph Goebbels — Däemon einer Diktatur*, Stuttgart (1949)
Sturm, Hubert, *Hakenkreuz und Kleebatt: Irland die Allierten und das Dritte Reich 1933-1945*, Frankfurt a.m. (1984)
Stuart, Francis, *The Victor and the Vanquished* (1954)
Taylor, A. J. P., *The Origins of the Second World War* (1961)
Trevor Roper, H. R., *Hitler's War Directives 1939-45* (1964)
Wagner, G., *Lagevorträge des Oberbefehlshabers der Kriegsmarine vor Hitler 1939-45*, Munich (1972)
Warlimont, W., *Inside Hitler's Headquarters* (1964)

Welles, S., *The Time for Decision* (1944)
Von Weizacker, E., *Memoirs* (1951)
West, Nigel, *MI5: British Security Operations (1909-1945)*, Toronto (1981)
West, Rebecca, *A Train of Powder*, (1955)
Wheatley, R., *Operation 'Sealion'*, (1958)
Wheeler-Bennett, J. W., *The Nemesis of Power* (1954)
Wilmot, Chester, *The Struggle for Europe*, New York (1952)
Young, A. P., *The 'X' Documents: the Secret History of Foreign Office contacts with the German Resistance 1937-39* (1974)

Index

Abdication crisis in Britain, xvi, 2, 12
Abercorn, Duke of, 100
Abwehr (Military Intelligence Service), xvi, xvii, 52, 55; pre-war information gathering, 57, 58; in dark about Ireland, 59-63; connections with IRA, 65, 82, 117, 118, 149-50; link with McCarthy, 152, and Goertz, 153, 180-1; Hempel's contribution to, 162, 163; lays down conditions for agent insertion, 197-8; *see also* Pfaus, Oscar C.
Abyssinia (Ethiopia), 23, 256
Academic Exchange organisation, *see* Clissmann, Helmut
Achilles, Bruno, 249
Acts of Parliament: Irish Nationality and Citizenship Act 1935, 12; External Relations Act 1936, xvi, 2, 12, 39, 72; Offences Against the State Act, xvii, 47, 68; Defence Forces Act, xvii; Treason Act, 47; Prevention of Violence (Brit.), 147
Adamandious Georgandis, 110
AEG, 63
Africa, 6
Aiken, Frank, biog., xiii, 44, 48; failure of US arms purchasing mission, 130, 141, 157, 182; Roosevelt loses temper with, 171; on neutrality, 177; listens to MacNeill, 181; alleged Goertz broke into his house, 189, 253
Air Raid Precautions (ARP), 44
Alsace-Lorraine, 65
American-Irish Defence Association, 171
American League for the Unity and Independence of Ireland, 133

'American Note', xviii, 226-7; *see also* Gray, David
Amery, John, 252-3
Anderson, Sir John, 101
Anderson, Karl (Walter Simon), xvii, 155
Andrews, Joe, 196, 198-9, 208, 234
Anglican Pacifist Fellowship, 80
Anglo-Irish, the, 40
Anglo-Irish relations, 1, 14, 20, 36, 39; circumstances in which Ireland would seek British aid, 40; convoluted nature of, 69-71; trade, 84; strained by threats of conscription in North, 140, 141; pre D-day tensions, 225
Anti-Comintern Pact, 37
Anti-conscription campaign, 48
Anti-Imperialist League, 56
Anti-partition, 1, 47
Anti-semitism, 12, 17, 18, 30, 33, 42, 82, 170, 214, 238
anthrax, Churchill's plan for use of to extirpate Nazis, 270
appeasement, Anglo-French, 37, 108
Arcadia, 76
Archer, Colonel Liam, 99, 100, 207
Ardennes offensive (Battle of the Bulge), 89, 231, 233-4
Army Comrades Association, 17
Army, Irish, *see* Defence Forces
Arnhem, Battle of (Operation 'Market Garden'), xviii, 237
Astor, Lord, 83, 108
Athenia, 76
Atlantic, Battle of, 136, 160, 234, 236
Auslandsorganisation, 14, 23, 24, 52, 56, 62, 63, 162, 163
Australia, 20, 135